THE ORIGIN
OF THE
MODERN JEWISH
WOMAN WRITER

D1069366

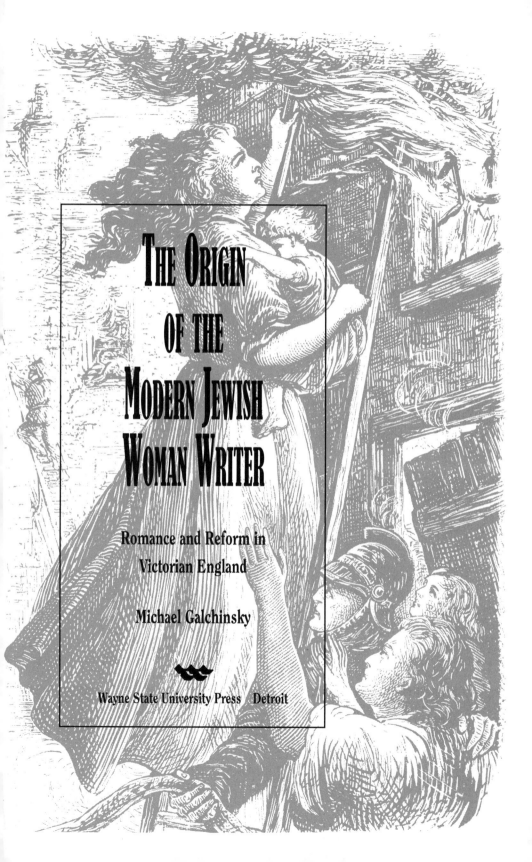

The Origin of the Modern Jewish Woman Writer

Romance and Reform in
Victorian England

Michael Galchinsky

Wayne State University Press   Detroit

99 98 97 96   5 4 3 2 1

Library of Congress Cataloging-in-Publication Data

Galchinsky, Michael.
    The origin of the modern Jewish woman writer : romance and reform
in Victorian England / Michael Galchinsky.
        p.   cm.
    Includes bibliographical references and index.
    ISBN 0-8143-2613-7 (pbk. : alk. paper).—ISBN 0-8143-2612-9
(alk. paper)
    1. English literature—Jewish authors—History and criticism.
    2. Jewish women—Great Britain—Intellectual life—19th century.
    3. Women and literature—Great Britain—History—19th century.
    4. English literature—Women authors—History and criticism.
    5. English literature—19th century—History and criticism.
    6. Aguilar, Grace, 1816–1847—Criticism and interpretation.
    7. Judaism—Great Britain—History—19th century. 8. Jews—Great
Britain—History—19th century. 9. Jewish women in literature.
    10. Judaism in literature. 11. Jews in literature. I. Title.
PR120.J48G35   1996
823'.8099287'089924—dc20   95-41199

To Sarah Galchinsky, who learned all she could of Judaism in her *shtetl*, Trisque, by listening outside the window of her brother's school, while waiting to take him home.

To Rose Gvirtz, who taught three daughters how to be Jews, the only Jews in the pioneer town of Fort Collins, Colorado.

My wish in the following very simple story, was to pourtray a Jewess, with thoughts and feelings peculiar to her faith and sex, the which are not in general granted to that race, in Tales of the present day.

Grace Aguilar,
"Adah, a Simple Story"

Contents

Preface

During my research in London, my attempts to recover materials relating to women's experience of Jewish modernity were frequently fruitless. As it turned out, I was sometimes luckiest when I was not trying. One afternoon I walked into the Jewish Museum of London with no other intention than to see the famous paintings of Moses and Judith Montefiore. Since the curator seemed amenable to talk, I happened to mention that I was interested in the writings of the Victorian Jew, Grace Aguilar, not expecting him to have heard of her. But on the contrary his eyes lit up, and he told me that the museum had been in possession of all of Aguilar's tributes, diaries, and unpublished poetry and fiction manuscripts since the early part of this century. The papers had been donated by a historian, Rachel Lask Abrahams, who had gathered the material from the personal papers of Aguilar's mother Sara. Nothing I had read had even suggested that this material existed. Unfortunately, the curator continued, from the time the documents had come to be housed in the museum, they had been inaccessible to scholars, because the institution did not have facilities for scholarly research. Just three months before I arrived, however, the museum had arranged to transfer the documents to the Manuscript Library of University College London, where if I was so inclined I might go directly that afternoon. The curator said he would be happy to write me a note of recommendation, if I cared for one.

A month later, I put in a request for the sole surviving copy of Marion Hartog's *Jewish Sabbath Journal,* the first Jewish women's periodical anywhere in the world in modern history. The Jewish Studies librarian at University College London returned an hour later to tell me that after an extensive search, he had concluded that the copy had been irretrievably lost. This was a blow, for I suspected that the *Journal* would illuminate many of the most difficult questions raised by the study of the Anglo-Jewish women's literary community. For example, how had the community come into being? and what purposes had it served for the women involved? I put an advertisement in the following week's *Jewish Chronicle,* looking for Hartog's ancestors.

9

No one responded. Two weeks later I had almost given up when, as I was sitting in the library, the telephone rang. It was the librarian. He had been in a basement in another part of the library searching for something else when, of all things, he had come upon the *Journal,* sitting in a stack of unrelated seventeenth-century documents. Did I still want to see it? I rushed over to the Manuscript Library to find a frail, brittle, and water-damaged sheaf coming apart in tiny bits in my hand. By the end of the day, the bits had covered my shirt. So this was what was meant by "recovering" history.

Like the archaeologist, the archival researcher knows that history is comprised of the material objects extant from the past. In the case of Jewish women's literary history, archival resources are more limited and exhaustible than in other areas, because women were exempted from participating in the intellectual life of Jewish communities for most of Jewish history. Yet many more documents relating to women's experience of Jewish modernity remain extant than scholars have generally recognized. Because earlier historiographical models neglected or underestimated the differential effect of Jewish modernity on men and women, the substantial wealth of nineteenth-century fiction and periodical literature dealing directly with that subject has remained largely unexplored. This lack of attention to basic sources in turn has meant that larger synthetic studies purporting to tell the story of Jews' modernization repeated the absence of gender as an analytical category. Over the last ten years or so—in studies of French, German, American, and English Jews—there has been a recognized need among feminists and other scholars interested in gender to return to the archives and recover what has been neglected.

This book focuses on a critical but forgotten moment in the development of Jewish women's writing, the moment in which modern Jewish women transgressed their traditional "exemption" from literary endeavor and began to publish books. Between 1830 and 1880, Jewish women in England became the first Jewish women anywhere to publish novels, histories, periodicals, theological tracts, and conduct manuals. In their own time, Grace Aguilar, Marion Hartog, Judith and Charlotte Montefiore, and Anna Maria Goldsmid were acknowledged by Christians and Jews alike as the most significant theorists of English Jews' entrance into the modern world. Their romances, some of which sold as well as novels by Dickens, argued for Jews' emancipation in the Victorian world and women's emancipation in the Jewish world. These texts served as emblems of Jews' desire to become acculturated to modern English life while simultaneously maintaining a distinct collective identity.

This study analyzes Anglo-Jewish women's momentous entrance into print in relation to Victorian literary history, women's cultural history, and Jewish cultural history. In the context of Victorian literature, it offers revisions of the development of the English novel as well as a reevaluation of such well-known novelists as Scott, Edgeworth, Disraeli, Dickens, Thackeray, and Eliot. In addition, its analysis of Christian responses to Jewish women's romances provides new perspectives on Victorian liberalism, orientalism, and conversionism. In the context of feminist approaches to women's cultural history, this study offers new interpretations of Victorian domestic ideology, the feminization of religion, and the advent of feminist political and literary institutions. Finally, this study attempts to show that, when approached through a gendered lens, modern Jewish cultural history looks remarkably different than it does in traditional histories of the period. English Jews' approach to gender roles, as well as their campaigns for emancipation and religious reform, were profoundly shaped by women's writing in ways that until now have not been fully understood or appreciated.

Drawing for the first time from the *Jewish Sabbath Journal* and from overlooked articles, tales, and midrashim published in standard Victorian Jewish periodicals such as the *Jewish Chronicle,* drawing for the first time in nearly a century on the Grace Aguilar MS, this book's aim is to reconstruct the lost subculture of the Victorian Jews.

ACKNOWLEDGMENTS

During the research and writing of this book, a community co-alesced to see the project through to completion. Fellowship and grant support was provided by the Mellon Foundation, Millsaps College, the Chancellor of the University of California at Berkeley, the Berkeley Graduate Division's Humanities Graduate Research Grant program, and the Koret Foundation. The librarians at the Manuscript and Jewish Studies libraries of University College London, the British Library, and the Newspaper Library in Colindale, and the curator of London's Jewish Museum provided generous and prompt assistance. The Jewish Museum graciously permitted me to quote from the Grace Aguilar manuscripts.

I would like to thank Catherine Gallagher for supporting a Jewish cultural studies project in an English department. Thanks also for frequently reminding me of what I had meant to say before I had ever managed to say it. Steve Goldsmith's generous, expansive criticisms of the manuscript, his nurturing mentorship, and his willingness to discuss the minute implications of my work, both practical and impractical, were invaluable. David Biale's unwavering support for the project buoyed up my belief in its legitimacy as Jewish scholarship, and his sharp criticisms improved the historiography and the chapter organization. Critics whose editorial comments materially strengthened the arguments were David Sorkin, Robert Alter, Chana Kronfeld, and Murray Baumgarten. The editorial staff at Wayne State University Press guided me through the revision and publication process with thorough, gentle, and sure hands.

Catherine Gallagher's Victorian dissertation group was the prod, the testing ground, and the *havruta*. Over the years, its members included Laura Green, Bill Cohen, Judith Rosen, Laura Camozzi-Berry, Peter Logan, Kate McCullough, Daniel Hack, Catherine Robson, Cheri Larsen Hoeckley, Alyson Bardsley, Rebecca Steinitz, and Irene Tucker. The *Msrepresentations* gang, particularly my partners in crime Elise Marks, Kim Drake, and Simon Stern, helped me laugh at critics and become one.

Thanks to Rachel Luft, whose curriculum on Jewish women enlightened me, and whose painstaking pruning of the manuscript was accomplished with kindness. She is a teacher. Thanks to the Jewish women whose wisdom, commitment, and power were a constant source of inspiration: Jennifer Sylvor, Rebecca Weiner, Ruti Kadish, Sharon Friedman, Diane Bernbaum, Rachel Wolff, and Sue Grayzel. And thanks to the Jewish men who have taught me that it is possible to love and respect women, while loving and respecting oneself: Steven Stark, Mike Richman, Marshall Richman, Duke Helfand, Brad Friedman, Doug Abrams Arava, Natan Margolit, Lewis Aframi, Michael Taller, David Franklin, and Daniel Lev. Crucial typing support was provided by Arlene Galchinsky, Joel Bashevkin, Sharon Friedman, Marshall Richman, and Rebecca Weiner. Thanks to Catherine Davidson and Michael Dunn for their assistance in gathering and reproducing the photographs.

The encouragement of my father and mother, Herb and Arlene Galchinsky, my sister and brother-in-law, Cindy and Howie Sales, and my grandmothers, Sarah Galchinsky and Rose Gvirtz, has been indispensable, as has that of my nephew and niece, Benjamin and Brinna Sales. Throughout the years of excitement and disappointment, rejection and accomplishment, Elke Davidson has been my touchstone. She tirelessly reread the text. She appeared as a witness at every talk in every city. Her immense editorial acumen, ability to synthesize, and capacity to suggest a different strategy improved and in some cases changed the shape of the project. She provided emotional support at every phase of the roller-coaster ride, even when we were both motion sick. And her belief in the value of the work sometimes exceeded my own. Her imprint is on every page.

INTRODUCTION:
A NEW APPROACH TO MODERN JEWISH LITERARY HISTORY

Among the many valuable works relative to woman's capabilities, influence, and mission, which in the present age are so continually appearing, one still seems wanting.

Grace Aguilar,
Women of Israel (1846)

THE DEVELOPMENT OF THE
VICTORIAN JEWISH PUBLIC SPHERE

During the nineteenth century, Jews constituted the largest and fastest growing non-Christian minority living on English shores. Their community grew by 1200 percent between 1815 and 1900,[1] and during the same period, they began to produce a voluminous Jewish public sphere comprised of periodicals, novels, philosophical and apologetic tracts, theologies, histories, and etiquette manuals. Many of the productions of this burgeoning public sphere were written by women, a circumstance that makes Anglo-Jewry unique among all Jewish communities in the world at that time. Between 1830 and 1880, Jews wrote in order to defend and debate the two salient movements gripping the community—the movement to emancipate themselves from the legal and political disabilities from which they still suffered as British subjects, and the movement to reform their religious institutions and practices. Their demand for emancipation produced such heated debates in Parliament over the nature of English national identity—ought Jews to be allowed full rights in this Christian nation?—that at one point the debate between the Lords and the Commons over the emancipation question threatened to dissolve the government.[2] The debate over religious reform threatened for a time to fracture the community irreconcilably. Yet despite this remarkable increase in visibility; the challenge Jews posed to the identity of an increasingly liberal, yet professedly still Christian nation; the bitterness of the reform debate; and the intriguing presence of women in the Jewish public sphere, historians and literary critics of Jewish modernity as well as of the Victorian period have until recently paid little attention to this community.

The population increase of Victorian Jews was remarkable given that only two centuries before, England had been all but depopulated of Jews. After Edward I expelled them from England in 1290, Jews were (officially, at least) absent from English territory for four hundred years. In 1656, Oliver Cromwell readmitted a small group of Spanish-Portuguese Jews led by an Amsterdam-based theologian named Menasseh ben Israel, in the hope that Jews might aid him in increasing commerce as they had the Dutch and the Italians.[3] From that point until 1815, the number of English Jews increased slowly—the Spanish-Portuguese, or Sephardim, came first, then gradually during the eighteenth century, the German-Polish, or Ashkenazim. At first these two communities were quite distinct. The Sephardim had fled from the Spanish and Portuguese Inquisitions and upon arrival were quite often wealthy. The Ashkenazim were likewise fleeing from persecution by Cossacks, Poles, and Germans, and at first were mostly poor. During the eighteenth century, the religious and cultural differences between the two groups meant a great deal, so that the earliest English Jews had built two separate communities, which rarely interacted and differed in synagogue practices, clothing, and even languages spoken. As the Anglo-Jewish population began to grow—from a few families to 20,000 persons in London and the provinces by 1815—these two communities gradually became one more or less unified group. By 1880, there were 60,000 Jews in Britain, an increase accompanied by a geometric growth in the number of Jewish communal institutions.[4] By the end of the century, due to the mass immigrations following in the wake of Eastern European pogroms of the 1880s, British Jews numbered 250,000.

These Victorian Jews were not merely melting into the British pot upon arrival, Israel Zangwill's play *The Melting Pot* notwithstanding. Between the start of Jews' agitations for relief from political disabilities in 1830 and the mass waves of Ashkenazic immigrants that began fleeing Russian pogroms to England in 1880, English Jews began building and maintaining a distinct communal identity, with autonomous institutions and an articulated set of priorities. They began to develop a "subculture," a term David Sorkin has used to describe a minority culture that "is largely composed of elements of the majority culture" but that "is nevertheless distinct and functions as a self-contained system of ideas and symbols."[5]

During this fifty-year period—called the Anglo-Jewish Enlightenment, or *haskalah*—Jewish literature and journalism played a crucial role in the development and maintenance of a minority culture with a self-contained system of ideas and symbols. When Maria Polack's novel *Fiction Without Romance; or, the Locket-Watch* appeared in 1830— the first novel to be published by an English Jew, in the year of the Jews' first efforts at parliamentary emancipation—the Jewish public sphere was nonexistent. But during the next fifty years, Jewish women, including Polack, Grace Aguilar, Marion Hartog, Celia Levetus, Anna Maria Goldsmid, and Judith and Charlotte Montefiore published scores of novels, short stories, etiquette manuals, and philosophical, historical, and apologetic tracts. Moreover, the Jewish public sphere grew to include at least a dozen periodical publications in English, Hebrew, and Yiddish. These included Morris Raphall's *Hebrew Review and Magazine of Rabbinic Literature,* which appeared between 1834 and 1836. Jacob Franklin published the *Voice of Jacob* between 1841 and 1847. The *Jewish Chronicle,* which eventually became the standard newspaper of the community, also came into existence in 1841.[6] Marion Hartog's *Jewish Sabbath Journal,* the first Jewish women's periodical in modern history, appeared for a short time in 1855. And from 1859–60, Marcus Bresslau's *Hebrew Review and Magazine of Jewish Literature* made its appearance. In part due to English Jews' increase in population, and in part due to their desire to acculturate while remaining distinct, the Anglo-Jewish public sphere began to flourish.

FIVE WAYS TO MAKE ANGLO-JEWISH LITERARY HISTORY DISAPPEAR

Until quite recently, this large and well-developed Anglo-Jewish public sphere has received scant attention, from historians of Victorian

Jewish culture, from historians of Jewish modernity in general, or from literary critics of the period. These scholars have missed out on the community's literature because they have practiced at least five different forms of historical erasure.

First, historians of the Anglo-Jewish *haskalah* have usually treated the male segment of the community as if it were the whole.[7] Because they have focused on men's achievements, these histories have typically either completely neglected or trivialized and dismissed the production of Anglo-Jewish literature, the vast majority of which was written by women.[8] Most histories of the period never mention women, unless it be Judith Montefiore, and then only in her capacity as travelling companion to her famous husband Moses. They have tended to tell the story of the men's agitation for emancipation from legal, political, and economic disabilities. Or they have told the story of the movement for religious reform, as the men imported it from Germany. With some recent exceptions, those literary critics who have attempted to address the importance of Victorian Jewish women's literary production have tended to lose sight of the contemporary community by focusing on a single individual (primarily, Grace Aguilar or Judith Montefiore); to minimize the work of women in relation to that of men; or to underappreciate the importance of gender in the emergence of an Anglo-Jewish literary tradition.[9]

Yet the role played by women is precisely what makes this history and this literature so unique and interesting. In their publishing activities, Anglo-Jewish women differed from every generation of Jewish women that preceded them. When early Victorian Jewish women began to publish books, they were breaking a centuries-old taboo against Jewish women gaining and displaying learning. Women were not prohibited from intellectual work in the framework of Jewish law, or halacha—they were rather "exempted" from the study of Torah, as they were "exempted" from the observance of all time-bound positive commandments. Their work in the economic and domestic spheres was deemed more significant in traditional Jewish gender ideology than their work in the liturgical or analytic spheres. From time to time a woman such as the Talmudic sage Beruria, married to a great scholar or the daughter of one, would come forward as an intellectual and be recognized for her learning. Glückel of Hameln, a wealthy seventeenth-century businesswoman, managed to write her memoirs while seeing to the fates of fourteen children. But these women were exceptional.[10] For most women, the exemption had the force of a taboo. More typically, an Ashkenazic woman would publish a book of daily meditations, or *tekhinot,* a form of women's writing sanctioned by the traditional male authorities.[11] But, except for those few Anglo-Jewish women who could read Yiddish, most of these *tekhinot* were in a language inaccessible to them. Because of this inaccessibility, when Jewish women in England began to publish, they were for the most part creating a Jewish women's literary tradition from scratch.[12]

They not only had few historical models to work from, but they had no contemporary examples to follow. Anglo-Jewish women writing in the 1830s preceded women elsewhere in Europe and the United States into print by fifteen years. Even in Germany, where Jewish salonières like Rahel Varnhagen were entertaining German literati,[13] or the United States and France, where the movement for religious reform was likewise taking hold and offering women more of a public role—even in these places Jewish women in the 1830s and 1840s were not publishing books. But Anglo-Jewish women became active as novelists, poets, polemicists, and speakers in the modernizing Victorian community in these decades. The Anglo-Jewish *haskalah* witnessed the emergence of the Jewish woman into modern literary and cultural history.

These writers are not only interesting today as historical curiosities. They laid the groundwork for the increase in Anglo-Jewish women's education and communal participation and influenced their American, German, and French Jewish counterparts; they were some of the most important theorists of the English Jews' emancipation and reform movements; and they produced an indigenous literature that played a significant role in the invention and maintenance of an Anglo-Jewish subculture.

All of these women's activities make the Anglo-Jewish *haskalah* different from versions of the *haskalah* being played out elsewhere. The study of the *haskalah* is the study of the Jews' movement from aliens to citizens, from a more traditional autonomous community to a more integrated and assimilated community, from the middle ages into modernity. In any given European country, the *haskalah*'s hallmarks are debates over emancipation and reform. Because these are the subjects of Anglo-Jewish women's writing, their literary production provides a unique opportunity to understand how Jews' entrance into modernity differed for women and men. The Anglo-Jewish women writers with whom this book deals—principally, Marion and Celia Moss, Grace Aguilar, Charlotte Montefiore, and Anna Maria Goldsmid—reveal much about the disparity that existed in men's and women's experience of modernity, at least in a liberal nation. The very existence of their work raises important questions that have never yet been entertained much less answered: What combination of influences compelled these writers to do what almost no other Jewish women before them or contemporary with them were doing? What influence did their books have on contemporary Jews and non-Jews? And why were they and their works almost immediately dismissed and forgotten? The first way to make Anglo-Jewish literary history disappear is to treat its primary writers, women, as if they did not exist.

The second type of erasure bears a structural resemblance to the subsumption of women's history by men's. Historians of the European Jews' *haskalah* have tended to subsume Anglo-Jewish history under the German-Jewish experience. Until the last decade, most historians of the *haskalah* took the German-Jewish example as a model for the whole, even though, as the Anglo-Jewish historian Todd Endelman has demonstrated, the assumption that the German-Jewish experience is paradigmatic for all Jews' experience is inadequate.[14] The processes of emancipation and reform took place at different times from one location to another and were not precisely the same from place to place. The Anglo-Jewish emancipation and reform movements began half a century after the analogous German-Jewish movements, and emerged into a different context. While Jews' emancipation in Germany was limited by anti-Semitism and required Jews' religious reform, emancipation in England took place in a more tolerant context, and did not require Jews' religious reform. England served as the liberal vanguard of Europe, at least as regarded subjects living within its domestic borders.

The Anglo-Jewish model offers an alternative history of Jews in Europe to the German-Jewish model: specifically, it offers the history of a flourishing Jewish culture in an increasingly liberal and imperialist state. If part of the value of a given history is its relevance to the context of those who recount it, the Anglo-Jewish experience seems in many ways more analogous to the current American or Western European Jewish experience than does the German-Jewish case. The latter's particular brand of entrenched religious and political anti-Semitism often leads historians to point teleologically from the German *haskalah* to the Holocaust. Anglo-Jewish history offers instead a model for understanding the development of liberal and reform Jewish communities, who struggle with the less extreme dilemmas of maintaining Jewish identity in a tolerant context. Victorian Jews' issues of assimilation and the changing roles of men and women seem similar to current issues faced by Jews in Western democracies.

The third form of erasure of this literature and history has been practiced by scholars of Victorian literature. In most cases, literary critics' neglect of the Victorian Jewish public sphere is comprehensible as simple ignorance, because the Victorian canon has definitionally excluded non-Protestant members of the British dominions—not only Jews, but also Gypsies, Catholics, Arabs, West Indians, and East Indians. Those scholars who have taken an interest in Jews have for the most part chosen to focus on Christian writers' representations of Jews rather than on Jews' own literary productions. Literary critics interested in the "Jewish Question" have tended to turn to the depictions of Jews by Walter Scott, Maria Edgeworth, Charles Dickens, Matthew Arnold, or George Eliot.[15] The best of this criticism has argued that these representations are moments in English Christian writers' negotiation of English national identity in a liberal state. But by focusing only on Christian writers' vision of Jews rather than seeing these representations in relation to the literature written by Jews themselves, these critics have left out half the available dialogue on the "Jewish Question." They have assumed that the responses of actual Jews (as opposed to fictional ones) are either nonexistent, unimportant, or unliterary. But, as Nancy Armstrong has suggested, Victorian culture is "a struggle among various political factions to possess its most valued signs and symbols."[16] By neglecting to record the various factions, these critics have been unable to represent Victorian culture fully.

One might expect a difference here between those critics in support of the traditional canon and those who have argued for expansion of the canon. But the latter critics have often neglected literature by and about Jews as well. While feminist literary critics of the period have grown increasingly attuned to class and race differences between groups of women, they, too, have tended not to account for religious or subcultural differences not based on race or class.[17] Those feminist scholars who have attempted to deal explicitly with religion have tended to focus only on Protestant and Catholic writers. For these critics, "English woman" still appears to mean "English Christian woman." The assumption of Christianity's universality is the fourth type of erasure.

The fifth type of erasure is the subsumption of Jews as "orientals." Those critics of the canon's "orientalism" who have considered Jews have, for some good reasons, treated the "Jewish Question" largely as a particular aspect of the "orientalist" conundrum: can an Oriental people be integrated into an Occidental nation? As biological determinism became more popular, expressed in such "sciences" as racist anthropology and England's own social Darwinism between the 1840s and 1890s, Victorian Christians (as well as a small number of Jews and converts from Judaism such as Benjamin Disraeli) increasingly categorized Jews racially, not as "white," but as "semitic."[18] This categorization meant that English Jews were seen as "eastern" or "oriental." Because of this categorization, Victorian Christian novelists and missionaries used many of the same hegemonic strategies to depict, persuade, and convert Jews as they used on other "orientals."[19] Yet Victorian attitudes toward Jewishness revealed particularities that have eluded scholars of orientalism as well.

None of these five types of critics and historians has adequately proposed or resolved the important questions raised by the Anglo-Jewish subculture's phenomenal growth and development during the nineteenth century. How did this subculture come into existence, and for what purposes? Were these purposes different for women than for men? And if so, how?

GENDERING MODERN ANGLO-JEWISH HISTORY

If this study is to answer such questions, it will need to provide an alternative to the men-only story that has up to now been transmitted as the history of the Anglo-Jewish *haskalah*. It will need to show how and why Anglo-Jewish women's experiences of and attitudes toward historical movements like emancipation and reform often differed from men's.[20] Most importantly it will need to show why men's attitudes toward these movements led them to produce very little writing, while women's attitudes led them to break the taboos of centuries and publish books. To lay the groundwork for these inquiries, here are two historical sketches—a sketch of the standard history of Anglo-Jewish men, explaining their reticence, followed by a sketch that suggests what a revised history might look like when taking women's experiences and production of literature into account.

First Sketch: Anglo-Jewish Men and the Desire for Union

When Jews were readmitted into England in 1656, a few scattered Sephardic families returned with Menasseh ben Israel who had been crypto-Jews—that is, Jews who had survived the Spanish Inquisition by pretending to be Catholics while secretly continuing to practice Judaism. These wealthy Sephardim were the original members of the new Anglo-Jewish community. By the end of the eighteenth century, the majority of English Jews were Ashkenazim. These two communities remained distinct until the controversy in 1753 over the Jewish Naturalization Bill (or "Jew Bill"), which would have enabled a small number of wealthy Jews to become naturalized. The bill passed through Parliament, but engendered a bitter pamphlet war and several violent incidents. Pamphleteers denounced the "Judaising" of the English nation. The incidents resulted in the bill's repeal a year later. In the wake of this experience, the Sephardic and Ashkenazic communities began to correspond sporadically and informally, finding that they shared a set of interests, at least as regarded gaining emancipation from the external Victorian world. After 1760, the two groups sporadically communicated with each other to represent themselves as a single group to the Christian government. In 1817, the Board of Deputies of British Jews, the cross-communal institution for liaison with the state, was formalized.[21] The necessity of representing themselves to a Christian government that, not recognizing the differences between them, expected them to speak as a body, pressured Ashkenazim and Sephardim to find a common voice for the purposes of diplomacy.

The formation of a cross-communal institution served them, for like other Western European Jewish communities during the early nineteenth century, the Anglo-Jewish community was beginning to modernize. That is, it was beginning to undergo the two transitions of emancipation and reform. Reformers in Germany and France were completely revamping their communities—dismantling the communal systems of government, changing the practices and architecture of the synagogue, altering the education systems, and introducing new literary forms such as the sermon into Jewish life. Perhaps most importantly for the purposes of this study, continental Jewish reformers' pens were busy in the service of their cause: they produced an enormous number of tracts, histories, novels, sermons, and periodicals arguing for various reforms. Parallel with this internal revolution, Jewish men were attempting to revolutionize relations with the external world, the dominant cultures of their host countries. Emancipationists were arguing for the removal of all legal, political, economic, and social disabilities from which Jews suffered at the hands of European governments. Like religious reformers, these emancipationists produced an enormous number of books and tracts.

Compared to their continental contemporaries, Anglo-Jewish men produced very little in the way of polemical writing about either of these movements. In fact, several prominent historians of Anglo-Jewish culture have claimed that English Jews produced no significant emancipation movement because they produced little emancipationist theoretical or polemical writing. Rather, the argument goes, the English Jews were much more practical than their continental brethren, preferring to stand for office rather than to write a book, or to use their influence and wealth to gain emancipation rather than to use the public press.[22] If they did not experience an emancipation movement that required manifestoes, the standard history argues that English Jews did not experience a reform movement that required them, either. Traditionalists and reformers basically overcame their differences after a short period of troubling debate with a few pragmatic alterations in synagogue decorum. According to this argument, in both the external movement for emancipation and the internal movement for religious reform, English Jews were pragmatists, not ideologues or writers.

It is true that Anglo-Jewish *men's* pragmatic approach to gaining emancipation did not call for a great deal of polemicizing. For the most part, they felt that emancipation was a much less urgent affair than did their continental contemporaries. Nor did reform in England, in their estimation, require a great deal of polemic. Their relative equanimity can be explained by their comfort in the increasingly liberal English context. By 1830, when English Jews first began to argue for the removal of civil and municipal disabilities, their community was for the first time beginning to feel comfortably settled. As V. D. Lipman explains, Victorian Jewry, "though containing a number of recent immigrants, was, in the main, a community of some standing; the bulk of its members was of families settled over fifty years, due to the most marked period of immigration having been between 1750 and 1800."[23] This settledness marks a fundamental difference between English Jewry of the period and other West European communities as in Germany and France, who were undergoing a period of profound instability and change. Reformers in these communities were struggling against centuries-old national, communal traditions. By contrast, the Anglo-Jewish community in 1830 was only just reaching a size that would permit the men to begin the process of *creating* communal structures. Early nineteenth-century Anglo-Jewish men were the architects of a period of growth, homogenization, and consolidation. In creating communal structures they did draw on reformist ideas of their German and French coreligionists. Still, unlike the continental reformers, the Anglo-Jewish men did not necessarily feel that they needed to reject their heritage first before they could build the community. Relatively small and young as their community was, they did not have to fight well-established communal traditions in order to form it.[24]

Indeed, at first, the community-building effort was not in the least driven by a desire to reform the traditional ritual and synagogue practices. Rather, the effort was driven by the desire to overcome religio-cultural diversity between Sephardim and Ashkenazim within the community and present a unified front to the government. The formation of a common institution for contacting the external world enabled a crossover in social contacts in the internal world, perhaps best measured by the number of Sephardic-Ashkenazic intermarriages that began to appear. Already by 1850, the Sephardim and the Ashkenazim were substantially integrated, with 38 percent of brides at Bevis Marks (the Sephardic synagogue) of Ashkenazic descent.[25] Other cross-communal institutions including the Jewish Board of Guardians (1854) and the Jews College (1855) were soon formed. The Sephardic and Ashkenazic communities brought very different cultural heritages to England—but as both groups had reason to seek to be recognized as "British Jews," both were increasingly able to reinterpret their differences so as to support union rather than dissension. The desire to build a strong "Anglo-Jewish" community increasingly outweighed the desire to maintain religio-cultural particularity.

Although both Ashkenazic and Sephardic men emphasized union, they did so for different reasons. The Sephardim were the oldest, most settled, and most wealthy segment of the community, having almost wholly comprised the small Jewish community in England from resettlement in 1656 until the beginning of the eighteenth century. Having descended from crypto-Jews or New Christians who fled from the Inquisitions in Spain and Portugal to Amsterdam and from there to England, they were undergoing a process that has been called rejudaisation. That is, they were rediscovering and claiming their Jewish heritage. One result of this rediscovery was their desire to create a

Jewish communal structure. Forced to hide their Judaism from the Holy Office of the Inquisition, they often took full advantage of the opportunity to bring their Judaism into the open in more liberal and tolerant countries. Their experience as crypto-Jews led some Sephardic expatriates to convert to Christianity in their new homes, if only because of the practical gains to be had by conversion, and because over time they came to feel estranged from Jewishness.[26] But those crypto-Jewish men who did not convert were not so invested in denigrating traditional Judaism as, say, German-Jewish reformers. As Spanish and Portuguese Jews, they looked back for heroes to the Golden Age of Spain in the tenth through twelfth centuries, and found their "enlightened" example in Maimonides, the medieval Sephardic philosopher, commentator, and teacher. Their rejudaisation supported a sense of solidarity with other Sephardim, and with other Jews.

On the other hand, rejudaisation did not necessarily mean adopting the traditional religious or communal practices. Having experienced the effects of persecution firsthand, Sephardim in England were likely to adopt from their new host country a liberal ideology that emphasized tolerance of minority groups—indeed, some historians argue that crypto-Jews invented the ideology of liberalism.[27] At the very least, crypto-Jews had brought with them from Amsterdam a philosophy emphasizing skepticism, tolerance, and individual choice over communal authority. This liberal approach affected the way they structured their community. When they first arrived in England, Anglo-Sephardic men did reproduce the kind of coercive communal structure traditional to Sephardic communities, with severe regulations called *Ascamot*. Perhaps this was a last attempt to preserve the traditional Jewish structure of halachic communal regulation. But this structure was in tension with their liberal approach, and could not last in a liberal environment like England. By 1830, they were rejecting this form of communal life.[28] They increasingly wanted to create a community in which institutions would rely on Jews' voluntary contributions and support. This desire was supported by the structure of most Protestant communities in Victorian life. Sephardim tended to use liberal means to make their voices heard—though a minority of English Jews by 1830, they were prominent among the founders of the Anglo-Jewish public sphere, creating journals and literary institutions, and writing books meant to be consumed both by Jews and by the general public.[29] Among men who did publish, they were at the top of the list. Increasingly, although they showed a religio-cultural pride that almost amounted to a sense of nobility at various times,[30] their liberalism meant a desire to become emancipated and anglicized— that is, free of political and social disabilities and reflecting in their customs and manners an "English" national identity. It also meant a toleration for the differences between them and the Ashkenazim. Both their desire for acceptance as full citizens and their toleration of differences among themselves were necessary elements in their ability to create a voluntary British community.

Like the Sephardim, the Anglo-Ashkenazic men were substantially less interested in reform than their counterparts in Germany or France. Although the earliest immigrants to England were Spanish and Portuguese Jews, they had been followed by German-Polish Jews seeking economic and political opportunity. By the 1830s there were a number of wealthy or middle-class Ashkenazim in London. English Ashkenazim found that they already enjoyed greater toleration than did their coreligionists in Germany. David Sorkin has argued that the Jewish emancipation and reform movements in Germany depended heavily for their momentum on the partialness of German toleration in an anti-Semitic context. In contrast, he argues, English toleration was virtually already on the books and in the streets, even though there were still a few restrictive laws and occasional incidents of social discrimination.[31] Consequently the Anglo-Ashkenazic men felt less need to reform themselves in order to prove their worthiness to be included in the general public life than did their German and French coreligionists. If, like the Ashkenazi editor of the *Hebrew Review and Magazine of Rabbinical Literature* (1834–36) they cited as a precursor Moses Mendelssohn, founder of the German-Jewish Enlightenment, they also translated great portions of the *Shulchan Aruch,* the fifteenth-century code of traditional Jewish daily ritual observance.[32] If, like the editor, Morris Raphall, they denigrated the legends and lore called Aggadah within the Talmud, they praised the legal debates called halacha "and the discussions connected with them,—conducted with profound wisdom and acute logical reasoning." Like Raphall, if they called some comments of the rabbis into question, they also declared, "we are neither innovators nor reformers."[33]

As a whole, then, most Anglo-Jewish men from both segments of the community had a greater level of comfort with traditional Judaism and a greater desire for a voluntary semiautonomous Jewish communal structure than did the German Jews. Not that the movements for reform and emancipation shaking the continent were ignored by

Anglo-Jewish men. On the contrary, they did import these movements, but altered them for their own purposes. When the most radical of the reformers among both the Sephardim and Ashkenazim joined together in 1841 to build their own synagogue, the West London Synagogue for British Jews, there was indeed a grave splintering within the community. The Chief Rabbi responded by excommunicating the reformers, an exceedingly rare move in the history of Anglo-Jewish responses to "heresy." But although it seemed for a while as if the debate might produce a wide gulf between Jews, for men the debate seemed to resolve itself rather quietly after several heated years. Although they were formally split, the two factions were not as far apart as they seemed. The break had more to do with uniting the Sephardim and the Ashkenazim as "British Jews" than with theoretical distinctions between orthodoxy and reform.

In the first place, most Jewish men who styled themselves "orthodox" were lax in their ritual observance, and had greatly assimilated English manners, speech, and fashions.[34] Moreover, as the period progressed, the "orthodox" synagogues came to seem more and more like the "reformers'." As Cecil Roth puts it, the reformers' "influence on the conservative majority, though unacknowledged, was nevertheless considerable. Synagogue decorum improved, organized choirs were introduced, the vernacular sermon became the rule, education was reorganized, and ministers of religion began to replace the old type of synagogal factotum." Even when the break between traditionalists and reformers occurred in 1841, the difference between the two groups "was one rather of presentation than of dogma."[35] The radical reformers in England were not nearly so radical as their German counterparts. Because the groups were not so distinct as in Germany, the men often felt that the two camps had more in common than in dispute. By 1870, the official breach between the two camps had been smoothed over, the reform synagogue invited to join the United Synagogue, the umbrella community structure. In other words, for Anglo-Jewish men the continental agitation for reform was not a point of intense controversy. They had less of an inner drive to reform Judaism, which meant that they had less to say about it. Their quiet pragmatic approach to reform meant a relatively small written production in the form of polemical tracts, fictional, or poetic texts.

They were also relatively tacit on the subject of emancipation, but for different reasons. Whereas the German Jews saw the reform and emancipation movements as complementary, Anglo-Jewish men from both sections of the community felt the movements were separate and required different responses, neither of which were "ideological." The reform movement in Germany was tied to the movement for emancipation in that the German Jews felt they must regenerate themselves and their "degraded" religion via reform before they could be emancipated and admitted as full members to German society. As they saw it, emancipation required them to rethink their communal structure, rituals, authorities, and beliefs. In other words, the responsibility for centuries of persecution was their own, a problem with their own selves and culture.[36] In contrast to this formula of "regeneration for rights," as David Sorkin has expressed it, Anglo-Jewish men tended to feel that their continued debarment from full civil and municipal participation was a sign of their Christian neighbors' degradation rather than their own. The greatest spiritual injury done them was a "cramping" of their individual and communal "energies," implying much less self-blame. Neither the Anglo-Ashkenazim nor the Sephardim, who had experienced English toleration for generations, felt they had to "emancipate" themselves from the "degradation" of centuries of anti-Semitic persecution and rabbinic tyranny. In a more pragmatic and less self-denigrating vein, they felt they had to "agitate for the removal of disabilities."

If, as Todd Endelman has suggested, Anglo-Jewish men did not produce an indigenous theory of emancipation, it was because they had no autonomous community whose breakdown they had to theorize and explain. Nor did they have to fight a large social or political anti-Semitic ideology. Rather than requiring a renewed vision of Judaism (a reform movement), Anglo-Jewish men's emancipation required the setting up of an Association for the Removal of Jewish Civil and Municipal Disabilities, repeated lobbying of Parliament, and the standing for election to Sheriff, Mayor of London, and MP to challenge the laws. If Anglo-Jewish men responded to the prospect of reform by quietly changing their synagogues and liturgical practices, they responded to the challenge of emancipation no less pragmatically by exercising influence and standing for office. This is the usual history of English Jews in the period of emancipation and reform.

Second Sketch: Anglo-Jewish Women and the Desire for Equity

But this picture is not complete. A major component of the history of the Anglo-Jewish *haskalah* is missing, for women wanted different things than men from the emancipation and reform. First of all, if for men the two movements were separate and unrelated, for women the movements were inseparable. The external emancipation of Jews from England's oppressive laws suggested to them the possibility of an internal emancipation of women from Judaism's oppressive laws. External emancipation thus inspired and dictated the kind of internal reforms they called for, including among other things, a place in the synagogue next to the men, access to biblical and other Jewish texts through translation, increased female education, perhaps even a ceremony commensurate to the Bar Mitzvah in the life of Jewish girls. For example, Grace Aguilar focuses attention on the emancipation while calling women to read and interpret the Bible:

> A new era is dawning for us. Persecution and intolerance have in so many lands ceased to predominate, that Israel may once more breathe in freedom; the law need no longer be preached in darkness, and obeyed in secret; the voice of man need no longer be the vehicle of instruction from father to son. . . . The Bible may be perused in freedom. . . . Free to assert their right as immortal children of the living God, let not the women of Israel be backward in proving they, too, . . . have a station to uphold, and a "mission" to perform, not alone as daughters, wives, and mothers, but as witnesses of that faith which first raised, cherished, and defended them. . . . [37]

Aguilar follows this peroration on Jewish and female freedom with a specific set of proposals, bemoaning the "sad scarcity of religious books amongst us, in modern tongues" (2:34), and arguing that "the religious as well as the moral duties of the law are . . . equally incumbent on *woman* as well as man" (1:180). If most men felt the reformist controversy was a rather minor debate over synagogue decorum, which flared bright but quickly died down, many women felt they had a great deal at stake in the reform movement, which was not about decorum but about gender inequality. Unlike men, women were hardly silent on the issue. For writers like Marion Hartog, Anna Maria Goldsmid, and Grace Aguilar reform was not primarily about religious dogma or practice, but about women's roles in the new community.

These women often found that Jewish men attempted to dissuade them from claiming such "modern" freedoms. In the relatively few essays, commentaries on biblical texts, and novels they produced, Anglo-Jewish men depicted Jewish women as undereducated, a sign that women were a "weakness in our camp."[38] While men argued for increased female education (if only so that women would be qualified to impart the tradition to children at home), they did little to achieve this goal, and censored women's attempts to educate themselves. Reformists and traditionalists alike agreed that women and men should occupy separate spheres, which they feared might collapse if women were educated. In response, Jewish women often wrote stories in which young women represent the "modern" stance, while old men tend to represent the traditionalist stance. Anglo-Jewish women writers often imagined that female education and empowerment and the religious and communal reforms required by modernity went hand in hand. If for Anglo-Jewish men, reform required a gentle critique of an older generation, for Anglo-Jewish women it required an often stinging critique of Jewish patriarchal notions of women's sphere. It required them to transgress the "exemption" on women's intellectual work and publish books.

This desire to critique sometimes meant that women were more outspoken than men on inequities occurring within the Jewish community. If men were attempting to produce union rather than dissension, women writers were sometimes the only voices in the community willing to describe publicly the differences between segments of the community. This was true, by and large, of Jewish women writers' outspoken defense of reformers, women, and the poor. For example, Charlotte Montefiore, noted essayist and member of one of English Jewry's wealthiest and most distinguished families, attacked conversionist exploitation of the Jewish poor in *Caleb Asher* (1845) and she attacked the Jewish class system in *A Few Words to the Jews. By One of Themselves* (1853). Marion Hartog consistently argued for redress of the inequities women suffered in the *Jewish Sabbath Journal* (1855). While Anglo-Jewish men did have disagreements among themselves, they preferred to deal with them quietly rather than publish them in forums open to the purview of Christians, who Jewish men feared might use Jews' internal dissension as an excuse to deny them rights. Women, on the other hand, felt that unless they raised the issues of class and gender discrimination within the Jewish community, they and those they spoke for would continue to suffer from them. This provided additional incentive for women to publish.

Just as women were more serious about reform than men and understood its aims differently, they also approached Jewish emancipation from a different standpoint. Unable to stand for office or hold meetings with the prime minister, Anglo-Jewish women still wanted to be involved with the attempt to gain Jewish emancipation. Like German-Jewish salonières such as Rahel Varnhagen, upper-class women in the community exerted influence by holding great parties to which they invited non-Jews important to the emancipationist cause. Perhaps such parties could be interpreted as female versions of the men's pragmatic approach.[39] With the exception of the very wealthy, however, women did not have the men's option of standing pragmatically for office in their approach to emancipation. Middle-class women adopted the only other instrument available—the pen.

It is significant that most of the emancipationist novels and polemics by women proceeded from the middle classes, whereas wealthy women's productions tended to address Jewish-only audiences, as with Judith Montefiore's etiquette and recipe book, or Charlotte Montefiore's tracts and the tales in her Cheap Jewish Library. Middle-class women like Celia and Marion Moss and Grace Aguilar tended to be bolder in their criticisms of the Christian Victorians. Perhaps they assimilated the emboldened stance of their middle-class English Christian female contemporaries, who were outspoken as social reformers and novelists.[40] Since such female reformism was not as prominent on the continent, that would also help explain why middle-class Jewish women elsewhere did not adopt the same example. By the time the first wave of mass Jewish immigrations to London from Eastern Europe began to arrive in 1880, changing the character of the Anglo-Jewish community completely, Jewish women had been producing these critiques for half a century.

THE ORIGIN OF JEWISH WOMEN WRITERS' GENRES

Driven in part by their desire to establish a particular communal vision of reform and emancipation, women began to publish books. Yet why did they gravitate toward the novel? The English novel was a secularized Protestant narrative form, foreign to Jewish literary history.[41] Why didn't Jewish women draw on Jewish literary history? To some degree, they did. Sephardic women drew on the crypto-Jewish heritage of women passing down the oral history of the Inquisition. They used the crypto-Jewish experience of passing as Christians as a metaphor for the anglicization they themselves were undergoing. A small number of Yiddish-speaking Ashkenazic women drew on their heritage to produce volumes of *tekhinot*. Both groups drew on the ancient Jewish literary form of Aggadah, creative retellings of biblical narratives with contemporary relevance, examples of which they read in Anglo-Jewish male periodicals such as the *Hebrew Review and Magazine of Rabbinical Literature* (1834–36). And both groups drew on the tradition of biblical women's possession of superior prophetic powers to justify their didactic and polemical appeals for justice, both to Jewish men and to non-Jews. In other words, Anglo-Jewish women did look to Jewish literary history for forms and tropes they could adopt, only to alter these forms and tropes so as to be relevant to their gendered experience of the modern movements for emancipation and reform.

Yet they also wrote novels. The bare fact that they did suggests two important insights about the state of the Anglo-Jewish community. First, it suggests that English Jews encountered a liberal dominant culture in which the novel was a literary form through which many concerns about the place of the Other in society were circulated. Second, it suggests that the Jewish community was itself trying to be liberal and was interested in forming bonds with the dominant culture that went beyond submission to or resistance against coercive measures.

In order to understand why Jewish women felt compelled to write novels, we need to understand what "liberal" meant in Victorian England. Jews and other minorities posed a difficult problem to Anglo-Saxon Protestant Victorians struggling to preserve the myth of an English homogeneity even while their domestic borders were increasingly flooded with peoples of many colors, religions, and nationalities. This influx of heterogeneity was due to the combination of imperial British military and economic expansion abroad with the promise of tolerant liberalism at home. In addition to the diverse groups that had been struggling within the British dominions for centuries— Normans, Saxons, and Jews; Catholics and Protestants; Scots, Welsh, and Irish—the dominant English were experiencing an influx of Indians, West Indians, Arab Muslims, and Gypsies. During the Victorian period, then, dominant white Protestants in Britain increasingly confronted difference, not only in their colonies abroad, but on what they thought of as their own shores.

Theories of what to do with these diverse populations ranged from Carlyle's defense of the white Protestant character of the nation to

J. S. Mill's proposal to persuade Jews and others to adopt an "English" set of customs, fashions, etc., to T. B. Macaulay's principle of liberal toleration. In relation to other peoples and nations abroad, the English seemed quite able to support violent practices in order to secure subjugation. In relation to minorities at home, however, Victorians across the spectrum had been so affected by the ideology of liberalism that they no longer supported explicit forms of coercion to secure compliance with dominant cultural expectations. To be sure, there were still members of an old guard who voiced support for severe measures on occasion. Yet, as could be seen in the Catholic Emancipation Act of 1828, the abolition of the slave trade, and the various Jewish emancipation acts, the trend was toward increasing toleration.

The word *toleration* should be used advisedly, however. While it might mean the abrogation of legal and political disabilities, it did not mean the complete social acceptance of minorities, particularly of Jews. No doubt their coreligionists in Germany or in Eastern Europe still faced a great deal more persecution of the explicit type—murder, extortion, disability under the law. English Jews increasingly faced a different sort of dominant culture—a liberal culture that, having decided not to support coercive measures, still exerted noncoercive pressures on minorities to conform to dominant standards. This "persuasive" attitude toward Jews emerged during the seventeenth century, when Puritans like John Milton and George Withers practiced what they called "philo-Semitism." Like "toleration," the term was misleading. It did not mean loving Jews; it meant using love as a political strategy to persuade Jews to convert. The end goal was the same as that of the Holy Office during the Inquisition: Jews' conversion. Jewishness still had to be eradicated, but now the individual person hidden in the Jew was supposed to be "reclaimed" with self-respect and dignity intact. Philo-Semites can thus be distinguished from other kinds of conversionists by their belief in and use of persuasive carrots rather than coercive sticks. As the old Anglo-Jewish joke had it, "What's a philo-Semite? An anti-Semite who loves Jews."[42]

By the early nineteenth century, this sort of persuasive conversionism had taken a broad hold. Victorian Jews faced several powerful conversionist societies (such as the London Society for the Promotion of Christianity Amongst the Jews, established 1807, and the Philo-Judaeans, established 1820), which were sanctioned by the Crown as well as by prominent politicians on both sides of the aisle. These conversionists were among the greatest supporters of Jews' political emancipation, on the theory that Jews would see how enlightened and moral their Christian neighbors were and would be encouraged to convert. In essence, they offered Jews a bargain: in return for the individual's agreement to shed his or her mark of difference, tolerant liberal Christians promised full social and political integration.

Jewish women were specifically targeted by "tolerant" conversionist societies. Conversionists attempted to persuade women in a number of specific ways. They referred to Jewish women's "malleability" and "impressionability," which was assumed to be part of the charm of their "oriental" natures. In order to undermine women's allegiance to Judaism and to their families, conversionists also repeatedly called attention to Judaism's inegalitarian stance toward women: since Judaism (and moreover Jewish men) oppressed women, the plea went, women should be eager to embrace a religion in which they were held in the highest esteem. Indeed, conversionists insisted that under their ideology, religiosity was woman's innate gift and the inculcation of religion to children was her most important task. The dominant Victorian Christian domestic ideology from which conversionists drew this sentiment considered the public sphere of business and government as the "secular" sphere, while the private domestic sphere was considered the sphere of spirituality and emotionality. Women were thus increasingly identified with religiosity—and women were to be caretakers of a higher, more spiritual feeling than their husbands could afford for themselves, their hands constantly mired in the muck of the marketplace. Feminist scholars of the period have begun referring to this belief in women's special aptitude for spirituality as the "feminization of religion."[43] Since all women were assumed to tend toward true religiosity anyway, conversionists might well target Jewish women and merely lift the obstructing veil of Judaism from their eyes.

From a literary historical standpoint, this philo-Semitic sort of "toleration," with its emphasis on using persuasive methods, had crucial effects on Christian novelists' representation of Jews. One of the most visible persuasive methods conversionists developed was the romance of Jewish identity. Conversionist romances pitied Jews' plight and invited them to join English society fully through "radical assimilation" or conversion.[44] They particularly targeted Jewish women, typically depicting a Jewish woman abandoning her family and community to convert and marry a charismatic Christian suitor. They drew on the Shakespearean conflict between the Jewish father and daughter in *Merchant of Venice,* but they no longer cared about Shylock; instead, they increasingly focused on, pitied, and sought to win over Jessica. The Jewish woman was depicted as alien, sensual, "oriental"—and above all, as malleable to the suitor's persuasive efforts. Moreover, she was increasingly seen as an emblem of the Jewish community as a whole. That is, the Jewish community was understood to be female, in the sense that it could be "conquered" and "wooed" to the truth that is in Jesus by the gentle yet firm persistence of a "tolerant" liberal Christian culture.[45]

All of the earliest Anglo-Jewish women writers felt that they had to respond to the romance genre. Maria Polack published her anti-romance, *Fiction Without Romance; or, the Locket-Watch* in 1830; Aguilar wrote her historical romance *The Vale of Cedars; or, the Martyr* between 1831 and 1835 centering on a Jewish woman in the Inquisition in Spain; and the Mosses published the *Romance of Jewish History* (1840) and *Tales of Jewish History* (1843), romances that directly assimilated the conversionist romances in order to transform them. In addition, several other Anglo-Jewish women writers, including Judith Montefiore in the preface to her recipe and conduct book *The Jewish Manual* (1846), and Charlotte Montefiore, in her *A Few Words to the Jews. By One of Themselves* (1853) took stands against romance. There are at least three reasons for this extended engagement with romance by Anglo-Jewish women. First of all, the romance form, as it appeared in Scott, Edgeworth, Thackeray, Bulwer Lytton, and Lewis, seemed to target Jewish women in particular for conversion. Secondly, since Jewish women frequently appeared in romance, it was a dominant cultural form in which they already occupied a legitimate position. Their adoption of this dominant cultural form was seen by many of them as an entry-ticket into full cultural participation in the Victorian world. The assimilation of the romance form itself is for many of them the emblem of the movement of Jews into the modern world. Finally, romance was frequently aligned with reform in the Jewish community, both the genre and the religious ideology honoring individual freedom over duty to traditional communal affiliations. By adopting or writing against the genre, then, Jewish women could position themselves along a continuum of Jews as traditionalists or reformers.

Women writers thus used the novel to argue not only for women's emancipation in the Jewish world, but for Jewish emancipation in the Victorian world. Adopting literary strategies from the non-Jewish world was an aspect of their attempt to persuade non-Jews to accept them as full English subjects. On the other hand, adopting literary strategies from Jewish men was an aspect of their attempt to persuade men to accept them as full Jews. In both cases, they not only assimilated the forms they inherited, but altered these forms to meet their needs as women. The tensions between their needs as women, as Jews, and as English subjects created a fluid and dynamic identity in which their gender, subculture, and nationality were often influencing their decisions about literary genre.[46]

This fluidity makes these texts crucial sources in the current critical debates over whether and how various aspects of a multifaceted identity reinforce and obstruct one another. At some points these writers' Jewishness suggests one course of action or interpretation of their position in the English nation, while their gender suggests a contradictory course or interpretation. For example, as Jews, these writers would like to refute the conversionist accusation that they are undereducated so as to prove to Christians their worthiness to be accepted as English, while as women they want to agree with the conversionists' claims so as to persuade Jewish men to provide them with greater educational opportunities. At other points, subculture and gender reinforce one another against nationality. For example, the experience of English national oppression is shared by Jews and women as Victorian subgroups—indeed, the experience of agitating for Jewish emancipation inspires some women to agitate for women's emancipation. Each writer's experience of history and choice of genre depends not only on subcultural, national, and gender affiliations, but on her class, religiosity, and on how long her family had been settled in England.

To revise Victorian Jewish cultural history with attention to all of these categories of identity is to rediscover the dialogues that took place between Christians and Jews about what should constitute English national identity. It is to rediscover the dialogues—so often lost—that took place between Jewish women and men at the doorstep of modernity. This commitment to rediscovering dialogues rather than telling a history in only one voice proceeds both out of a profeminist commitment to women's various and unique articulations of their processes and experiences and out of a progressive Jewish commitment as old as midrash to the possibility of multiple legitimate contending perspectives. Progressive Jews and feminists agree with one another that pluralistic dialogues over contested categories of identity provide the fullest sense critics can achieve of a diverse collective past.[47]

This is not to suggest that feminism and Judaism are always in concordance with one another. In fact, the dilemma which is at the heart of this study demonstrates that the two often coexist in tension. For, finally, how does one place a value on the development of an Anglo-Jewish women's novel-writing tradition? When looked at from the standpoint of gender, the history of Anglo-Jewish women's writing looks like the history of empowerment—from a feminist perspective, a positive development. But if one looks at Anglo-Jewish women's assimilation of the novel form from the standpoint of Jewish cultural continuity, with a late-twentieth-century perspective on the efficacy of the assimilationist model, then the development of the Anglo-Jewish novel looks like a potentially negative result of hegemony. The two views appear to contradict one another. In fact, since they result from two different positionings, they have no power to cancel each other out, but rather coexist uneasily. To write within this dilemma is the task of profeminist, late-twentieth-century Jewish cultural history.

ONE
WALTER SCOTT AND THE CONVERSIONISTS

Why did Victorian Jewish women in the 1830s and 1840s pick up the pen? And what resources did they bring to the task? This chapter begins to answer the first of these questions by exploring the pressures acting on Anglo-Jewish women from the dominant culture in the late eighteenth and early nineteenth centuries. Specifically, it argues that non-Jewish writers depicted Jewish women using the representational techniques of "orientalism": they depicted their heroines as dark, sensuous, malleable, and amenable to persuasion. And they saw these heroines as emblems for the Jewish community as a whole.[1] It was these charges—of Jewish women's impressionability, of their capacity for conversion—to which Jewish women writers came to feel they had to respond.

These charges were given a forcible new life when Walter Scott published his historical romance *Ivanhoe* (1819), depicting a spiritual Jewish woman, in thrall to her materialistic father but attracted to a charismatic Christian suitor. A series of conversionist romances followed, revealing that dominant English culture was undergoing a shift in perspective toward Jews. Rather than using premodern coercive means such as torture, extortion, or threats of expulsion to force Jews into radical assimilation, Victorians such as M. G. Lewis in *Jewish Maiden* (1830), Amelia Bristow in *Rosette and Miriam* (1837), Edward Bulwer Lytton in *Leila* (1837), and William Makepeace Thackeray in *Rebecca and Rowena* (1843) were attempting to use persuasive means—that is, fiction—to achieve the same end. Believing that Jews who felt invited into Victorian culture would choose to join it fully through conversion, these novelists came to see a particular kind of romance novel as a persuasive political instrument. To see why and how is the work of this chapter.

SPEAKING THE JEW

Aside from the readmission of Jews in 1656, and the Jew Bill controversy of 1753, the first thirty years of the nineteenth century saw more attempts by Christians to rethink the role of the Jew in British society than during any time in English history. By 1815, for the first time since the Expulsion, an Anglo-Jewish community was developing that was large enough to be visible, to have its own identity, and to have an impact on non-Jewish society. The passing of Acts of Parliament enabling Dissenters and Catholics to hold office and vote in the 1820s served as a catalyst for Jews seeking the removal of Jewish disabilities. Beginning in 1830 and continuing for the next thirty years, Jews stirred up a pamphlet and press flurry on the issue that at one point was so controversial it nearly brought down the government.[2] As Jews saw it, the fate of their bid for full citizenship was connected to the fate of other marginalized religious and racial groups in the Victorian period. As a result, they advocated for both Catholic Emancipation and the end of the slave trade. Emancipationist Jews were thus natural allies of Christian liberals, and at least some Christian liberals, such as Thomas Babington Macaulay and Robert Grant, acknowledged the alliance.[3] It was no accident that the first Reform Bill was passed just two years after the Jews began to agitate for removal of disabilities. Removal of Jewish disabilities and liberal reform were part of the same cultural movement toward increasing the number of marginalized groups who could exercise influence over the direction of Victorian society. Thus as the nineteenth century continued, it became increasingly necessary for non-Jewish Victorians to rethink the role of the Jew in England, if only because it was necessary to think through the role of liberalism in England. As Thomas Carlyle put it in his anonymous antiemancipationist pamphlet "The Jew Our Lawgiver," allowing Jews into Parliament would be a disastrous result of "Infidel liberalism," and would lead eventually to the total franchise of all men in England.[4] The figure of the Jew was one of the tropes by which the English would understand themselves as a nation.[5]

While Victorian Jews allied themselves with Christian liberals, most of them understood too well that liberalism did not necessarily offer them full coexistence. Rather, Christian liberals frequently believed that Jews ought to convert. This sort of conversionist liberalism could and often did fuel an enormous energy on behalf of Jews' "betterment." Out of such love philo-Semitic activists founded Hebrew Christian Free Schools for poor Jews. There, Jews were given food and shelter, were taught sewing and basket weaving, and by the bye, were introduced to the Gospel. It was likewise no accident that many of the liberal MPs attempting to extend the franchise to Jewish men, open the city of London to Jewish commerce, and remove obstacles from Jews' holding political office were also members of conversion societies. Liberals were convinced that by taking pity on Jews' suffering and removing their legal and economic disabilities, Parliament would demonstrate the superiority of the English Christian character, being exposed to which Jews would naturally desire to convert. "Toleration" translated into a specific set of political practices. These liberal reforms enacted out of philo-Semitic motives were the political ground in which the non-Jewish "novel of Jewish identity" developed.

When Jews in philo-Semitic writings were not being pitied, persuaded, and converted, they were being made into metaphors—for the virtues as well as the excesses of the modern Christian nation. In nineteenth-century English literary history it is virtually always true to say that when non-Jews write about Jews, they are really writing about themselves. Quite flexibly, Jews were made to represent selfish materialism (Carlyle), romantic wandering (Coleridge, Wordsworth, Byron), legalism and the market (Blake), Jacobinism (Burke), capitalism (Scott), criminality (Dickens), pauperism (Mayhew), and philanthropy (Cumberland, Edgeworth, and Dickens). For these writers the Jew served as a projection of their fears and hopes for those ideologies and institutions that defined their own secularized Christian existence.[6]

Of all the various strands of non-Jewish thought about Jews that appeared during the late eighteenth and early nineteenth centuries, a single genre elicited more fictional and polemical responses by Jewish writers than any other: the romance novel that took as its starting point the plot of Shakespeare's *Merchant of Venice*.[7] Victorian novelists casting about for a plot to examine "the Jew" most frequently looked to Shylock and his daughter Jessica. The romance genre basing itself on Shakespeare's plot portrayed the Jewish community in some complexity, addressed it explicitly, and introduced a Jewish female character. There were two basic novelistic uses of *Merchant,* one of which elicited polemical responses from Jews, the other of which elicited fictional responses.

First, there was the attempt, made by Richard Cumberland in *The Jew* (1794), Maria Edgeworth in *Harrington* (1817), and Charles Dickens in *Our Mutual Friend* (1871) to rehabilitate the image of the Jewish man by replacing the stereotype of the dirty moneylender Shylock with that of the benevolent philanthropist. It is difficult to tell what kind of impact the earliest of these representations had on Jews, since the Jews had no public press until 1834, and no press committed to relations with the non-Jewish world until 1841. But Jews looking back on these representations from later in the century seemed to dismiss their impact on the Anglo-Jewish community's vision of itself.[8] The revision of the moneylender as benevolent philanthropist was welcomed by Jews as a relief, but the shrewder among them saw that it was simply replacing one stereotype with another equally unreal, or as the Anglo-Jewish poet and novelist Amy Levy was to put it in discussing the Fagin/Riah pairing in Dickens, the novelist "tries to compensate for his having affixed the label 'Jew' to one of his bad fairies by creating the good fairy Riah."[9]

Still, these novels could not be dismissed out of hand, since they did tend to introduce a female character to whom Jewish women novelists would feel it necessary to respond. Drawing on the sketchy existence of Jessica in *Merchant,* these novelists tended to endow their moneylender-turned-philanthropist with a daughter, one who could be seen as a role model by the Anglo-Jewish writers who were looking to the dominant culture to provide models. But these revised Jessicas—who, unlike their source, did not steal their father's money and marry out without his permission, but were rather spiritual and beautiful—disappointed the Jews. When a Jewish woman did appear, like Berenice in *Harrington,* she usually turned out to have been Christian all along. All in all, when one cast one's eyes over the whole field, as Amy Levy did in 1886, there did not seem much to which Jews could relate. Taking even *Daniel Deronda* (1876) into account, Levy argued, "There has been no serious attempt at serious treatment of the subject; at grappling in its entirety with the complex problem of Jewish life and Jewish character. The Jew, as we know him to-day, with his curious mingling of diametrically opposed qualities; his surprising virtues and no less surprising vices; leading his eager, intricate life; living, moving, and having his being both within and without the tribal limits; this deeply interesting product of civilization has been found worthy of none but the most superficial observation."[10] Perhaps because of this feeling that non-Jewish novelists of Jewish identity failed to grapple with the complexity of Jewish life, few of these novels elicited a fictional response from Jewish writers. Those that depicted negative stereotypes of Jews did, however, elicit multiple polemical responses. Famously, both Edgeworth and Dickens were persuaded to write novels in atonement for their negative portraits of Jews when called to account by Jewish women readers.[11] In addition, there is at least one recorded instance of Dickens having changed his plan of giving a public reading of *Oliver Twist* in response to appeals from the *Jewish Chronicle.*[12]

There was, however, a strand of representation of Jewish identity by a non-Jew, a revision of *Merchant of Venice,* which exercised Jewish women repeatedly in the 1830s and 1840s to give a fictional response. This was the representation of the relationship between father and daughter in Walter Scott's historical romance *Ivanhoe,* and in the numerous revisions of that text, which followed in the 1830s.[13] There was something in Scott's romance that felt "real" or significant to Jewish women writers. As chapter 3 will show, Jewish women assimilated the father/daughter plot and the genre of *Ivanhoe* and its successors, only to transform it so as to represent their view of Jewish reform. So how did Scott's historical romance speak to them?

Victorian romance emerged from centuries of Christian European engagement with the genre in a variety of forms—the medieval chivalric poem, the eighteenth-century criminal romance, the gothic novel, the romantic poem, and the historical romance. According to Gillian Beer, each of these subcategories is related to the others by giving "repetitive form to the particular desires of a community, and especially to those desires which cannot find controlled expression within a society."[14] Romances tend to have the feeling and function of dreams—improbable coincidences fulfill otherwise unspeakable fantasies. In the Victorian period, the romance provides a fantasy fulfillment of one dream in particular—the legitimation of a forbidden love affair between the hero and the heroine to which social expectations and the heroine's father are generally represented as the main obstacles. The hero and heroine generally hail from different classes, races, countries, or religions, and their coming together represents a fantasy of breaking through the barriers of prejudice that separate them. The hero generally belongs to the dominant group, the heroine to the marginalized group.[15]

Perhaps the Victorian romance can best be described in contrast to the realist novel that increasingly superseded it. Though the romance may deal with issues similar to those explored in the realist novel (i.e., the recognition, negotiation, and legitimation of heterosexual love), romance differs from realism in several ways. It exhibits a greater tolerance for types (e.g., the Outcast Hero, the Oppressed Daughter, the Tyrannical Father) over well-rounded characterizations. It prefers melodrama and simplicity over ambivalent moral, political, and emotional plotlines. It conventionally includes improbable coincidences and character choices rather than strictly plausible actions, feelings, and events. Finally, it legitimates individual desire and conscience over the norms and the laws of the communities in which the characters live. This last aspect aside, for Victorians, the romance was politically and religiously a reactionary form, while the realist novel was understood to be a progressive, liberal form. Romance's "tendency to simplify and allegorize character" (69), to suppose that characters were not socially constructed and could transcend social regulation, especially identified the genre with premodern Christian literature.

The realist novel, by contrast, was the form of modern secularized Protestantism, and was often thought by Christian liberals to be progressive. It assumed that characters' subjectivities were formed through negotiation with social discourses seeking to regulate them. As Beer says, "Until after Spencer the romance was still very much the dominant form of fiction. . . . With the gradual rise of the realist novel, however, it tended to be . . . in *reaction*" (7).[16] One of the ironies of Anglo-Jewish women's writing is that the Jews attempted to use the romance form for politically and religiously progressive aims. They assimilated a form that already wore the code of the Christian past for Christian readers, in order to argue for far-reaching communal and social reforms among both Christian and Jewish liberals.

The particular subcategory of the romance genre that Anglo-Jewish women writers were most drawn to adopt was the historical romance— a romance set in the context of a historical event, such as the Inquisition or the destruction of the Second Temple, and generally including historical personages as characters in the action, such as Queen Isabella or Titus. It was just this type of historical romance Walter Scott made available with the publication of *Ivanhoe*. His plot was inordinately popular among non-Jews, inspiring eleven operas and five stage productions, as well as numerous fictional imitations.[17] It was in *Ivanhoe* that for the first time the Jessica figure became the center of concern.

Scott sees the drama of the Shakespeare plot for modern readers not in the reversal of the Jewish male stereotype, not in the plot twist of making the daughter a Christian all along, but in the conflict within *Merchant* between the Jewish father and his wayward Jewish daughter. He takes this conflict and alters it in ways that turn out to be tremendously significant for Jewish self-representation. Isaac is a typical materialistic, dirty, moneylending, worldly Shylock. He is a hypocritical Jew who invokes his God only when he can secure some business by doing so. He uses Jewish ritual to forward materialistic aims; his representation is in line with a typically intolerant Christian view of Jewish ritual as in itself too material, too concerned with the formalistic letter and not concerned enough with the spirit of the law. But there are some differences between Scott's Isaac and Shakespeare's Shylock. For one thing, in himself, Isaac is much less sympathetic than Shylock, his motives those of a stock character without a "hath not a Jew eyes" speech to complicate them. On the other hand, unlike his literary progenitor, Isaac is not a tyrannical father to Rebecca, for "out of reverence for her talents . . . [he] permitted the maiden a greater liberty than was usually indulged to those of her sex by the habits of her people" (276). Most Jewish women are oppressed by their fathers, according to Scott, but not Rebecca. Perhaps this leniency is why Rebecca, unlike Jessica, bears her father such intense loyalty.

That she does so is indisputable. Not only does she remain with Isaac to the end, she defends him from his critics. In responding to Bois-Guilbert's description of Jews as money-grubbers, she says, "Thou hast spoken the Jew as the persecution of such as thou art hast made him."[18] Her defense of Isaac is a curious one in that, like Bois-Guilbert, she assumes that Isaac is indeed degraded, merely apologizing for his degradation by blaming it historically on Christian persecution. The Jewish man's degradation appears a foregone conclusion. Scott assumes that his moneylending, the economic basis for capitalism, is an inherently unspiritual occupation.

But Rebecca's defense of Isaac can only raise the question: If "the Jew" is degraded by persecution and by the taint of money, how is it that Rebecca is not degraded? If Bois-Guilbert has "spoken the Jew," he does not at all seem to have "spoken" Rebecca. How is it that she has evaded history? When she says that Bois-Guilbert has "spoken the Jew," she seems to have erased herself. For Rebecca is emphatically not your typical Jessica, running from her father, taking his money, and marrying out. Scott is rewriting the daughter's role in Shakespeare's father/daughter plot. Besides sticking with her degraded father to the end, Rebecca is "endowed with knowledge as with beauty" and is "universally revered and admired by her own tribe, who almost regarded her as one of those gifted women mentioned in the sacred history" (276). Her knowledge is of medicine and Jewish lore, her beauty is "Eastern" and "exquisitely symmetrical"[19] and "might have been compared with the proudest beauties of England" (93). Given Scott's emphasis on the importance of "race" to character formation in this novel, this last detail seems particularly important; he seems to be struggling to come to grips with the possibility that a Jewish woman could be English. In fact, the whole romance between her and Ivanhoe is set up to foreground this possibility. This Anglo-Jewish daughter seems infinitely more sympathetic than her father, who is simply unredeemable. In *Merchant*, Shylock has moments of great sympathy, but his daughter barely appears. In *Ivanhoe*, Scott has altered the focus of the Shakespeare plot from the materialistic older man to the spiritual younger woman.

What makes Rebecca so spiritually superior and how did she get to be that way? To begin with, she runs behind her father undoing his usurious acts with her generous acts of benevolence. For example, when Isaac cheats Gurth of ten zecchins, Rebecca repays that and gives Gurth an extra ninety (125–27). Here and elsewhere she goes to great lengths to show that not all Jews are materialists. Along with her benevolence, Scott describes other aspects of her moral goodness, such as the "gentleness and candour of her nature" (280) that are revealed when Ivanhoe becomes ill and she nurses him to health even though she knows he despises her as a Jew. Further, she manages to convince him of the truth of ethical monotheism, "that a Jew may do good service to a Christian, without desiring other guerdon than the blessing of the Great Father who made both Jew and Gentile" (281). It appears that she has such self-possession and such spirituality, because this spirituality is her "nature," her inborn gift, impervious apparently to the same history of persecution that degrades Isaac. His ontology is historical, hers essential. It is in her nature to understand that monetary transactions taint one with worldliness and bring about anti-Semitism, and that what makes one spiritual is the belief in the universalistic Great Father rather than any particularistic ritual acts or creed. Her ethical monotheism is a stance that was not available to any Jewish woman of the period in which Rebecca is supposed to have lived, given that it was an innovation of reform Judaism and the secularized Protestantism known as liberal humanism of Scott's own period. According to legend, Rebecca was in any case modelled, not on a medieval Jew, but on a modern Jewish woman—on Washington Irving's description of the American Portuguese Jew, Rebecca Gratz, who in the 1820s and 1830s founded both the Female Hebrew Benevolent Society and the first Jewish Sunday School in the United States.[20] Her modern spiritual superiority consisted in the knowledge that the letter killeth and the spirit giveth life. The distinction between spirituality and a materialism that encompasses both money-mindedness and legalism was itself a traditionally Christian one that Scott had secularized so as to make it appear modern, unproblematic, and universal. In fact, during the medieval period in which the novel's action is supposed to take place, the spirit/matter binary was of very little significance to Jews. It was only when, as the Anglo-Jewish novelist Benjamin Farjeon was to put it in *Grif,* "home became earth's heaven," when reformist Jews had begun to separate out the spiritual from the worldly, the religious from the secular, the domestic from the public, that the distinction between spirituality and materiality came alive for Jews. This was not yet the case in England when Scott first published his novel. His depiction is drawn, then, not from Jewish self-representation, but from a projection of his Protestant categories onto them. He bequeathes Rebecca a secularized Protestant morality that is embarrassed by what it deems worldliness (Isaac) and drawn to what it deems the universal morality of ethical monotheism.

Although from a contemporary Jewish perspective Rebecca would have been seen to be a reformer like her American namesake, Scott does not seem to have had much knowledge of modern-day or even medieval Jews, representing their rituals in ridiculous ways. He has them engage in monetary transactions in Hebrew, for instance, which, since Hebrew was not a spoken language at the time, would not have occurred.[21] Given this, it does not seem likely that he is promoting a Jewish reform movement in his romance novel. Rather, he is promoting a move toward a secularized Protestant morality, in which the individual derives a moral code for himself or herself by consulting Scripture individually. But even were a Jew to accomplish such a self-formation, it does not appear that Scott would accept her as fully

English, for he seems to understand Rebecca as a member of the Jewish race with a Protestant nature. And when forced to choose between race and nature, race is the more important for Scott. For although he flirts with the notion that a Jew could be an English-woman, ultimately, what counts is that she is born a Jew. Although he draws her with enormous sympathy, even bringing his Englishman to fall in love with her, in the end, he sees her as the test case for how far liberalism will go—will it go so far as to tolerate non-Christians? The conservative Scott is certainly no supporter of a monarchy divested of its Christian ties. Once one admits Jews—even those Jews whom, unlike the materialistic Isaac, one finds spiritual or romantic, even Jewish Protestants like Rebecca—one threatens to undermine the Christian foundations of the country. Because Scott equates Rebecca with liberal reform, he ultimately cannot commit himself to seeing the romance between Rebecca and Ivanhoe fulfilled, for the bottom line is that the Christian character of the nation must be preserved, and Rebecca is of the Jewish race. When he sends Rebecca and Isaac into exile at the end of the novel, he implies that Rebecca's liberal position—that the Great Father recognizes the ethical acts of both the Jew and the Gentile—is attractive but finally incorrect.

He makes this decision even at the expense of his novel's closure, for the romance form, which highlights individual desire over the prevailing social conventions, seems to have a tendency within itself toward individualism. It is a tendency Scott can only overcome by writing Rebecca out of the country. In the end, the Normans and Saxons have "formed intermarriages with each other" (464) "as a pledge of the future peace and harmony betwixt two races, which, since that period, have been so completely mingled that the distinc-tion has become wholly invisible" (463). These "intermarriages" have required a kind of conversion, for "the Normans abated their scorn, and the Saxons were refined from their rusticity" (464). But the Jewish "race," as Rebecca calls it, remains distinct, unintermarried, and un-converted at the end of the novel. Rebecca and Isaac go to Granada. Apparently, not only may Jews not intermarry, but they must leave the country rather than stay and be treated on equal terms. Why is this? When Rebecca questions Ivanhoe's chivalric code, his love of battle and glory, he tells her, "Thou wouldst quench the pure light of chiv-alry, which alone distinguishes the noble from the base . . . . Thou art no Christian, Rebecca" (295). Although she is humanistic, ultimately for Ivanhoe as for Scott, to be a Jew means to "quench . . . chivalry." Rebecca the romance heroine subverts romance.[22] But while many contemporary readers may have been able to follow the logic, the whole telos of the novel suggests another ending, for which Wilfred's marriage to Rowena can only seem a poor substitute.

As popular as Scott's rewriting of the Shakespearean father/daughter plot was, the ending was unsatisfying to many members of the non-Jewish Victorian audience, precisely because it did not fulfill the merging of the Jewess and the knight promised by the rest of the novel. For example, Thackeray wrote: "Of all the Scottish novels, . . . that of which the conclusion gives me the greatest dissatisfaction is the dear old *Ivanhoe.* . . . I feel sure the story can't end where it does. I have quite too great a love for the Disinherited Knight, whose blood has been fired by the suns of Palestine, and whose heart has been warmed in the company of . . . Rebecca, to suppose that he could sit down contented for life by the side of such a frigid piece of propriety as that icy, faultless, prim, niminy-piminy Rowena."[23] Through his military conquests, Ivanhoe has undergone a change: he has lost some of his English frigidness in the suns of Palestine. What makes the "Eastern" Jewess so attractive is the warmth of Palestine in her body, her sensuality. The imagined sensuality of the Eastern woman goes hand in hand with an attempt to colonize her land. The exotic land is a woman who beckons the frozen soldier— this orientalizing myth of the Jewish woman is the basis for Ivanhoe's attraction to Rebecca, and he can no longer return to his frozen state.[24] Thus, according to Thackeray, his marriage to Rowena must fail. Scott himself recognized the dissatisfaction with his ending. As he explains in his retrospective introduction of 1830: "The character of the fair Jewess found so much favour in the eyes of some fair readers, that the writer was censured because when arranging the fates of the characters of the drama, he had not assigned the hand of Wilfred to Rebecca, rather than the less interesting Rowena. . . . [T]he prejudices of the age rendered such a union almost impossible" (xiii–xiv). Given that earlier in this introduction he has eschewed historical realism, however, his defense that the "prejudices of the age rendered such a union almost impossible" must have seemed forced at best. A slew of revisions by Christian writers followed, setting the father/daughter plot of *Ivanhoe* in the modern world, and exposing some of its more hidden anachronisms, especially the anachronism that such a daughter as Rebecca could have lived in the Middle Ages.

FORMING THE HEROINE OF ROMANCE

No, Jewish Protestants did not live in the Middle Ages, according to those of Scott's followers who were conversionists. Jews were then both too "bigotted" and too persecuted by Christians to think of converting. Jewish Protestants lived in Scott's own time, they were the men and women who called themselves reformers—and they were more likely to be women than men. This was the message conversionists promulgated between 1809 and 1880. These millenarian evangelicals of the London Society for the Promotion of Christianity Amongst the Jews and allied organizations believed that tolerant policies and persuasive speech that recognized the greatness of Israel's ancient past, while pitying the unfortunate decline of its postcrucifixion past, present, and future, would succeed better in bringing about Jews' conversion than intolerant policies, persecution, and hate speech.[25] The London Society was no fringe organization. Founded by the convert Joseph Frey who under the auspices of the London Missionary Society had already been proselytizing for some years, the society "enjoyed the support and patronage of both evangelical churchmen and Nonconformists."[26] An end paper to Rev. John Harding, "Mercy for Israel, a sermon preached on behalf of the London Society for the Promotion of Christianity Amongst the Jews" in 1866, claimed the following statistics: the society's income for 1866 was £34,992. It employed 134 agents, 60 of whom were Hebrew Christians (converts from Judaism). It occupied thirty-three stations, two in England, the rest in Europe, Asia, and Africa. It circulated 449,595 portions of Scriptures in Hebrew, and two million copies of other books and tracts. Since its establishment in 1807, 1,087 converts were baptized in the society's chapel in London; 1,500 Jewish children were educated in its schools; and "upwards of 20,000 Israelites have embraced Christianity, during the present century, as the result of the labors of this and other societies."[27] These statistics are inflated, but the society did spend over £850,000 on its work between 1810 and 1858, and did enroll between three to four hundred Jewish and Christian children in its Free School, and did provide adult education to converts, instructing them in candlewick making, basket making, and other trades. The conversionists targeted the poor, often appealing to their economic need to persuade them to convert.[28]

But if the conversionists felt they were more likely to net the poor than the rich, they also felt that they were more likely to net women than men. Conversionists targeted Jewish women because they perceived them to be oppressed by Jewish men, and therefore more likely to be reformers. In "Jewish Women," an article in the 1877 edition of *Israel's Watchman; A Hebrew Christian Magazine,* the editor sees conversion as an attempt "to remedy some of the grievous disadvantages under which Jewish women are placed by . . . the rabbis" who teach "that woman is not be regarded as man's companion, but as his inferior."[29] The editor goes on to castigate "the shackles of Rabbinism," pointing out the facts that Jewish women are trained differently from Jewish men; there is no ceremony in the life of Jewish girls commensurate with Bar Mitzvah; Jewish women are exempt from minyan and from worshipping with their fathers or husbands; and most Jewish women, never having been taught Hebrew, could not follow their own prayers. The result of their lack of education is that Jewish women are "superstitious." Amelia Bristow's Jewish female character, biblically named Eliphalette, is "spiritual" precisely to the extent that "she devoted much of her time to studies of a description hitherto unknown to Jewish females."[30] Immediately upon perusing a New Testament, she converts, for she has "a mind that had so long and eagerly sought a more excellent and more spiritual worship than the heartless ceremonies Judaism presented!"[31] The perception that Jewish women were both oppressed by Jewish tradition and by nature more "spiritual" and heartful than Jewish formalism could bear led the London Society to found a Hebrew Christian Girls' Free School, to which conversionists would attempt to persuade poor Jewish girls to come for instruction, arguing that they were being provided little in the way of religious education by their Jewish community. In addition, conversionist presses opened their pages to Jewish women writers, in some cases when the writers could not be published in Jewish presses or only with extensive editorial emendations. The conversionists reviewed Jewish women's work, taking it seriously even when they critiqued it. When Rabbi Isaac Leeser made extensive editorial arguments against Grace Aguilar's *Spirit of Judaism* in his footnotes to her text (which he published), conversionists castigated this procedure as an example of Jewish men's oppression of Jewish women. Marion Moss also published in the conversionist press—the *Jewish Herald and Record of Christian Effort For the Spiritual Good of God's Ancient People* ran a poem she wrote criticizing conversionists, and in the next issue, a Hebrew Christian wrote a poem in response.[32]

The conversionists hoped to see their reward in the spiritual enlightenment of the Jewish women, and often speculated as to their success.

51

In Aguilar's work, "We cannot help thinking that we see the influence of Christianity. . . . It shows the silent and unseen influence of the gospel." This Christian influence, the reviewer goes on to speculate, shows that "she belongs to the more spiritual, the more religious section of the Hebrews. . . . She manifests a deep concern for the purity of her religion and inveighs against tradition."[33] Conversionists saw reform as the "spiritual" side of Judaism, the Judaism in which God, purified of his [sic] materialistic and legalistic Talmudic dross, was finally recognized for what he was: Love. Reform was the modern Jew's step toward Christianity. They saw Jewish women as spiritual, as at the forefront of reform, and as one step away from conversion. Jewish men, by contrast, were rooted in the letter of the law, and were the "leaders of unbelief, and even of the most godless Materialism."[34]

With this ideology actively promoted, it ought not to seem surprising that Scott's romance, which foregrounds the Jewish daughter in a way Shakespeare did not, was latched onto by many novelists, though they had to adapt it to their own ends. For if Scott's romance left the reader dissatisfied because the love between the Jewish woman and the Christian man could not be fulfilled, conversionists could easily rewrite it so as to effect the desired conclusion. The solution, the daughter becoming a Christian, had already been available in the examples of Gotthold Lessing's internationally popular *Nathan der Weise* (1779) and Maria Edgeworth's *Harrington* (1817); in both of these texts it is revealed at the last moment that the spiritual Jewish woman was really Christian-born.[35] The revelation of the daughter's birth enables the consummation of the romance deferred in Scott's novel. After Scott, however, the Jewish woman tended to need to undergo a conversion ceremony before she could be acceptable, as in M. G. Lewis's *Jewish Maiden* (1830) or Bulwer Lytton's *Leila* (1837).[36] In *Rebecca and Rowena* (1843), Thackeray's "Romance upon Romance," Ivanhoe, off at the wars again after Rowena's death, rampages through Eastern and Western Europe cutting off the heads of Saracens and other infidels. Along the way, remembering Rebecca, he ransoms numerous Jews being mistreated by intolerant Christians and Moors, like a good Victorian philo-Semite. Through this activity, he finds Rebecca, who meanwhile has been imprisoned by Isaac for declaring herself a Christian out of love for Ivanhoe. Ivanhoe rescues her, and they are married—according to Thackeray, not altogether happily. Many such revisions of Scott's triangle of materialistic-Jewish-father/spiritual-Jewish-daughter/chivalric-Christian appeared in the 1830s and 1840s. The conversionists take the traditional father/daughter plot of Scott's Isaac and Rebecca—which looks back to Shakespeare's Shylock and Jessica—and refocus it on the daughter.

M. G. Lewis's *Jewish Maiden* (1830) is a revision of *Ivanhoe,* which alters it to better fit the philo-Semitic conversionism available during the period.[37] Glanville the Christian hero gets himself into debt in trying to support a wife who is devoted to fashion. He must borrow money from one Solomon Schreiber, a "stock-jobber and money-lender," a "dingy" and "shrewd" fifty-year-old German Jew with a large nose, an olive complexion, curly hair, a "monstrous dialect" of English ("Ah, mishter Geddin, I am sho habby yo have honoured my poor housh vid your gombany"), and an attitude of "extreme servility." Schreiber's offices are dirty beyond description, "the floor was covered with impressions of dirty shoes" (1:160–67), and his house and dress are gaudy. His business practices, which he does not scruple to perform after returning from services on the Sabbath, are "acts of chicanery and overreaching covetousness" (1:179). He is stingy, clannish, "the proud Jew at heart" (1:180). Like Scott's Isaac, Schreiber is a Shylock, divested of Shylock's sympathetic moments. Unlike Isaac, Schreiber is not redeemed by his leniency toward his daughters.

When Schreiber invites Glanville to dinner at his house, the Christian man finds that the broker has a dandified son trying to be a fashionable Englishman to the hilt (he eventually dies of malaria), and two daughters, Miriam and Rosetta, whom Schreiber announces "carelessly . . . without bestowing on them further observation" (1:173). Their mother is dead. The daughters are simultaneously neglected and suppressed, for they are "shut up like nuns" (1:187), allowed no contact with anyone and no converse with the world, except when their father brings clients over, at which time they are trotted out for display like show ponies. The only time they feel truly autonomous is when they "escape to the uncontrolled freedom of their own apartment" (1:189), and read romance novels, which are a "freehold of imagination," and in which they find men unlike their father and brother who do not "view them as objects calculated to be useful and ornamental in their homes" (1:192). If they feel ugly in comparison to the heroines they find in the romances, those with "the fair cheek, blue eyes, and golden tresses of some Christian girl" (1:190), still this self-hatred is better than being chained to their father's house with no education and no means of attaining it. When Glanville finds Miriam home alone one Sabbath, he thinks, "how very wrong and how unfortunate . . . to bring up children like wild beasts, in cages, without affording them any opportunity of studying that world on which they must one day embark" (1:221). Miriam is much more naturally spiritual sitting at home on the Sabbath than her father who is at the synagogue hypocritically praying for gold.

When he finds Miriam alone, Glanville strikes up a conversation with her on Byron and gives her a list of "secular" books to read, discovering in her a "mind that required only a little forming and cultivating" (1:232). Unlike Christian anti-Semites, who attempt to persecute Jews into converting, this tolerant man uses, not coercion, but persuasion, to achieve his ends. In short, he introduces her to the "world." But it is not the great world with which his wife Honoria is too much enamored; it is not the world of fashion. It is rather that world refracted through a spiritualizing medium—it is the world of romance. "Her romantic heart panted to be one of that graceful world, where rare beauty, splendid genius, fascinating accomplishments, unmeasured generosity, sterling honour, and stainless virtue" exist in novels (3:21). Still, there is no danger that Miriam's taste will be as lavish and worldly as Honoria's; having grown accustomed to so little, the extravagance of the romantic world cannot harm her. But to join this world, she will have to find a way to leave her father's house. She will have to apostasize.

This narrative of the dominant masculine figure persuading the minority, figured as a powerless woman, to undergo "radical assimilation," is a standard narrative of orientalist discourse, as both Said and Bitton-Jackson have suggested.[38] The responsibility for the oppression of Miriam is displaced from the dominant society onto another Jew, her tyrannical father. A hegemonic narrative is thus mapped onto a romantic marriage plot, in which standard Christian oppositions between spirituality and materialism are played out in the antagonism between daughter and father—with the Christian suitor leading the daughter to true spirituality. Little by little, Glanville wins Miriam's heart without either of them knowing it. He "flung the first ray of knowledge over her prisoned intellect" (2:200), and she treats him as an "oracle . . . , his slightest wish executed the moment it was expressed" (2:201). For her, he is a window on the world from which she is debarred by her tyrannical father. She reads all the books he suggests (including Shakespeare, Homer, Virgil, geography, French, and Italian—and especially Byron), and he teaches her how to draw. She is, in short, becoming a drawing-room lady, to whom he is attracted because she is tractable to his advice, unlike his wife. She is his fantasy of a younger subservient daughterish woman. One evening, at sunset, he apostrophizes her: "You were formed to be the heroine of romance . . . so young, so solitary, so inexperienced; living in this dark and gloomy edifice, without one congenial mind, with your bright imagination, and your guitar, and your diamond pencil, to write love-verses on every window: now, you only want a silken ladder, and a lover, and a moonlight night to render you the heroine you appear" (2:180). In Glanville's imagination, Miriam becomes an imprisoned damsel of chivalric romance, a Rebecca who writes "love-verses" with her "diamond pencil" as an escape from the horrible situation in which she finds herself. This is not how she describes herself—this is how the Christian hero describes her. He has made her into a fictional character, a "heroine" of his own imagination. And what he imagines her, she willingly becomes. His imagination creates reality. His charisma persuades and transforms. He is the inspiration for the love verses she writes. Perhaps this myth of the Jewish woman inspired by a philo-Semite to write and convert is the conversionist myth of the origin of the Anglo-Jewish woman writer.

But if Miriam emerges from an oppressed and materialistic upbringing to become a writer and heroine of romance, Glanville himself emerges from a lowly upbringing, from monetary distress, and from a bad marriage, to become a romantic hero. He is spiritualized by relieving himself of the taint of worldliness. When he complains to his friend Gethin about his wife's dissoluteness, Gethin replies, "Ah, my dear friend, you were formed to live in the golden age, when every woman was an angel, and every man a hero" (2:186). The parallel form of address ("you were formed") emphasizes his innate bond to Miriam. Again, the act of uttering the romance myth transforms reality: Glanville becomes the myth. He becomes a knight in order to save his damsel from distress locked up in her father's dirty tower. With its nostalgia for lost social forms, the chivalric romance merges with the romance novel. As in *Ivanhoe*, the chivalric romance is implicit in the romance novel, informing and directing its plot.[39]

It takes some time for these two romantic characters to find their way toward one another, for Miriam, though "imperfectly acquainted with her own imperfect creed," is "reared in all the bigotry of her sect" (3:32). Deprived of education by the oppressive Jewish patriarchy represented by her father, she asks Glanville to explain the tenets of

Christianity to her—and he does, "in very simple terms, suited to her comprehension" (3:34). He speaks of the glory of ancient Israel and the "degradation into which . . . he described them now fallen" (3:35). By this mixture of courting, condescension, pity, and rational exposition of the errors of Judaism, so characteristic of philo-Semitism,[40] Miriam is converted in heart. Before they can marry, there is still the little matter of Glanville's wife, who in her worldliness has neglected their sick child. The child's convenient death provides the occasion for their separation; and Honoria's subsequent death leaves Glanville free. But it is only after Solomon's death has given occasion to his auditors, and his monetary crookedness has been confirmed, that Miriam can think of leaving the house. And it is only after Glanville has told Miriam that "the truly religious heart knows nothing of the prejudice of sect" (4:189), that the way is opened for the two of them to acknowledge their love.

But if Glanville's "truly religious heart" sounds similar to Rebecca's expression of ethical monotheism, in which the particular creed is less important than the individual's moral goodness, it appears that Protestantism is still of some importance. Miriam is still brought to convert at the end before the two of them solemnize their vows. Protestantism is not understood to be a particular creed but the expression of the universal truth. Just as Scott finally rejects the radical implications of ethical monotheism for his characters, and therefore exiles Rebecca, so Lewis finally rejects the idea that "good" people need not regard particular religious upbringing, and reasserts the importance of that upbringing. Again, the imperatives of the romance novel—that individual choice ought to be more important than the "bigotry" of social convention or religious prejudice—are compromised in the conclusion, because Protestantism is not understood to be a religious prejudice, but the ground of truth. In Scott's case, the compromise of exile at least does not require the Jews' apostasy; on the other hand, Lewis's apostasy at least does not require the Jews to uproot themselves. Apostasy or exile—the choices in themselves constitute a rejection of the universal toleration one might imagine would be advocated by a truly "tolerant" humanism.

Lewis's novel was less popular than Scott's but her conclusion—conversion—provoked a greater response from Jews. Indeed, there is evidence that while Jews deprecated Scott's portrait of Isaac, they welcomed *Ivanhoe* as a revision of other troubling aspects of Shakespeare's version of the father/daughter plot, in which the Jewish family is torn asunder by an ungrateful daughter's apostasy; in other words, they welcomed Scott's revision of Jessica as the devoted Rebecca.[41] The Jews reacted to novels like *Jewish Maiden,* on the other hand, with anger and fear. It may be said that the form of this novel was understood by Jews, both men and women, to be the most important strand of non-Jewish thought about Jews to have emerged in the first third of the nineteenth century. The most typological way of phrasing this plot would be: Male Jewish Materialism struggles against Suppressed Female Spirituality and the result is the Death of Materialism and the Birth of the Spirit through Conversion. *Ivanhoe,* the novel that introduced the plot that made these novels possible, is actually a significant variation because it leaves Rebecca unconverted at the end.

These Victorian Christian novelists of Jewish identity are participating in a large and ongoing cultural shift in perspective toward Jews from a relation of coercion to a relation of persuasion. The shift had been taking place since Puritan philo-Semites engineered the official readmission of Jews to the country during the seventeenth century, and certainly since Richard Cumberland's benevolent philanthropist Sheva made the scene in the 1790s. In a relation of coercion, it makes ideological sense to depict one's adversary as an evil figure, one powerful enough to call out the use of force. Since cultural power resided primarily in men during the Middle Ages and the Renaissance, it made sense to portray the primary Jewish adversary as male. Thus, as in *Merchant of Venice,* the father figure was played up, the mother written out, and the daughter nearly absent. There would be no son to carry on the tradition. In a relation of persuasion, however, it makes sense to depict the Other as a figure not evil but merely misguided, and willing to learn. Since cultural power still resided, in the Victorian period, primarily with men, it seemed to make ideological sense to "feminize" the Other, in other words to depict the Other in a position of relative weakness. Jews would no longer be forced to convert or be killed; they would be "tolerated," pitied and badgered. The fathers would not be subjected to beatings—but they would be written out of the plot, either through "voluntary" exile or a timely and convenient death. The daughter, meanwhile, would figure in a narrative in which she converts as part of a typical romantic marriage plot. Jewish women who were already married were clearly excluded from the possibility of conversion through marriage, so they still had to be written out.[42] In addition, it was still difficult to write in a son who might possibly carry on the tradition. As in M. G. Lewis's *Jewish Maiden,* the son tended to attempt "radical assimilation" and either convert offstage or die.

This family romance is, then, the major plot and the ideological perspective that early Victorian Jewish women confronted in the dominant cultural context. But the shape and content of their response will not be fully comprehensible unless the forces impinging on them from within their subculture are also taken into account. The next chapter attempts to discover how Anglo-Jewish men were "speaking" the Jewish woman.

Two
The "New Woman" and the
Emergence of the Modern Jewish Man

Studies of Victorian Jewish men have for the most part focused on the men's political and practical achievements as they entered modernity. Scholars have been concerned to describe men's attempts to gain emancipation in Parliament; to free Syrian and Rumanian Jews from persecution; to respond to the secession of a group of prominent members of the community to establish a reform synagogue; and to form such Anglo-Jewish institutions as Jews' College, the Jews' and General Literary and Scientific Institute, and the Board of Deputies of British Jews. While such an approach succeeds in illuminating the activities that preoccupied men in the "public" worlds of the synagogue and the Parliament, it leaves in shadow the effect of modernity on men's perception of their roles in the "domestic" world. It does not adequately describe men's perceptions of the changing relations of men and women, or of their changing experiences and definitions of masculinity.

Between 1830 and 1875, in more than thirty-five articles in eleven periodicals, Jewish men repeatedly acknowledged that their behavior toward women was less than ideal and that their approach to their own gender needed revision. While defending themselves against conversionists'—and Jewish women's—charges that they oppressed Jewish women, they nonetheless began to call for increased female education and greater access for women to communal privileges. At the same time, even men who supported these reforms began to fear that creating a more egalitarian community would mean the loss of male power and privileges. Worse, the merging of the separate spheres threatened to undermine men's sense of what made them separate and unique—in a word, their masculinity. These fears, along with men's concern that communal integrity and continuity had to be maintained, prevented them from altering their behavior or opening their educational and synagogal institutions to women to any large degree, even when they acknowledged the necessity for doing so. In a few cases, the fear of change prompted even reformist men to censor the most prominent evidence of women's educational advancement—their books. If Jewish women were being subjected to a conversionist campaign from the dominant culture, they were also the subject of a rather fearful and confused effort among Jewish men to limit the penetration of egalitarian ideas into the domestic recesses of communal life.

In such a contentious milieu a scholar of Victorian literature might have expected a number of Jewish male fiction writers to have worked through the changing roles of men and women in novels. With only a few exceptions, however, Jewish men did not tend to think through their cultural cruxes in fictional terms. They did not publish many novels or tales or stories, finding such forms trivial or un-Jewish. The exceptions only appeared toward the end of the struggle for emancipation in the late 1850s, when Jewish men began to assert that the novel form was the cultural literary form that, when assimilated, would enable them to be fully accepted into dominant culture. These late fictional efforts—late since women had already been publishing fiction since 1830—definitely addressed the issue of men's relation to women, as the discussion of Matthias Levy's *The Hasty Marriage; A Sketch of Modern Jewish Life* (1857) in this chapter demonstrates.

But if Jewish men were late in adopting fiction from the dominant culture as a legitimate means of Jewish male expression, they did write midrashim—interpretive retellings of biblical and Talmudic stories—which bore the cast of their Victorian acculturation; and many of these midrashim spoke to the issue of women's roles in the community. Not surprisingly, most of these stories depict the relationship between men and women as a relationship between fathers and daughters. Desirous of assimilating English forms wherever possible, Anglo-Jewish men structured their midrashim similarly to the father/daughter conflict found in the romances of Scott and the conversionists. They could do so without feeling that they had betrayed Jewish tradition, for there was an ancient Jewish custom of referring to all women as "Daughters of Israel" in relation to their fathers, husbands, and the Almighty Father. Drawing both on the English Christian romance, and on Jewish patriarchy, these midrashim disclosed a benevolent paternalism with a barely concealed coercive underside.

SEPARATE SPHERES: TRADITIONALISTS

The Jewish male presses responded to the conversionists' accusations of Jewish women's oppression and vulnerability with angry rebuttals. Both traditionalists and reformers resisted the idea that Judaism oppressed women, although the two groups resisted on rather different grounds. In 1846, a long article in Jacob A. Franklin's traditionalist periodical the *Voice of Jacob,* entitled "Position of Israel's Women," argued that "It has frequently been asserted, that Judaism does not award the same justice to the gentler sex that other religious systems do." On the contrary, says the editor, the Jewish woman is treated better in Judaism than women were treated by the Greeks and Romans, "which were wont to admire, or perhaps to ridicule, in an over sensitive chivalry." Judaism was not a romantic tradition—that is, as Franklin understands the term, not a tradition based on a man's placing a woman on a pedestal for her beauty alone—but rather a tradition in which all things, including love and issues of sexual equality, were based on a communally authorized moral vision that was primarily expressed in the performance of mitzvot, or commandments derived from rabbinical interpretation of the Hebrew Bible. To show how the Jewish tradition is different from romantic chivalry, he points to the biblical examples of Miriam, who had greater powers of prophecy than Moses, and Deborah, who shows that "a woman was not thought incapable of exercising the highest functions (those of Judge), in the then Jewish Commonwealth . . . [women] are always represented as the equals of men." Women are not on pedestals for their beauty; their judgment and insight are respected. If most of the prophets and judges were men, this does not undermine the principle that they may be women. To prove this the editor adduces biographies of learned Jewish women, and discusses the characteristics of the good woman to be found in Proverbs 31.[1]

This sort of double message—women may be learned and prophetic, but need not be—is characteristic of Franklin's attitude toward

women's roles. Franklin criticizes some halachic sages' "misunderstanding of female character," arguing that their sexism was due to the
fact that they lived in the East and were influenced by Islamic customs. By denying the conversionist commonplace that English Jews
are "orientals," he is able to deny Anglo-Jewish men's sexism. At the
same time, he justifies the halachic exemptions of women from time-
bound positive commandments on the grounds that these exemptions
are "founded on some physical disability or impropriety." The disability is women's "weakness," the "natural" excuse for exempting women
from heavy labor. The greater number of exemptions are justified by
reference to a particular ritual act's "impropriety," meaning that the
act would conflict with women's need to fulfill duties in the home.
What appears to be inequity can be explained from the Jewish notion
of the separation of spheres.[2] The Rabbis, he argues, did not exempt
women from learning Torah, but only from "the more abstruse points,
not of religion, but of the subtleties of theology." For this traditionalist
writer, the difference between religion and theology appears to be the
difference between ritual actions, and the theory behind them. Men
learn the abstract theory and are responsible for most ritual acts. For
women, most rituals would compete with "the discharge of women's
particular duties"—that is, child rearing and running the domestic
economy. In terms of education, women are responsible for knowing
only their limited number of duties, which are so time-consuming
that to take time out to learn the theory behind them would be
"improper." Moreover, women are innately holier than men, and therefore need study less. Besides having greater powers of prophecy than
men (i.e., women's intuition) as Miriam had, women make better
martyrs. Franklin claims that "at the expulsion of the Jews from Spain,
it was the women . . . who encouraged their husbands, sons, their
parents, and their brothers to prefer exile with its horrors, to the
preferred alternative [conversion]." More aligned with Scott than the
conversionists, he believes Sephardic women the least vulnerable to
conversion.[3] But paradoxically, this strength is due to the fact that,
just as the conversionists argued, Jewish women are more spiritual
than Jewish men. This traditionalist Jewish man agrees with the conversionists that Jewish women are more spiritual; he disagrees with
them about how that spirituality ought to be interpreted.

The next year *The Voice of Jacob* attacked the conversionists' "chivalry" again, arguing that Jewish women were held in much higher
esteem than Christian women were in the days of Christian chivalry,

when Christian mothers were "little more than an upper servant." Chivalry, which for Scott was at the heart of romance, is heartily disliked by a traditionalist magazine, for it turns out that romance is the code word for reform in the Jewish subculture, and all that pertains to reform is anathema.[4] Accordingly, Franklin argues that in Judaism, the love between a man and a woman is based on a model that differed from that promoted by romance. Neither degrading nor elevating the role of the woman, the Song of Songs "proves that Judaism, much as it has been assailed, . . . fostered a very high regard, if not a deep and tender respect, for man's best friend, his help-mate; and for the home, . . . the seed-bed of all happiness." While to a late-twentieth-century feminist, this description of the married woman in her home may make her sound more like a treasured pet than an equal, the writer insists that the Song of Songs shows that "the lover and his loved one are placed on the same high level. They feel, they manifest, reciprocal regard and passion."[5] Both choose in this model of mutuality. Both choose, even though the male is still the "lover"—the active one—the female "his loved one"—the possessed object of his desire. Both choose, but one of these equals clearly does more of the choosing than the other.

When the editor's idea of reciprocity between men and women is challenged by a regular contributor, Amicus Veri, who points out the inequities of polygamy, levirate marriage, divorce, and adultery laws in Deuteronomy, as well as a host of other passages where women's inferiority is alleged, the editor replies in a more careful vein: "We did not contend that the Jews as such place the female on the same footing with the male; but we endeavoured to show that the Jewish law does not, as has been said, pronounce woman the mere attendant of man. We argued that the law of Moses regards woman as an independent being, having rights and duties, both religious and social—and moreover that as a human being she is of equal importance with man in the eyes of the Lord: for instance, it is just the same crime to murder a woman as to murder a man."[6] Women's equality in the eyes of God for purposes of being murdered does not, however, translate into equality of rights and duties because of the separation of spheres. Indeed, the traditionalist men's idea of reciprocity, such as it was, ultimately did not extend to such areas of Jewish life as education.

Still, traditionalist men's ideas of the separation of spheres, although echoing Jewish tradition's exemption of women from learning, had been altered by their confrontation with the modern world—and specifically with the very different Victorian ideology of separate spheres. In the Judaism that existed in autonomous Jewish communities of the Middle Ages, both the man's and woman's duties had been equally religious, but had taken place in different locations—the man's religious duties took place in the yeshiva, the woman's in the home and in the market. "Secular" duties did not exist. Judaism was a total ideology comprising law, ethics, politics, economics, gastronomy, philosophy.[7] But as Judaism confronted the modern world, Anglo-Jewish men modified this notion that men and women tend separate, but equally holy, gardens. Assimilating the non-Jewish Victorian model of separation of spheres, they now asserted that women were the primary religious providers, while men were the primary "secular" providers.[8] Now religion was concentrated in three places, in the synagogue, in acts of charity in poor neighborhoods, and in the home—the latter two of these being women's sphere. The public sphere of business and politics was divested of religiosity, became "secular," and became man's. The woman at home was the mainspring of religiosity, "grafting" religion onto her children's hearts. The Victorian traditionalist separation of spheres, which distinguished men's and women's spheres as secular and religious, respectively, is not the same as the traditional separation, which distinguished men's and women's spheres as separate but equally religious. Traditionalists assimilated Victorian Christians' "feminization of religion," the phrase historians have begun using to describe the evangelical domestication of religion during the period.[9] As one traditionalist man succinctly put it, "The chief honour of a female is religion."[10]

To B. H. A., a regular traditionalist contributor to M. H. Bresslau's reformist *Hebrew Review and Magazine of Jewish Literature,* this ideology of separate and unequal spheres had important consequences for Jewish women's education: "The ultimate aim of education in all ages has been to render mankind perfect in their spiritual nature," he writes in 1859. "But as nature has assigned different avocations to the male and female, so has it laid down an especial rule for the guidance of men, and a separate system for the education of women. . . . Female education should have no other aim . . . than the development of the feminine qualities with which *woman* is endowed. Her feelings, wishes, sympathies, should have full scope for action; whilst, on the other hand, the masculine virtues of firmness, seriousness, and self-dependence, must be inculcated upon the mind of man."[11] But this separation of educational ideals does not mean that women should not be educated at all. In fact, quite the opposite, given that "The chief honour of a female is religion." Since the primary site of religiosity is shifting during the period to the home and to charitable action, and since the home and charities are assigned to women, women must be spiritual providers while their husbands bring home the secular public bread.[12] B. H. A. remarks that Jewish women can only "engraft" religion "on the heart of their tender offspring" and on the hearts of the "humble" if they are educated themselves. In other words, as traditionalist Victorian Jews assimilate Anglo-Christian forms of religiosity, women's religious education becomes increasingly important. B. H. A. goes on to propose a condescending three-fold system of education for women: (a) a "thorough, clear, easy, and abridged history of the creation," (b) "an equally abridged and instructive history of our religion and nationality," and (c) "a compact, well-digested, and authentic course of the ethical dogmas and principles of our religion as laid down . . . by Moses Maimonides." Like Glanville, the philo-Semite in M. G. Lewis's *Jewish Maiden,* this Jewish man would provide Jewish women with nothing too difficult or abstract—just enough to make them the equals in religiosity of their female Christian neighbors.[13]

But lest one should think from the condescending tone of his proposals that he is not serious, he outlines the grave consequences of neglecting this type of women's education. He disagrees with the editor of the *Voice of Jacob* that Jewish women's constancy is sufficient, for he argues that Christian hegemony is extremely strong: "The Christian youth meets with encouragement by the worldly grandeur of his persuasion; the whole civil constitution is so peculiarly arranged as to interweave with his actions and regulations the ideas of the prevailing religion. How different, however, is it with our youth. Externally restrained by a peculiar position, and tempted by allurements of apostasy,—internally agitated by the difficulty of the tenets of his religion." If young men will be tempted, young women, whose minds are more malleable, will be more so. Indeed, some women have already been influenced, if not by apostasy, then by the other dangers posed by Christian cultural hegemony—fashion and romance. One man complains of the "excessive love of dress and finery . . . which characterises so unmistakeably the female portion of our community." Among the upper classes, this fashion consciousness is a direct result of "the mysteries of 'Lady Audley's Secret,' 'No Name,' and 'Cary's Confessions,' . . . 'Edith the Captive.' " Romance-novel reading is connected to fashion and this is connected to the neglect of duty. "In the meantime the household duties are neglected; the education . . . is overlooked; . . . the money that was so hard to earn is swiftly squandered away; and in many cases . . . bankruptcy, and ruin crown this awful evil."[14] Such are the least of the evils springing from a neglect of women's proper education.

But if the consequences of neglecting women's education are romance reading, fashion consciousness, neglect of duty, and apostasy, another writer, the translator of Mendelssohn's *Jerusalem* into English and a Talmudist, argues that there are equally severe consequences for teaching Jewish women too much. "He who crams his daughter's brain with a prolix exposition of the Mosaic or ceremonial law, teaches her something unsuitable to the calling of a woman" inasmuch as she becomes "an impertinent reasoner, who at last neglects her duties as a housewife."[15] A measure of education is necessary in order to maintain the new separation of spheres in which women are primarily responsible for infusing religion into their children, but too much education will dissolve the separation of spheres altogether, inasmuch as women will become "impertinent reasoners." A delicate balance must be achieved.

MALE CHAMPIONS: REFORMERS

In seeming contrast to this doctrine of separation of spheres, Jewish men interested in reforms in the community argued that women's education was a central point to be achieved.[16] In his inaugural sermon, David Woolf Marks, the founding rabbi of reform's home in Burton Street, the West London Synagogue for British Jews, attempts to sketch out "what the house of worship once was, and what it can become in our days." Among other things, he argues that in biblical days, religious instruction was not "limited to either age or sex. Indeed, there were certain periods, when it was compulsory upon all the women to attend the holy house, to hear the word of God expounded," he argues, quoting the passage in the book of Nehemiah where Ezra reads before men and women.[17] Woman is "in every way [man's] equal" and is endowed "with wondrous perceptions, that she might participate . . . in the full discharge of every moral and religious obligation." Note that he does not say that women might participate in every "legal" obligation; reformers' demotion of halacha, their promotion of Judaism as a moral or religious ideology, rather than as a total ideology encompassing law as well as ethics, opens the space to promote a nontraditional view of women's role. His suggestion to ameliorate women's current lack of knowledge is to have them attend his sermons on the Sabbath, or in lieu of that, to read the published versions of them, so that they may provide "home instruction in matters that appertain to the essentials of the Mosaic faith."[18] Women's active understanding of the ethics underlying Scripture is one major difference between the goals of reformers and traditionalists. The ethically informed woman will make a good educator of small children.

But while reformist men made several efforts at educating girls and women, these efforts were rather paltry and unenthusiastically undertaken. M. H. Bresslau published a series of meditations on the weekly Torah portion in a book called *Sabbath Evenings At Home,* primarily directed at educating women. And the Jewish Association for the Diffusion of Religious Knowledge distributed didactic tracts for women's use. But, as will become apparent in the next chapter, it was primarily Anglo-Jewish women who both polemicized for the expansion of female education efforts in their writings and spearheaded the practical realization of a Jewish Girls' School and Jewish women's literature.

More frequently, reformers contented themselves with applauding the efforts made by women. Beginning in 1856, Abraham Benisch, the reform-leaning editor of the *Jewish Chronicle,* began to recognize the prevalence of women writers dedicated to women's education. Benisch looked around him for signs of a developing Anglo-Jewish literature and was amazed. In a review of *Imrei Lev, Prayers and Meditations for Every Situation and Occasion in Life,* Hester Rothschild's translation and adaptation of *tekhinot,* or women's daily prayers, he exclaimed:

> It is a remarkable phenomenon on the horizon of Anglo-Jewish literature that it is women, not men, that shine there as the principal stars. The translations of Miss Goldsmid and the original writings of the late Miss Aguilar and Mrs. H. Montefiore, are productions of which the community may well be proud. It is in vain that we seek for an explanation of this phenomenon. We cannot look for it in the nature of our literature, for its abstract character and gravity seem to hold out little attraction to the female mind, nor can we discover it in precedent, emulation, or example set elsewhere, for female authors have been comparatively rare in Jewish literature, nor is this field at all cultivated by continental Jewesses. Teeming as the modern German and French Jewish presses do with literary

productions, we are not yet acquainted with one which proceeded from a female mind. This distinctive mark seems to be wholly and entirely reserved for the Anglo-Jewish literature.[19]

For Benisch, "literature" primarily meant translations of Talmudic and biblical text and commentaries, but here he includes as well the fictional and polemical productions of Grace Aguilar, Anna Maria Goldsmid, and Charlotte Montefiore. Still, Benisch and other reform-ist men showed signs of anxiety about women's initiative.[20] Benisch's response to this "remarkable phenomenon" was to found a Jewish men's literary club and offer prizes for the best essays. As the years passed, and still no Jewish male champion of letters stepped forward, he continued to lament the lack.

Women's emergence as writers continued to produce praise mixed with anxiety among reformist men over the next three decades. In 1858, and again in 1860, 1867, and 1887, the *Chronicle* reprinted a list of short biographies of historical "Learned Jewish Women" by Dr. Carmoly.[21] The *Chronicle's* anonymous "Communal Weekly Gossip" took one occasion of the reprint of the article to make the following observation:

> This [list] of learned Jewish women furnished by Dr. Carmoly . . . is far from being complete. It might be carried on to great advantage . . . to our own time. Our own England, in our age, takes the lead of them. There is at present not a country which either absolutely or relatively can boast of so many distinguished daughters of Israel as Great Britain. In fact, it is our women who at this moment represent Anglo-Jewish authorship; nor do they unworthily represent Anglo-Jewish learning, piety, and zeal. But for the mental activity displayed by them, but for the ardour of Jewish feeling manifested by them, the history of Anglo-Jewish inner religious life and higher aspirations would present a blank. Jewish men have in our own time performed comparatively little; but Jewish women have excelled.

Perhaps by praising these women and reprinting the article the *Chronicle* hoped to fend off criticism by conversionists and Jewish women themselves that reform-minded men in the community had for the most part neglected to keep their promise to educate women.

Although ostensibly reforming men were committed to the goal of women's education, it was difficult to find them taking the issue seri-ously, even as late as the 1860s. Many reformers were finally no less committed to the separation of spheres than their more traditional contemporaries. Michaelis Silberstein, translator from German of Herder, a life of Mendelssohn, and other "enlightened" texts, argues that "There is nothing that makes women more unpleasant, and consequently more unhappy, than if they overstep the charming contrast of the sexes, in assuming the occupations and the cares of a man, and in usurping his sphere of activity and education." He goes on to point to the prayer in the Birkhot Hashachar, the morning blessings, thanking God that man is not a woman and exclaims: "what man on earth would not utter such a prayer? who would not thank God most fervently that he has not made him like a woman, but that he has girded him with strength, to go forth as a valiant defender of his fatherland, as a righteous judge. . . . What prayer would the learned editor utter in time of need and danger, if a beloved wife, a mother, a sister, or any other of the weaker sex, looked up to him for protection?"[22] The difference between Silberstein and a traditionalist is that where the traditionalist is disgusted by chivalry as a Christian invention, the reformer here invokes chivalry to support the Jews' anglicized version of the separation of spheres.

Even those reformers who supported a less severe separation than Silberstein tended to invoke the chivalric paradigm. On November 8, 1861, in an editorial possessively titled "Our Women," Benisch claimed that "Ungallant men assailed the fair sex" as frivolous, mercenary, extravagant, and conversionist. Women responded with a "brave defense made by the women themselves." By this "brave defense" he seems to mean the literary production of Aguilar, Charlotte Montefiore, Hester Rothschild, Anna Maria Goldsmid, Maria Polack, and the Moss sisters. The men's time having been, until 1858, taken up with securing the removal of Jewish disabilities in Parliament, they have not been able to attend to the issue of the conversionist attack on women. But now it is time, he says, for "male champions" to come "into the field." Like Silberstein, Benisch is not troubled by metaphors derived from chivalry, as his more traditionalist counterparts are, for he is committed to anglicization, to appropriating the forms of English Christian thought, as he sees them, wherever possible. These romance categories of male champions defending members of the fair sex are, in his perception, the English way to think about men and women. Romance is intimately connected with anglicization; anglicization is intimately connected to reform.[23]

As a male champion, Benisch argues that the charges against Jewish women by their men are false. Still, he finds himself having to admit that women,

> in a religious point of view, unfortunately constitute the weakness of our camp. . . . Whilst in all denominations around us the females frequently form the broad arteries in which the religious life circulates, and always the capillary vessels through which it is carried into the households, . . . our own women, as a rule, are devoid of religious enthusiasm, and not rarely indifferent, if not absolutely hostile, to all religious aspirations. . . . Just compare the number of female worshippers attending the synagogues on Sabbath with those crowding the Churches on Sundays. Just compare the amount of Biblical and religious knowledge possessed by our women with that acquired by our neighbours. . . . Those acquainted with the communal history will have no difficulty in tracing many, if not most, of the losses [i.e., apostasies] sustained by the Jewish body to the pernicious influence exercised by women in their capacities as wives or mothers. This is a phenomenon perceived only in modern time.

According to Benisch, modern Jewish women not only are culpable when members of their family convert, but also are more easily drawn to Christianity than Jewish men because they are "less satisfied with the abstract than with the concrete, loving to individualise their ideal, whilst yet placing it beyond the bounds of the human." Loving to individualize an ideal is a necessity in adopting Christianity, which has in the person of Jesus individualized the ideal of divinity. To prevent Jewish women from needing such a crutch, he argues, they must be educated in the theory of Judaism just like the men: "We must begin by unrolling before the female mind the glorious principles upon which Judaism is based"—including the unity of God, Israel's mission, the halacha, and history. "We must fill the female heart with an ideal Israel. . . . Once convince the intellect . . . and enthusiasm is sure to come." At any rate, such an outcome is "much more likely" than if they are expected to follow "mere mechanical injunction." Benisch's desire that the Jewish community should stand up to Christian standards of religiosity drives him to argue for expansion of women's intellect beyond the traditionalists' inculcation of acts without theory. To aid this education in abstractions, Benisch calls for the creation of "a popular religious literature in the vernacular" (his own translation of the Pentateuch being a prime example), and for the institution of a Bat Mitzvah, arguing that "our females will feel themselves raised to the equals of men, and proud of the distinction of having been received into religious fellowship."[24] The need to produce Jewish women who are just as religious as Christian women, and to secure a separate religious sphere safely in the home, pushes Benisch to argue for what many considered radical reforms. The next several issues of the *Chronicle* were filled with angry responses to his editorial.

As Benisch's editorial shows, by the 1860s the Woman Question had made it to the national agenda in Victorian England, and had begun to affect the Anglo-Jewish community. Ever alert to the new requirements of anglicization, the men began to alter their paradigms for thinking about women's roles in the community. Even some nominally orthodox Jewish men began to see that female education and religious reform were necessary to head off the conversionists and maintain the faith in an age in which religious affiliation was voluntary. For all the rhetoric of equality, these reformers showed that they still held onto the Victorian separation of spheres—but this did not preclude them from proposing radical alterations in women's opportunities. In fact, quite the contrary; the separation is the reason for making radical alterations. An article in the *Chronicle* "On the Education of Israelitish Girls" on April 18, 1862, sums up this position nicely when it argues that female education is more important than male education since women are the keepers of Jewish spirituality in the home. The writer continues that the rabbis of the Middle Ages reversed the priority because they were persecuted and did not have their minds clear. But Christians know that Jews still maintain this backward system, and so "It is the women . . . towards whom the efforts of the conversionists are daily directed; these seducers knowing well that this is the best means, sooner or later, to draw over whole families to their side." In biblical times, women were taught with men, but the "Judaism of the middle ages has . . . abandoned women." The writer essentially agrees with the conversionist assertion of Jewish women's oppression. But whereas the conversionist sees the way out of this problem in conversion, the reformist writer sees women's oppression as a major justification for religious reform. He asks which of the two traditions regarding women—the more permissive of "ancient Mosaism" or the more restrictive of "the middle ages"—modern Jews are to choose. For him, as for reformers across the continent, this is a nonchoice; or rather, it is the difference between following God's revelation, "the great law of Sinai," and the mere musings of biased rabbis, "the human law." This reformist writer assumes the Talmud is not divine law.[25] The answer to his question is therefore obvious: "Fathers

71

and Mothers! instruct your daughters not in the science of superficial formalism, but in the great principles of the religious idea."[26] Talmudism, in this typical reformist view, is a set of formalistic laws. What is needed is a more flexible, more spiritual tradition, that of a Jewish ethical monotheism emphasizing "the great principles of the religious idea." This reformist philosophy contains the same ambivalence between particularism and universalism involved in Lewis's or Scott's invocation of the idea, but as an ethical philosophy independent of halachic tradition, it need not be held back from women. Victorian Jewish male members of the reform movement argued that a just solution to the Woman Question required the redefinition of Judaism away from a halachic framework.[27]

This male champion of Jewish women's education was expressing the position that reformist Anglo-Jewish men had reached by the 1860s. Although based on a recognition that Jewish men had treated Jewish women unequally in the past, it remained in seeming accord with traditionalism's separation of spheres, restricting women primarily to the home and to charitable activities. If reform meant, in part, bringing liberal ideals to bear on Jewish practice, democratizing the synagogue officeholder procedures by introducing elections and dispensing with payments for various honors on the Sabbath, it seemed to mean as well at least paying lip service to bringing equality between the sexes. Jewish emancipation in the external world might mean at least a measure of women's emancipation in the Jewish world. For men, however, this emancipation did not mean an equal distribution of duties, rights, and privileges.

CENSORSHIP

If reformers like Benisch were theoretically in favor of extending religious education and a certain amount of intellectual equality to girls and women, they did not intend that this "equality" should practically entail any diminution in their own power. The same men who argued for the modernization of women's roles in the public institutions of the synagogue, the school, and the press often experienced such modernization as a disruption of their own roles. By far the most acute feelings of disruption were inspired by women's entrance into the world of publishing. The fact that the synagogue and the educational system were fast ceasing to be male preserves in Jewish life was upsetting, but Victorian domestic ideology demanded that men should accept women's participation in church and school if they wished to be accepted as citizens. The idea that women should break up Jewish men's monopoly in learnedness and publishing—the achievements that since the Middle Ages had constituted the very definition of Jewish manhood—was on the other hand intolerable. The fact that women's publications outnumbered and outsold men's argued that men had somehow become "unmanly." This feeling was exacerbated by the fact that many men disapproved of the direction in which women writers were pushing the community, but were unable to do anything about it. They seemed unable, that is, to form a literary response that could compete in the marketplace with women's novels, those specimens of a modern genre that was foreign to Jewish literary history. As one man said of Aguilar's novel *Woman's Friendship,* women's use of the form seemed to prove that they were becoming "Jewish Protestants," just as conversionists claimed. Yet men seemed unable to displace the novel form with their more traditional midrashic, philosophical, and aggadic productions.

For these reasons, the men's desire to allow women more of a part in Anglo-Jewish public life was simultaneously accompanied by a desire to intimidate women out of public life. This charge is borne out vividly in two cases of male relations with Jewish women writers. In both cases, the men were the most well respected scholars and editors of their day—Benisch and Philadelphia's Isaac Leeser. Both (after repeated suggestions by Grace Aguilar) had published English translations of the Bible. Both edited important periodicals, the *Jewish Chronicle* and the *Occident.* Both solicited work by Jewish women. And both exercised a punitive form of authority over these women's texts.

Isaac Leeser, rabbi of Mikveh Israel in Philadelphia, encouraged women's writing. He solicited women writers, helped find them publishers, and provided a means for communication between Jewish women in England and America when there were no women-run publications that could serve the same purpose. But when it came down to questions of theology and philosophy, perhaps he felt that as a rabbi he had the duty to act as critic and censor. As he declared in a sermon on women's education, "It is not to be denied that it is almost entirely useless for the female to become learned in the strictest sense of the word; it would unsex her."[28] The most blatant example of his censorship is his edition of Grace Aguilar's reformist meditation on Judaism's central prayer, the Shema, in *The Spirit of Judaism* (1842). Not only did Leeser insert editorial disagreements throughout the text, he appended an editor's preface in which he set forth the "chief points of difference between Miss Aguilar and myself."[29] The result is that one cannot read Aguilar's book without simultaneously reading Leeser's refutation of it.

The reactions to this editorial procedure varied in predictable ways. When *Spirit of Judaism* was published, the Jewish press was still in its infancy. Aguilar's book was the first by a woman to be reviewed. On April 1, 1842, Jacob Franklin, editor of the *Voice of Jacob,* called attention to women's increased visibility in the public life of the community, and connected this new female activity to the advent of the religious reform and emancipation movements: "This is truly becoming a printing age among our people," he began. "The spirit of former times is reviving and an imperious sense of duty is impelling many to step forth from the ranks, to enquire, and to inform." But Franklin did not view the results of this development entirely with excitement. With Aguilar's work before him, he asked, "Where are our *leaders?*" implying that because of her gender, Aguilar could not be one of them. He looked with favor on Leeser's editorial procedure because Leeser had "deeper research, wider experience, and, therefore, sounder judgment," while Aguilar is "a lady, and that too a young lady" who "by the iron rule of custom" had been "limited to fewer opportunities of acquiring information and experience." In 1842, Franklin was not prepared to admit that a Jewish woman's pen could make as important a contribution to Anglo-Jewish self-understanding as a Jewish man's.

The conversionists, on the other hand, who thought Aguilar's writing would "lead to the cross of Christ," felt Leeser's editorial procedure proved their assertion about the arrogance of Jewish men.[30] Aguilar herself seemed chastened by it, acknowledging that she was indeed undereducated.[31] Yet, if her knowledge was limited, she might have responded (and often subsequently did) that her limitations were only those that all Anglo-Jewish women experienced. If some of her work bore a Protestant cast, for example, it was because much of her reading on religious subjects was limited to Christian books, since these, and not Jewish books, appeared in English.[32] The prospect of a woman setting forth her views on Judaism seemed agreeable to Leeser—as long as those views accorded with his more traditionalist views. A woman could not simply speak from her own experience and expect to be supported for doing so.

The case of Abraham Benisch and Marion Hartog's *Jewish Sabbath Journal* is perhaps a more egregious instance of censorship, because while Leeser at least published Aguilar's book (and assured her a large sphere of influence), Benisch's censorious act had a measurably negative effect on a generation of women who followed Hartog. In July of 1854, Marion Hartog brought out a prospectus for a new periodical, the *Jewish Sabbath Journal; A Penny and Moral Magazine for the Young*. Hartog, along with her sister Celia Levetus, was already well known for her historical romances *The Romance of Jewish History* (1840) and *Tales of Jewish History* (1843), as well as for her occasional poems that appeared in the *Chronicle*. In her prospectus, Hartog advertised the *Jewish Sabbath Journal* in language that fully accorded with Victorian Jewish men's domestic ideology, which, as we have seen, placed the responsibility for religious instruction of children squarely on the woman's shoulders. "It is an undeniable fact," Hartog says, "that the frequent desecration of the Sabbath, more especially among the junior members of our community, is mainly attributable to insufficient religious teaching. Alas! the days are gone when the elders sat in the gate, and expounded the laws to all who sought to drink at the fountains of living waters; and none have arisen to supply their place. . . . The majority of Jewish children, especially boys, receive their education at Christian public schools, or from private Christian teachers." She is speaking in Benisch's language—the language of Jewish female home instruction of children—and he endorses her call for a public subscription, saying that "the cost will be so trifling, and the talents of the editress are so well known, that we consider it a duty to recommend it."[33] Not astounding praise, perhaps, but enough to give the project legitimacy in the eyes of the public.

Without his endorsement, perhaps, the *Chronicle* might never have received the slew of letters to the editor that followed in support of the *Sabbath Journal,* and had he not supported it, the *Chronicle* would probably never have published them. Although Hartog's justification had been that the journal would serve the purpose of "home instruction," almost from the beginning, the readers who wrote in (mainly women) understood that the *Journal* would not only address the young. In fact, ever since Haim Guedalla's failed effort to edit a Jewish literary periodical called *Sabbath Leaves* some years before, a literary publication had been a desideratum in the community. "An Expectant

Subscriber" (whose gender cannot be determined) imagined that the *Jewish Sabbath Journal* would be "the upholder of Jewish rights, the standard of Jewish literature, and within the reach of even the poorest!" An emancipationist journal for the young? A "standard of Jewish literature" for the young? The rhetoric of youth education clearly reads as a necessary but by no means sufficient cultural code for what Hartog was attempting. This supporter went on to say that "judging by the poems of Mrs. Hartog in your valuable journal, she is fully capable of undertaking the important office." "A Mother in Israel" wrote seeking to be on a women's committee to distribute the *Journal* free to the poor. "A Subscriber from the Beginning" opined that "a work of the kind is required, the active mind must be fed." Perhaps the fullest understanding of the role of a women's periodical in the community was expressed by "R. H. A.," a woman who was to publish many articles and stories in the *Journal* once it became a reality:

> we do indeed want words that will find their way into the home circle, sentiments that shall mingle amidst the doings of everyday life. . . . We thirst for the living waters that shall strengthen our faith, soften our feelings, ennoble our nature, and make us worthy of the name we bear. . . . The subjects must . . . be popularised and simplified, so as to find a ready acceptance in the humble abode as well as on the table of the wealthy. . . . It is a significant sign that this goodly work is undertaken by a female hand. More than one victory has been achieved by woman . . . —to plant the banner of religion where faith sleeps and is dormant, to root out coarseness and ignorance, to make room for intelligence and refinement, to draw closer the social bond, and teach Israel to feel and to know that he is Am Echad (one people). Such are some of the happy results to which this unpretending journal may help lead the way.[34]

In this view, women not only teach children, but popularize Judaism for adults, both rich and poor, in so doing strengthening the social bonds of a religiously and economically diverse community. The role of the Jewish woman's periodical mirrors the role of the Jewish woman writer, who was said to be "the moral governess of the Hebrew family."[35]

Despite these shows of support, subscriptions for the *Journal* trickled in slowly. It was customary among English Jews, as Benisch bewailed on a number of occasions, not to support literary pursuits in the community. Despite the slow start, Marion Hartog herself worked hard to win the public to her cause, placing notices of the number of subscriptions received in the *Chronicle* weekly. She also published "Lines Written on the Death of Grace Aguilar" (November 10, 1854), which in its final lines unabashedly called on the community to support her project:

> How long shall Israel's thoughtless great ones . . .
> (Who to be learning's patrons should be proud)
> Let living genius hopeless pine away,
> And waste their empty honours on a shroud.

The rich are being called on to support a community-wide effort: the fantasy is that the journal will provide a space in which the diverse classes of Jews will cohere into a single community. The poem was followed the next week by a letter lamenting Aguilar's death, and calling on mothers to support Hartog's efforts: "Another claimant now appeals to us for aid in a good and righteous cause; I trust she will not also have to complain of Israel's apathy. . . . Mothers . . . , will you refrain when . . . you may be the means of bringing the light of truth to the homes of the ignorant?" This writer has expanded Hartog's mandate to include not just the young but any uneducated or poor Jew.

Still, despite such appeals, the pace of subscription continued to be slow.[36] Hartog, who had placed herself more in the public light than almost any woman of her time, began to feel the strain, and wrote in saying "I am obliged to confess, that I fear [the publisher] Mr. Valentine's prognostic of failure will be borne out by the event, and that there is no support for Jewish periodical literature."[37] She promised to return all subscriptions if she had not received enough by the end of November. She was entreated by a group of thirty-four women in Liverpool not to give up the project (November 24, 1854). She continued publishing poems in the *Chronicle* that contained veiled hints about the *Sabbath Journal*.[38] At last, however, on December 8, 1854, Hartog wrote in that the project was under way, showing, too, how much of a strain being constantly before the public had been for her: "Sir,—A few weeks since, when I wrote to you respecting the 'Jewish Sabbath Journal,' it was in a spirit of despondency which nearly led to the abandonment of a project, the realisation of which has been the dream of more than half my life. Since that time I have received many letters on the subject, which have revived my courage." She had certainly been planning this project for a long time. But why did such a task require courage? It required courage because it was the first of its kind anywhere in the world—the first Jewish women's periodical in modern history.[39] Without models to work from, Marion Hartog was able to muster the courage and the funds to underwrite the project. On January 5, 1855, the *Chronicle* carried the announcement of the *Jewish Sabbath Journal*'s first appearance on February 22.

But then—weeks passed. As the first three issues of the *Journal* appeared, the *Chronicle* became silent and did not give the *Journal* any notice. Hartog grew anxious, hurt, and finally angry. In an editorial in the *Journal,* she complained:

> We have received letters from numerous correspondents, inquiring why our little serial has not been reviewed in the "Hebrew Observer" [the forerunner of the *Chronicle*]; and one Christian friend asks if we have neglected to send it to the Editor. We can but answer that we have been duly attentive to the courtesies usually bestowed on the press, and that we constantly advertize in that journal, but the Editor, for some reason unknown to us, has not even shown the common civility of acknowledging the receipt of the "Sabbath Journal." Is it forgetfulness on his part, or is it wilful? We know not, and we care not to inquire.[40]

The publication of these fatal words is a crucial moment for the understanding of gender relations between Jews in the Victorian period. Hartog, as an editor of her own journal, feels sufficiently at home inside her pages to be able to criticize one of the most powerful men in the community. The journal, she believes, provides her a zone of security—she speaks almost as if she were sharing an intimate conversation with a few friends. And indeed, by this point, with five numbers issued, the *Journal* had become a women's alternative to the other Jewish periodicals. The readership, the authorship, the editorship—all of these were almost solely the domain of women. Women who had never previously published stories began to submit. They wrote stories about women who become successful independent artists, free of their families. Women wrote sermons—among English Jews, heretofore exclusively a male genre. They wrote meditations on the mother/child and mother/daughter relationships, relationships that were unexplored in mainstream Jewish periodicals, which tended to concentrate on the father/daughter and father/son relationships. They wrote exposés of Hebrew-Christian Free Schools that drew in poor Jewish girls.[41] And the submitters received gentle criticism and encouragement from "the Editress."[42] In other words, what started off as an ideologically correct enterprise—a woman becoming a moral governess educating the communal children—quickly became something else. It quickly became a security zone, a women-only space, a place of female independence. Or at least it became the illusion of such a space, the articulation of the desire for such a space.

How little security and relative power Hartog had, however, became almost immediately apparent. On March 23, 1855, Benisch published his long-awaited review in the *Chronicle*. In it, he destroyed the *Journal*:

> The Editress of the above Journal in blaming us for not having noticed her publication, insinuates that our silence is the effect of unworthy motives. Now we must protest against the assumption that an Editor is obliged to take notice of every publication forwarded to him. It is obvious that he must exercise great discretion in the selection of subjects for notice, and that he is not at all obliged to state publicly the reasons which guide him in that selection. We should, therefore, have paid no attention whatever to the insinuations made, were it not attempted to make use of our silence as political capital, and to represent us as a wrong-doer. We will, therefore, depart from our rule, and state the reasons of our silence. We have left the production unnoticed, not because in the abstract we do not wish for such a publication. . . . We have left the "Sabbath Journal" unnoticed because we could not conscientiously recommend to the community the two numbers sent to us, since some of their contents appeared to us calculated to promote superstition, to pass off accounts drawn from profane sources as the word of God, and to lay down doctrines which we consider un-Jewish, and adopt views which, in their ultimate consequences, may lead away from Judaism. . . . [A] publication conducted by parties so little conversant with the principles of the religion which it is designed to inculcate, cannot be safely and conscientiously recommended to the community.

This was a remarkable review coming from a man who had encouraged Hartog, published supportive reviews of her earlier work, printed her occasional poems for years, and referred to her just months before as "talented." It was all the more remarkable because the Chief Rabbi of the British Empire himself had given his personal approval to the project.[43] Benisch's commitment to female "equality" seems to have had a short tether. In this crucial test of this powerful reformer's commitment to female emancipation, he censored a woman with little power when she misbehaved. He silenced her when she criticized. He did so by wielding charges to which women were vulnerable in the community and to which they could not respond: he called her uneducated, profane, superstitious, un-Jewish. In fact, he employed the same epithets typically directed at Jewish women by conversionists.

The result: Hartog's subscriptions fell off. She was no longer able to publish notices in the *Chronicle*. Despite the fact that many women expressed their support, Hartog resolved to close the *Journal*. The last number of the *Journal* ended with a poem "On the Death of My Beloved Child." Hartog lived for another fifty years, maintaining a boarding school with her husband and her sister. But except for a few occasional poems, she seldom published again. Her literary career was over.[44]

Women who published in the years following her debacle were timid. They were submissive to the point of obsequiousness. For example, when Miriam Mendes Belisario announced her intent to bring out a book on "Sabbath Evenings at Home"—a project similar in aim to Hartog's *Sabbath Journal*—she "begs to state, that she has submitted her humble efforts to the religious supervision of the Rev. D. A. de Sola, not feeling herself justified in proffering instruction of such vital importance to her young co-religionists, on her own unsanctioned authority."[45] "Little Miriam," the self-denigrating pen name of a woman who published a series of stories for youth based on biblical incidents, allowed her work to be published and edited under the auspices of the Jewish Association for the Diffusion of Religious Knowledge. Perhaps because she ceded authority for her texts to men, she became "quite an Anglo-Jewish institution of our day."[46]

Censorship and direct warnings were more visible during the 1860s and 1870s when the Woman Question was on the national agenda. An 1864 poem in the *Chronicle* called "Rights of Woman" set out to explain to women their roles:

> The rights of woman, what are they?
> The right to labour, love, and pray;
> The right to weep with those that weep,
> The right to wake when others sleep.
>
> The right to dry the falling tear;
> The right to quell the rising fear;
> The right to smooth the brow of care,
> And whisper comfort in despair.

The right to watch the parting breath,
To soothe and cheer the bed of death:
The right, when earthly hopes all fail,
To point to that within the veil.

The right the wanderer to reclaim,
And win the lost from paths of shame;
The right to comfort and to bless
The widow and the fatherless.

The right the intellect to train,
And guide the soul to noble aim;
Teach it to rise above earth's toys,
And wing its flight for heavenly joys.

The right to live for those we love;
The right to die that love to prove;
The right to brighten earthly homes
With pleasant smiles and gentle tones.

Are these thy rights? Then murmur not
That women's mission is thy lot;
Improve the talents God has given;
Life's duty done, thy rest is heaven.[47]

Here, the notion of "rights" is transposed from the legal realm to the realms of the domestic, the spiritual, and the social. The woman is imagined to be middle or upper class, tending to the needs of the poor and dispossessed. She is described as being responsible for children's education, but her "intellect" is not meant to be used critically. Here, the English doctrine of separate spheres particularly influenced Jewish men to demand that their Jewish sisters, daughters, and wives "murmur not."

The *Chronicle*'s lead article of 1875, "Faith and Its Influence on Women," revealed the ways in which suppression of women's opinions could be sought in less direct fashion. In the guise of an article on female faith, it quickly becomes a critique of the fledgling woman's movement. According to the editor, "possibly there is no feature of the age more dangerous or more distressing than the growing irreligion of women. It was formerly a fact, and it is at present a fancy, that women are more religious, more disposed to belief, than men. . . . That simple unquestioning trust in Revelation, which was one of the greatest charms and graces of womanhood, seems to be giving place to a hard philosophy." This "hard philosophy," which is complex and questioning, consists in the ideology of the New Woman: "The 'home' has ceased to be the sole stage on which they shine. They now seek to gain the glitter of the 'world.' The movements for the employment of women, and the education of women in spheres hitherto believed to belong exclusively to men, may have refined their minds, but have they preserved their hearts? . . . Are we training girls . . . in the paths in which our mothers were trained in those halcyon days when the examinations of Oxford and Cambridge were not held of so high account as the examinations of the Conscience?"[48] The nostalgia for the "halcyon days" before women were too secularly educated is accompanied by an increased call for "the religious education of the womanhood of the future." Religious education is perceived as synonymous with domesticity, while secular education is aligned with the New Woman. The article's very tone—not addressed to women, but to male readers who could share the feeling of loss over the end of male-only privilege—excludes women from its audience. Censorship could take the form of rhetorical exclusion as well as outright denial of "rights."

It could also take the form of positive reinforcement, as in the review of Mrs. Atrutel's *Book of Jewish Cookery,* in which the reviewer hopes "that the day has not gone by for Jewish ladies to superintend . . . the most agreeable and womanly duty of domestic management. . . . We trust that in the struggle for Woman's Rights and the anxiety which women manifest to attain and assume positions from which Nature herself . . . seems to bar them ladies will not recklessly abandon the humble household duties. . . . Cooking is surely more practically useful than Chemistry, and a girl should know as much about the production of a pudding as about the parentage of a Plantagenet."[49]

Besides using positive reinforcement to criticize the women's movement, the strategy of using a male editorial hand to control the public interpretation of a woman's text remained useful into the 1870s, as in the review of *The Hebrew Woman* by Constance de Rothschild, whose aristocratic family connections nevertheless could not entirely protect her from criticism. The editor at the *Jewish Chronicle* praises de Rothschild's portrait when she says that Jewish women should "minister to the happiness of the domestic hearth," but disagrees with her at any point in which she suggests that Jewish men have limited women's freedom. For example, when she suggests that rabbis in the Middle Ages deliberately placed women in a secondary and degraded

position, he counters that they were just "naturally sharing the dominant prejudices."[50] Women could identify limitations on women, but
this type of editorial control ensured that they could not seek to place
the blame for these limitations on the men who controlled the institutions that controlled their lives. Women could speak out, but they
faced chastisement for speaking out too critically, and men had a
variety of means to limit, trivialize, or undermine their statements in
the public sphere. These included using the editor's prerogative to
criticize their work, using the reviewer's prerogative to undermine
their attempts to establish women-only institutions, addressing only
men in their writings, directly refusing women legal rights, and moral-
izing on women's proper spheres.

ROMANCING THE JEWISH MAN:
THE CASE OF THE DISRAELIS

In order to assimilate the Victorian separation of spheres, Jewish
men began to see a need for women to be active, intellectual,
educated—if only to ensure that they would fulfill the standards of
good motherhood that Victorian domestic ideology demanded. But the
prospect of a community in which women were educated, published,
dispensing opinions, and influential frightened these men with visions
of usurpation of their masculinity and brought out the punitive underside of their benevolent paternalism. One might think that this ambivalence in all its complexity could be detected in the men's fictions, but
in the early and mid-Victorian period, Jewish men did not usually
engage in explicitly fictional production because they did not conceive
of fiction as a valid Jewish form. In fact, men who did write explicitly
fictional productions were deemed outsiders.

Jewish men defined literature as ancient biblical and medieval rabbinic literature. More modern forms such as novels were understood
by them to be distinctly foreign literary genres—and if one agrees
with Michael McKeon's argument in *The Origins of the English Novel,*
they were right: the novel grew out of medieval Christian chivalric
romances.[51] In fact, the earliest Jewish male periodicals rarely explicitly discussed modern Jewish life at all. Morris Raphall's *Hebrew Review and Magazine of Rabbinical Literature* (1834–36) contained

articles on the transmission of the oral law, on Maimonides, on the
Shulkhan Aruch, and other concerns traditional to the genre of the
moral weekly. When Raphall did break with tradition to discuss a
modern Jewish thinker, he did so in order to provide a picture of an
ideal path for modern Jewish men, and this ideal path did not include
writing fiction. His obituary for Arthur Lumley Davids, a leading
Anglo-Jewish male thinker who died young, praises him for having
written a work of Jewish philosophy and a work of philology, as well as
for delivering vernacular sermons and for his emancipation appeals in
the *Times*.[52] Other biographies of contemporary Jewish male heroes,
such as Isaac Lyon Goldsmid and Francis Henry Goldsmid (father and
brother of translator Anna Maria Goldsmid), emphasized their practical efforts on behalf of Jewish emancipation and their essays in that
cause.[53] Generally speaking, until emancipation was achieved, most of
Jewish men's energies were geared to the practical attainment of that
goal. Writing fiction, they felt, was not only impractical and therefore
trivial, but would feminize them in the eyes of a host culture that
directed its novels to young women. When, in 1844, several reformers
did desire to found a Jewish literary institution, they established the
Jews and General Literary and Scientific Institute (JGLSI). Besides
holding meetings on Moses Mendelssohn and Bishop Lowth, these
men were interested in such nonfictional topics as whether man is a
carnivore, the effect of Henry VIII's destruction of the monastic establishment on England, and the politics of Pitt.[54] When Abraham
Benisch established the Anglo-Jewish library in 1855, he set out to
collect works of history, biography, ethics, sermons, and ancient Judaism, but no fiction.[55]

Moreover, even these nonfictional "literary" projects met with little
support from the community. M. H. Bresslau, in an article entitled
"Have the Jews any Literature?" complained that "the smallest Jewish
book in England meets with every difficulty in selling it among his
bretheren, unless he offers it from house to house and turns literary
beggar!"[56] Literary men in the community regularly attempted to establish journals and institutions that just as regularly foundered for lack
of communal financial support. Such was the fate of Haim Guedalla's
Sabbath Leaves, the JGLSI, the Literary and Translation Society, and
the Anglo-Jewish library. If men were not willing to support such
traditional Jewish genres as translation of ancient texts or such newly
popular reformist genres as the sermon, they certainly were not ready
to participate in writing fiction.

Perhaps the limits on Anglo-Jewish male writers can best be perceived in relation to the fiction of two who had gone beyond its
boundaries. The community's most famous convert, Benjamin Disraeli, may have claimed a racial connection with Jews past and future,
but his novels demonstrate that his concerns and genres were quite
distant from those of men living within the social and political constraints of the Anglo-Jewish community of his day.[57] His father, Isaac
D'Israeli, had long before begun to put distance between himself and
the Sephardic community. The story of the father's rebellion against
the Sephardic regulations, or *Ascamot,* is well known (he refused to
pay a monetary penalty the elders required of him), as is his subsequent conversion of Benjamin and his sister when Benjamin was thirteen, the age of Bar Mitzvah.[58] What is less well known is the distance
Isaac D'Israeli had begun to place between himself and his Jewish
forebears before converting his children, not in the area of communal
affairs, but in the area of literature.

English Jewry's first "man of letters," Isaac D'Israeli was known in
the London of the 1820s and 1830s for his dilettantish anecdotes and
essays in his *Curiosities of Literature.* Most of these "curiosities" have
little to do with his Jewishness, but rather are concerned with the
criticism and creation of an English "national literature," in which he
hopes to play a prominent part. In "Drinking-Customs in England," for
example, he traces "a new era in this history of our drinking-parties
[which] occurred about the time of the Restoration."[59] This reference
to the Restoration as part of "our" history is intriguing because the
D'Israeli family did not arrive in England from Italy until 1748. In
order to claim belonging to English national history he feels he must
erase or distort his relation to Jewish familial and communal history.

Of all Isaac D'Israeli's writings (which fill seven volumes), one
volume squarely centers on Jewishness, *The Genius of Judaism,* published in 1833.[60] In this sustained attack on "rabbinism" and the Talmud, D'Israeli bids to become an English version of the German-
Jewish *Gebildeters,* or reformers. As continental reformers often did,
D'Israeli aligns himself with members of an important ancient off-
shoot of Judaism, the karaites, as well as with Protestants who read the
Bible according to their inner lights rather than in reference to established authority. As he says, "Jewish Reformers or Protestants, as the
Caraites may be distinguished, often arose to relieve themselves from
the degrading servitudes, and the bewitching superstitions of rabbinical Judaism" (10). But this karaite or "Jewish Protestant" not only

throws off superstitions, he attempts to throw off Jewish literary traditions and develop a new literary language. The language he wants to develop is the language of romance, as his tale of a "Jewish gentleman well known to the scientific world" indicates:

> A Jewish gentleman, well known to the scientific world, and moreover a lover of ancient romances, had often luxuriated in the descriptions of the splendid banquet of the "Peacock," so famed in the Romances of Chivalry. In an hour of fancy he had a peacock killed; the skin was carefully taken whole from the body, and when the bird was roasted and richly farced with aromatic spices, the skin was nicely replaced, and it was served up with its gorgeous plumage. A religious scruple suddenly haunted his mind that the demon *Trefo* sat on the peacock, and that its flesh was forbidden aliment. The Israelite despatched the brilliant fowl to the house of a neighbour, the Chief Rabbin, for his inspection. He told his tale, the Rabbin alternately looking on the gentleman and on the peacock:—at length the oracle! First he solemnly observed that there were some things of a doubtful nature, among which was the eating of peacocks. He opined that this bird was among the forbidden meats. "Be it so!" exclaimed the romantic Ritualist; "it was the fancy of a moment, and I have only lost a splendid bird; I have not transgressed. Since it is killed, I will send it as a curious dish to my neighbour, who, being a Christian, is not perplexed by so difficult a ritual as our own. He may partake of the feast of the peacock."
> "I would thank you for it myself," said the Rabbin.
> "For what purpose?" interrogated the Ritualist.
> "To eat it!" rejoined the master of sentences.
> "How! If forbidden meat for me!—You understand the consequence?"
> The Rabbin fixing his eyes on the Ritualist, and holding his finger up, as we mark our interjections in writing, to prepare the reader, (here the hearer,) for the notable wisdom forthcoming, and with an emphatic *distinguo!* thus opined the Opinionist. "Eating the peacock is, as I told you, among the doubtful things. One Rabbin is of one opinion, and another of another. You have required my opinion as your Rabbin; you are bound to abide by it. I opine that it is unlawful to be eaten. My father was of a different opinion, and therefore it may be eaten by me, because I act on my father's opinion. I accept the peacock, but I must not ask you to participate in it." (170–73)

The Ritualist wants to eat the peacock because of his "fancy," that is, because of an individual desire sparked by Christian chivalric romance. The mere existence of such an individual desire not immediately referred to communal authority indicates that he is measuring himself in relation to the Christian world, living somewhat outside the bounds of a halachic community. Yet this Ritualist is willing to let a reasonable and even-handed Jewish law override his fancy for romance. The seeming arbitrariness of the Rabbin's decision, however, seems to show that Talmudic formalism is full of injustice and superstition. And this is only one indication among many that Judaism in its rabbinic formulation has not respected the needs or the desires of the individual.

It has certainly not respected the needs or desires of women. "The Rabbins . . . have treated Wives with an utter recklessness of domestic feeling; and in their morning thanksgivings there is one to God, for not having been made a woman. . . . [T]he Rabbins [drew from Deut. 24:1–2] the monstrous inference, that a man may put away his wife if he think another to be handsomer than her; and it is even maintained, for they build their follies as children build houses of cards, that a divorce may be allowed, even when a poor creature has suffered her husband's soup to be burnt" (169). As a reformer, then, D'Israeli combines the twin aims of liberating women from unreasonable rabbinic reasoning and claiming for himself the genre of romance. Both aims spring from this "scientific gentleman's" desire to apply reason to Jewish law and to increase the autonomy of the reasonable individual in the face of seemingly irrational communal dictates. But while liberating women and identifying with romantic chivalry were deemed within the reformist men's purview, the writing of romances was not. When later in the century Philip Abraham named his collection of miscellaneous items of Jewish interest *Curiosities of Judaism,* he was implicitly suggesting that D'Israeli's "curiosities of literature" were lacking a crucial Jewish element.[61] D'Israeli's earlier forays into romance suggest, then, that his final act of rebellion against the Sephardic *Ascamot* was the culmination of many years of slow movement outside the acceptable realms of Jewish manhood.

In this context in which the writing of romance seems beyond the bounds even of reformers, Benjamin Disraeli's early historical romances such as *Alroy* (and later *Coningsby* and *Tancred*) seem to place him outside the norms of Jewish communal life.[62] But Disraeli employs this genre without appearing to feel either trivialized or feminized by it, suggesting that as a convert he had his literary tastes shaped by opinions other than those expressed in the Anglo-Jewish subculture. In fact, the young Disraeli seems to have developed his taste for romance by attempting to imitate Byron.[63] His twelfth-century Jewish "Prince of the Captivity," David Alroy, bears a great deal of resemblance to the *Giaour* or *Cain,* Byron's brooding dark heroes. Having no vocation, Alroy resolves to rescue Jerusalem from the Christian crusaders. With cabalist Jabaster's and prophetess Esther's help, he succeeds in building a Jewish army, infusing it with messianic fervor, regaining the scepter of Solomon, and reconquering the East for the Jews. He is the messianic but practical leader Daniel Deronda is supposed to be after the end of Eliot's novel. But then, just when he is about to rebuild the Temple, Alroy is influenced by Jabaster's worldly brother Honain to attempt to conquer Baghdad—and he loses the scepter and the kingdom. A fantasy of Jewish power gone wrong, *Alroy* already relies on a racist belief in the superiority of Jewish blood, a belief that only becomes more explicit in his later "Young England" novels as Sidonia praises the superiority of those with "semitic" blood. These romantic, nationalist, and racist fantasies were a way in which Disraeli could claim his connection to his Jewish heritage, counter his anti-Semitic critics, and at the same time maintain a distance from actual Jewish cultural life. They served complex purposes for him. But, from a historical vantage point, they exemplify the ways in which his interest in historical romance was more synchronized with that of women living within the Jewish community than with men. Ironically, as he rose to power as prime minister, Jewish men increasingly tried to claim his kinship: "Benjamin Disraeli belongs to the Jewish people, despite his baptismal certificate," wrote one in 1876. "His talents, his virtues and shortcomings alike, are purely of the Jewish cast."[64]

MIDRASH

While Jewish men mostly refrained from writing fiction, they did reprint and expand on biblical stories that spoke to them in a traditional Jewish men's literary form—midrash Aggadah. This genre consisted of interpretations of biblical and Talmudic narratives, retold so as to speak to contemporary conditions.[65] While recognized as a creative form in which the writer could leave the strict letter of the text behind, such midrash had been able nevertheless to attain the force of law in traditional communities. The Anglo-Jewish men scanned the Bible and the Talmud looking for ways to understand the remarkable leadership taken by Jewish women in their day, and looking for narratives that reflected their sense of the proper separation of spheres. This scanning procedure was one that women writers could not engage in, for they had no access to the languages or the texts from which most of these midrashim were derived. With midrash, men sought to maintain Jewish patriarchy in the midst of modern upheaval. And with midrash, they sought to maintain a link with past Jewish literary tradition in the land of the novel.

What their search revealed was a series of narratives casting men's and women's roles as a relation between a benevolent father and a submissive daughter. Such father/daughter plots rationalized Jewish women's continuing secondary status from a variety of angles—traditionalist, scientific, reformist, antifeminist. In these midrashic narratives, men tacitly assimilated the conversionist father/daughter plot and altered it for their own interests. Principally they altered it by displacing the sympathy for the daughter back onto the father. This choice represented a terse but deliberate attempt to respond to conversionist narratives in kind but in a comfortably Jewish genre.

It was a common practice of Morris Raphall's traditionalist *Hebrew Review and Magazine of Rabbinical Literature* (1834–36), the first Jewish periodical to appear in English, to take "Talmudic Allegories" or midrashic tales out of their context, translate them into English, and publish them as separate pieces. In a periodical that shunned "fiction" as un-Jewish or trivial, these legends were among the first published Anglo-Jewish stories. For many English Jews (particularly women and uneducated men), these translations were the sole means by which they could gain any knowledge of the Talmud and of the meaning of traditional Judaism. But because so few of these midrashim were ever published, the very choice of legends could influence Victorian Jews' understanding of their classical heritage disproportionately, with only a little embellishment by Raphall. For instance, "The Sun and the Moon," which appeared in 1835, tells the story of how the male Sun became predominant over the female Moon. The Moon, envious of the Sun's greater light ("Why do two monarchs occupy one throne? Why must I be the second, and not the first?"), has her power stripped away by the Almighty Father for daring to ask such a question, and when she repents and accepts her secondary place, "weeping over her fault," she is given back a few silvery rays of light. The moral of the story Raphall has added drives the point home: "Daughters of beauty, beware of envy. Envy has driven angels from heaven"—or, perhaps Raphall's fear is, from the house.[66] The fear that "daughters" might begin to question their heavenly "father" if given half a chance was one major reason why Anglo-Jewish men did so little to bring about Anglo-Jewish women's education. This midrash is an ethe-realized father/daughter plot.

The midrash is all the more interesting when compared to its traditional sources. A slightly different version of the same legend was published in Louis Ginzberg's *Legends of the Jews*. The legend contains the gendered sun and moon, the moon's attempt to gain greater light than the sun, her punishment and remorse, her reinstatement, a second attempt to gain greater light than the sun, and a renewed punishment. Even more interesting than the legend, however, is Ginzberg's note that the moon "became a symbol of Israel and the pious, whereas the sun represents Esau and the ungodly."[67] In the traditional midrash, that is, God has sympathy for the moon. He reacts too harshly to Israel's sins, and allows her enemies to dominate her. God even seeks to atone for his mistake by making a sacrifice of atonement on the new moon. By leaving out this context, Raphall has managed to divest the moon of all sympathy. Rather than representing all of Israel—that is, men as well as women—the moon simply represents the sinning daughters to be chastised by their fathers.

The father/daughter plot appears again in what is by far the most bizarre midrash on biblical narrative on women, "The Origin of Woman," which appears some twenty-five years later in the *Jewish Chronicle*'s series on the "Creation."[68] The series was an attempt to dispute Bishop Colenso's controversial claim, in light of geological discoveries about the nature of time, that the Bible could not be depicting the literal truth, especially as regarded the creation story. The writer attempts to make the creation story measure up to the standards of Victorian science, and nowhere more so than in the section on the creation of Eve from Adam's side, which he sees as "the most singular and interesting part" of the Pentateuch. He disputes the common idea that God took one of Adam's ribs surgically out of his body and proposes in its stead "a natural process" that is "known to physiologists"—"parthenogenesis." Specifically, he proposes that Eve grew from Adam's side by a process known "among some of the lower animals" in which "the offspring grow by *gemmation,* or budding from the parent stock, and when arrived at a certain stage of maturity, they become separated by a natural process, and assume an independent existence." The idea is worked out in quite remarkable detail:

The gemmation commenced by there being formed below the rib a minute eyst, or sack, enclosing the germ of the new organism about to be developed. We may imagine, that, after attaining a certain stage of maturity, this vessicle was, with its contents, while yet very minute, extruded from the centre of the left breast, to which it remained attached by an umbiblical [sic] vascular attachment, similar to that by which the human fetus is attached under ordinary circumstances. We may farther suppose, that the enclosed embryon drew all its nourishment from the body of the man, through this vascular attachment, in the same manner as the fetus draws nourishment from the mother. The only difference would be in the situation of the germinal sack, which, in this particular case, would appear to have grown and become developed outwardly, instead of inwardly, as in the ordinary case.

According to this view, it is probable that the process of development occupied the usual period of nine months, during the whole of which Adam's state of unconsciousness was prolonged . . . . The subsequent nourishment of the infant would probably be accomplished in the ordinary way by lactation, the only difference being the substitution of the breasts of the male for those of the female, as the source of supply. That such a substitution is not altogether out of the course of nature, where it is required, by the necessity of the case, is fully proved by more than one authenticated case of an infant, who had lost its mother, having been nourished with milk from the breasts of its father . . . The necessity of providing for the early nutrition of the first female, destined to be developed out of the first male, may thus be held as accounting for the existence of these organs of nutrition in the male.

This learned speculation—a not at all disguised fantasy of male conquest of the birthing power—"involves the smallest amount of departure from the ordinary laws of organic development." Indeed, this reasoned argument becomes the basis for supposing that all female "viviparous animals whatever" were gemmated from male creatures. That is, in all the "higher" organisms, women were only created secondarily. Like "The Sun and the Moon," this scientific midrash sets out in a general way to theorize women's inferiority to men. And like "The Sun and the Moon," the woman turns out to be a daughter. Adam is Eve's father, giving birth to her without a mother, and nursing her. As in the father/daughter plots of conversionists, the mother is once again written out of the narrative. But this time the father is not a tyrant, as he is in the conversionist plots, but a benign ("unconscious") life-giving maternal presence. One thing is certain: such a painless pregnancy and labor could only have taken place before the expulsion from the garden.

In some ways, the scientist and the traditionalist proceed very differently. The earlier writer, Raphall, addresses only other Jews, while his successor looks outward to justify Jewish belief to the host community—an indication of men's increasing acculturation. Raphall bases his vision of female submission on a traditional midrash, while the learned scientist stretches the midrash form to contain the modern discourse of reason. Raphall is homiletic and particularist, while the other is expository and universalist. Yet, while they differ on many points, both the modernizer and the traditionalist use their midrashim of fathers and daughters to theorize women's inferiority. On that, if on nothing else, they can agree with one another. One of the functions this midrashic father/daughter plot serves, then, is to unite an increasingly diverse male community at women's expense.

By far the most often revived biblical story of the day was the story of Jeptha's daughter, relatively obscure to most Jews today (except for feminists), but repeated incessantly by Victorians, Jews and non-Jews alike.[69] What Victorians found in this tale was an explanation for most of the emotional currents of the father/daughter relationship that concerned them so much. In the Jewish community, this tale particularly spoke to religious reformers of both genders, who saw in it a critique of a Jewish father who, with his reliance on the rigid Talmudic legal system of halacha, breaks faith with his daughter—and although she must pay for his mistake, he must live with the guilt.

Jeptha is a judge (Judges 11) who, in this Victorian version is not the child of a harlot as he is in the Bible, but rather the "child of a favourite handmaid" of his father's. This respectable judge makes a vow to offer up the first thing he sees to the Lord, if only the Lord will make him victorious in an upcoming battle. Upon returning to Gilead victorious, the first thing he sees is his daughter. Since human sacrifice is against the law, the elders order her exiled to Shiloh, "where, in perpetual virgin seclusion, her days must pass in the service of a tabernacle." This perpetual seclusion is quite a departure from the biblical text, in which she is indeed sacrificed—Victorian "respectability" would not allow for such barbarism. Although not a word of reproach escapes her obedient lip, "To her, this destiny was worse than death . . . thus to lose home, and all held dear. To see none else but strangers near her, brought to her young bosom a chill as if from the tomb." Still, she keeps her chin up, and having cheered her despondent father ("Remember, thou hast many honours, father! Thou art a Judge of Israel! . . . thou hast much to render life dear to thee"), she takes her female companions on a pilgrimage around the city's environs to say farewell. After she has gone, the daughters commemorate her loss every year by walking the same paths around the city that she had walked on her last day, singing a lament.[70]

Like the conversionists, the Anglo-Jewish male reformer who updated Jeptha's story also adopts a father/daughter plot to envision the contemporary Jewish community. But while the conversionists see the father as materialistic, this Jewish reformer sees the father as stuck in an inflexible Jewish legal system—he sees the father as too traditionalist. Jeptha as good as kills his daughter with the law, for the traditionalist elders feel that they can bend the law only as far as to allow her a deathlike lifetime seclusion. Still, if the reformer's critique of halachic restrictions on women is evident, the separation of spheres is likewise evident. Jeptha's daughter, named only in relation to her father, is a woman who knows her place in the world. Cognizant that she still owes obeisance to her guilty father, she is able to meet the crisis without a word of complaint—indeed, like the ideal Victorian Jewish daughter, she represses all of her own feelings to help her father overcome his conscience. While conversionists understand their heroines' inherent spirituality as a form of latent Protestantism, this reformer understands the daughter's spirituality as a form of reformism. He depicts her commemorating her oppression and her transition by creating a new ritual and a song, just as reformers marked girls' transition to Jewish womanhood by creating the new ritual of Bat Mitzvah. And like Bat Mitzvah, this new ritual is generalized so that all Jewish women may participate in it, year after year. The wrong done Jeptha's daughter by her father is generalized as the oppression all Jewish women suffer under the law. It becomes the occasion for the creation of community among Jewish women. Perhaps this male reformer understood the song of Jeptha's daughter as an emblem of the new writing being produced by Anglo-Jewish women in his own day.

Only a few years later, Jewish men were using biblical stories to respond to the challenge of the New Woman, still concentrating on the father/daughter relationship. One of these midrashim concerns the daughters of Zelophehad (Num. 27:1–11), who, upon their father's death, ask Moses whether they may inherit their father's property, since their father has borne no sons. The Lord rules that the daughters do inherit. When this tale appeared in 1868, women's ownership of property was one of the central legal questions of the day. Jewish fathers were able to support a daughter's inheritance of property as long as there was no brother to inherit it. Although this writer is able to support reforms for women, the relationship of father to daughter still suggests that women are not understood as full and equal citizens.

Three years later, the Woman Question was playing in earnest throughout the Anglo-Jewish community, as it was throughout the dominant culture. Tract No. 105 of the Jewish Association for the Diffusion of Religious Knowledge, a highly touted male-organized association concerned with educating the Jewish poor, was called "Esther and the Mission of Woman." It purported to elucidate "woman's rights and woman's mission, woman's culture and woman's work" using the biblical story. The moral of this tract was this: "Do not try to arrogate to yourself the rights of man; exercise worthily the true rights of woman— rights which are no less arduous, though they are more blissful in results than those of man."[71] Here, interestingly, is the first time a midrash on women has not invoked the father/daughter plot. Nonetheless, women's agitation for rights produces an unambiguously negative response.

From traditionalist to scientist, from reformer to antifeminist, Jewish men wrote midrash when other forms of narrative were unacceptable to place themselves within a range of Victorian Jewish male opinions on the question of women's roles. These midrashim appeared in the most visible Jewish journals in the young Victorian Jewish public sphere. Sometimes the midrash was direct, moralistic, and punitive, as in "The Sun and the Moon" and "Esther and the Mission of Woman"; at other times, as in "The Origin of Woman," the woman's secondary status was structurally assumed rather than being insisted on. These midrashim shared in common the assumption that women's secondary status was not to be challenged. Other midrashim, such as "Jephtha's Daughter" and "Zelophehad's Daughters," were written by reformers with a more critical voice, a voice that was perhaps unable to free itself from its traditionally patriarchal assumptions of women's subordination, but that was increasingly aware of the costs of those assumptions to women, and in a different way also to men. Perhaps the progress of these men toward a profeminist stance was arrested by the very metaphor they chose to help them think through the problem of men and women, the same metaphor that their more traditionalist male coreligionists chose, the metaphor imposed by both dominant culture and a long history of Jewish patriarchy—that of the father in relationship with his daughter.

Ironically, by continuing to reject the novel form for the midrash, men left the field of the novel open to women, who embraced it. Thus the very existence of these midrashim reveals that the pace and the genres of modernization were different for women than they were for men. Men were still emerging from a traditional system of education with a focus on classical Jewish literary genres, while women, having received little or no formal education, had little connection to traditional forms or resistance to modern forms. In England, even reformist men saw themselves in some measure as preservers of continuity with the past.

MATTHIAS LEVY'S *THE HASTY MARRIAGE*

Of the several exceptions to the rule that men did not write fiction, the most telling is Matthias Levy's *The Hasty Marriage; a Sketch of Modern Jewish Life.* This "sketch" appeared in 1857, just as the struggle for emancipation was coming to a close and Jewish men could afford to turn their attention inward. Levy was an officer in the Great Synagogue and was well known as the historian of several orthodox synagogues in London; he was not the type of Jewish man one would expect to descend into the female realm of fiction, much less the genre of romance. Perhaps because he felt uncomfortable with crossing the genre-gender line, he adopted the pseudonym Nathan Meritor. On the other hand, perhaps he was merely protecting his reputation, for like the hero of his novel, traditionalist Edgar Lavite, he believes that "there are occasions in life when it becomes necessary, for our own security, to conceal our names, partly because by revealing them we do not assist the cause in which we may be engaged."[72] Levy's cause is "to save families from disgrace and children from ruin"—particularly female children whom he believes are in grave danger of giving in to the temptation to convert. He hopes to "bring clearly before the eyes of our authorities, as well as the authorities of other religions . . . the temptations which are held out to [Jewish girls] by the church, and the brilliant prospects, painted in gaudy colors, which are set before their eyes, and which induce them, more or less, to enter into the marriage state, contrary to, and in defiance of, divine law" (iii). Levy entered the realm of fiction in order to engage with the Christian romances that depicted Jewish women leaving their tyrannical and materialistic Jewish fathers to elope with a charismatic Christian suitor. Levy agreed with conversionists that Jewish women were more likely to convert than Jewish men, but he attributed these conversions to a different cause than the persuasiveness of missionary Christian rhetoric. Levy found the cause in the advent of religious reform among Jews, and specifically in what he saw as reformers' alliance with the literary genre, the romance. By writing a romance in which all of the conventional expectations are turned on their head, Levy attempted to confront reformers with their own hypocrisy. Yet, although he was able to satirize novel writing and the romance form, he was not able to ignore the form completely. In order to reach his target audience— anglicized Jews who increasingly read novels—he had to write in their language. A traditional Jew would not have rendered himself impure by engaging in an un-Jewish form. But traditionalists like Levy were not traditional Jews—they had been affected by modernity as much as reformers. If they wanted to be heard, traditionalists like Levy eventually realized they would have to write fiction.

Levy did everything he could to deny that he was writing fiction. Denigrating "the laws of novel-writing" (iv), he says he has used methods "which may, or may not, be allowable by the rules of novel writing" (iv)—including interspersing his own opinions and ideas and criticizing Christian conversionism. He takes pride in claiming that the plot of his novel "is greatly deficient" and that it was written "in a few leisure hours" (v) and then not altered, to render it devoid of artifice. Indeed, from the first chapter, he denies any affiliation between his work and the gothic, provincial, and historical varieties of the romance novel. "It is not to a shady nook or quiet retreat, that I am about to introduce the reader. . . . [I]t is not on a dusty road, bounded on either side by the hawthorn and sweet briar, where may be seen two horsemen, riding gallantly forward; it is not in an ancient gothic mansion, situated in _____, in the county of _____shire, several hundred miles from the metropolis. . . . And finally, it is not either to a prison or a dark alley, or any other spot which partakes of a gloomy appearance. . . . This work will have nothing of the romantic" (1–2). Moreover, the London house in which the story takes place "is not in a fashionable street. . . . Altogether, it was a street about which there was nothing that partook of mystery, people were not afraid to walk there; there were no old stories attached to it; nothing monstrous or absurd connected with it. It was . . . an ordinary street" (2–3). And, if we have not yet understood his rejection of romance for realism, the narrator introduces us to "an every-day matter-of-fact sort of place, with an every-day matter-of-fact sort of gentleman for its owner" (4). Like Maria Polack, the traditionalist woman who some thirty years earlier had published the first Anglo-Jewish novel, *Fiction Without Romance,* Levy is concerned to deny any hint that he is invoking the traditions that in traditionalists' eyes are traced to Christian origins. Indeed, the project of debunking the romance form as a Protestant—or, what amounted to the same thing, reformist—invention was one that seems to have transcended gender lines among traditionalists.[73]

Although his orthodoxy may explain why Levy takes a stand against romance, it does not fully explain why Levy is so insistent that this is not a work of fiction, when he is in fact telling a story with characters, a plot, and a narrative voice that sound remarkably like those of conventional novels. Why does he end scenes just before the climactic moment, skip over years, introduce new characters late in the narrative, and in general do everything he can to undermine his own project? There are many reasons. First, Levy was suspicious of art that depicted profane events. His attempt to write, not a novel, but a "sketch," is in line with what Steven S. Schwarzschild has called "the theology of the slashed nose." Schwarzschild refers to the practice of Jewish artists, mindful of the Second Commandment prohibiting idolatry, of deliberately introducing an imperfection into their art so that no one could mistake it for a spiritual representation.[74] According to Levy, then, the lack of artistry is proof that he is no idolater; specifically, he "slashes" his text to prove that he does not worship modern life—which the romance, the very form he satirizes, represents.

He had nothing but disgust for those Jews who wore fashionable clothes, taught their daughters popular piano music, or in other ways assimilated cultural codes from dominant Victorian life. These fashionable people he called reformers. *The Hasty Marriage* is written to prove that such reformist behavior will "bring misery on" such families and subject them to "the invasion of the enemy" (11). Fashion equals reform, and both are forms of romance that destroy the Jewish family.

Then, too, by writing fiction, Levy was entering into a female realm, what Celia and Marion Moss called "the flowery paths of romance."[75] In order to prevent himself from being feminized, he needed to deny his investment in the romance form, while at the same time introducing a traditionalist male character whose manhood was apparent in the remarkable virility of his argumentative abilities.

In response to these inducements to write against romance, Matthias Levy produced one of the most ambivalent and unusual texts in the Victorian Jewish canon. Good-hearted but neglectful middle-class parents, Henry and Rachel Montague, have two daughters. Leonara, nineteen, is "a sensible girl" (6), irresistibly attractive, open, honest, gentle, obedient to her parents, and above all unromantic. She is "more the angel than the woman" (6), never talking about love, never reading novels. Her younger sister Caroline, on the other hand, is jocular but with "a dark gloomy interior, where intrigue, passion, and disobedience were the reigning monarchs" (7). The family is proud to be Jewish, but because they are reformers, "what they do is most inconsistent with common sense, and totally at variance with the prescribed orthodox faith" (8). What they do is pay lip service to the rituals of their religion, while at the same time attempting to adopt a life resembling that of their Christian neighbors. Specifically, after some resistance, Rachel agrees to Caroline's desire to learn to play the piano. Levy depicts this act of yielding to the hegemony of the drawing room as a tragic error bringing on the destruction of the family, and ultimately of the Jewish community. Caroline's desire to play the piano is characterized as romantic and proves that "for her religion she cared nothing; and when that is the case (more particularly in the fair sex), honor, affection, obedience, love—all, all are gone" (25).

The agent of the family's destruction is Caroline's Christian music master, either "Signor Pacheco Graber, or Herr Pacheco Graber—for he would answer to either of the two prefixes" (13). Graber's indeterminate Italian or German nationality marks him as all the more foreign and untrustworthy. True to his insincere appearance, Graber whisks Caroline away with promises of wealth he does not have, marries her in a provincial church that does not so much as ask whether Caroline believes in the Bible from which the minister is reading, and impoverishes her to the point at which she is forced to make a living as the actress Signora Graberini. The narrator has contempt for the church that allows such a farcical marriage to take place within its confines: how can a self-respecting religious establishment permit a union that is so clearly based on the young woman's naïveté? What calls out the narrator's greatest contempt, however, is that when Caroline's father discovers that she has left with Graber he begins to cry. In response, the narrator calls the daughter and the music teacher "worthless carcases" (69). Graber's acts of persuasion and Caroline's ungrateful abandonment of her father combine to feminize the patriarch. Whereas in conversionist novels the father's humiliation and the daughter's conversion are the goals of the narrative, in this Jewish man's revision these results are tragedies. And such tragedies may be avoided, the narrative suggests, by avoiding their source—romance.

Graber is the antitype to which Edgar Lavite is the type. Edgar is "strictly orthodox" even though "people sneered at him, fools joked at him; ignorant ones ridiculed the ceremonial part of his religion" (27–28). Edgar cares nothing for this disapprobation, for "wisdom came to his aid; reason lent her support; and with these two weapons he went fearlessly into the thick of the fight" (28). The female reason is secondary to the male wisdom because Edgar has not succumbed to what are in his mind "the flimsy ideas that Reform imparts to the mind, and the unsound and unstable doctrines which it inculcates" (28). Among these ideas is the notion that reason is the highest mental faculty with which Jewish men can interpret tradition. By maintaining an orthodox approach, Edgar has avoided being feminized by the Victorian culture of reason and progress. He can avoid reason with a clear conscience because he is confident that other, better minds have already done the work of thinking through tradition for him. As Edgar tells Caroline's father, "what would be the result, if every man were allowed to put his own construction on an ambiguous sentence. . . . We who spend our lives in a shop or a profession, how are we to be able to express an opinion contrary to that of men whose careers have been spent in theological studies?" (30).

Because his is not a merely traditional practice, but a traditionalist practice—that is to say, a stand against modernity—Edgar's anti-reformist position translates into a position against the forms of modern life, particularly fashion, romance, and individualism. Unlike Graber who dresses above his station like a gentleman, Lavite is an "ordinary young man" (29) who dresses plainly. Moreover, he ignores the offer of matrimony by the father of an upper-middle-class Jewish woman because they are a showy family who have changed their name to Johnson and keep Sunday as the Sabbath, and because their daughter is a votary of fashion who uses rouge. Instead of marrying her, Edgar proposes to Leonara Montague, Caroline's sister, because she shows no signs of romance, but rather speaks abstractly of love's ability to "elevate the soul, refine the mind, and prepare us for a future and a better world" (114). Leonara's and Edgar's ideal woman is "elevated to become an angel" (115) rather than succumbing to the temptations of modern life as Leonara's sister has, with tragic consequences.

Why does Caroline follow in the Shakespearean tradition of Jessica rather than in the tradition of Scott's Rebecca in *Ivanhoe*? Why, like the Jewish heroine of a conversionist novel, does this daughter betray her father and leave him for a foreigner? Levy might have maintained that Jewish women were converting and yet attributed the situation to a different cause. For instance, Jewish women writers agreed that their heroines were being subjected to pressure by conversionists, and they agreed that some women were accepting the conversionists' explanations and offers. But they attributed these conversions to a particular cause—the lack of Jewish girls' education. And they argued that increased female education was clearly the solution. Even Maria Polack and Judith Montefiore, the orthodox women writers of the group, took stands in favor of female education. "Perhaps I may be rather singular in my ideas of female education," says Polack's protagonist Mr. Desbro, in explaining his refusal to marry an uneducated woman,

> but I am not so foolish as to be frightened at what the *vulgar* term "a learned woman." Be assured, Sir, the female mind is equally strong and capacious with our own; and when a woman is ignorant, it is the fault of a man that she is so. It is a sort of vanity, or conscious superiority in our sex, that disdain to acknowledge an equal in the other. Many a brilliant imagination is cramped, and its finest ideas destroyed, for want of encouragement from those beings whom they are taught to love and look up to. And I firmly believe, that the frivolity, so often depreciated in women, would cease to exist, if they were properly encouraged in the pursuit of more rational amusements.[76]

Although many of Polack's positions are strictly within the realm of male traditionalism, her position on female education seems strikingly different from the male traditionalist. Indeed, just as emancipationists spoke of the "cramping" effects of Jews' legal and economic disabilities, she speaks of women's minds being "cramped" by neglect.[77] To argue her cause, she goes so far as to place her argument in the mouth of a man, who justifies female education with reference to the benefits it would have for men. Gender is where the orthodox Polack and the orthodox Levy part company. For Levy refuses to consider that Caroline's flight is the fault of her education, for she "had the benefits of a good, sound, *moral* education. But alas! she had made but sorry use of it" (59). Trained to be submissive and accept her separate sphere, it is Caroline's fault that she rejects her training and is lost to the "kind, good-natured, honourable family—whose members had always sustained a most irreproachable name" (62). Levy blames Caroline's restlessness, not on her education, but on her own romantic fancies, and on her mother's overweening desire to fulfill them. It is her mother's laxity in exposing her to modern life that leads to her flight and the dissolution of the family.

Actually, Levy invokes both mother and father when he says, "Parents! when will ye be taught that you bring misery on yourselves, and disgrace on your families, by pandering to every wish of your children" (11). But Rachel and Henry are faulted differently. If Rachel is faulted for giving in to her daughter, Henry is held responsible for the fashionable and romantic failings of both wife and daughter: he is faulted for not being dominant enough in his household. According to Levy, his laxity is not merely an accident of his character, but is endemic to his religious practice, is indeed endemic to the project of reform itself. For Montague is lax in exercising his domestic authority because his fashionable reformist religion is lax in respecting rabbinic authority—it tolerates diversity of opinion. Edgar dislikes reformers because "their religion . . . sowed dissension, created discord . . . took some from the orthodox faith; it left a vague and uncertain impression on their minds; and, from its own insecurity, did the same amount of injury as it expected to do good" (78). Reformers' tendency to "make Religion subject to their own convenience" (78), to erode the strictures of obedience in the name of reason, ultimately has the effect of weakening the patriarchal family structure. Romance and reform feminize the Jewish man, and are in that sense equally as dangerous to the community as conversionists. This is why Montague is to blame for his daughter's flight, why, in Polack's words, her frivolity is "the fault of a man." Edgar Lavite resists the "orgies" (77) of reformist tempters, feels secure in "the wisdom" of tradition, and has no interest in learned women. He maintains his manhood. One can be sure that, for as long as Leonara remains married to him, she will remain an Angel in the House and a "daughter of Israel."

FROM WITHIN AND WITHOUT

For the first third of the nineteenth century conversionists like M. G. Lewis and "tolerant" romance novelists like Scott depicted Jewish daughters as the spiritual half of the Jewish community, in contrast to their materialistic Jewish fathers—a spirit/matter binary that was itself a secularized version of a fundamental Christian dichotomy. Conversionists felt it imperative that the spiritual half marry out of this binary, which was tainting, limiting, and obscuring it, in a romance of a Christian man and a Jewish woman. Within this romance, individual fancy and Christian cultural hegemony would be respected over the dictates of paternal Jewish communal authority. According to conversionists, these romantic Jewish women were undereducated and oppressed within the Jewish community, and were therefore more easily brought into "the truth as it is in Jesus" than their oppressors.

In response, Jewish men, both for their own reputations among Englishmen as well as for the sake of Judaism, defended the role of women within Judaism. Yet, although they proclaimed women the spiritual equals of men, and the superiors of men in terms of prophecy and charity, although they assiduously wrote biographies showing women capable of learning within the Jewish tradition, they could not put the conversionists' accusations fully to rest. Traditionalists invoked a separation of spheres, even though the separation they argued for—between public secularity and private religiosity—was assimilated from Victorian Christian domestic ideology, and differed from the traditional Jewish separation between distinct but equally religious spheres. Many of these men accused Jewish women of being filled with romance, of being fashion-conscious, reform-minded, and in general weak soldiers in the Jewish camp. Under pressure to rethink their sexual politics, reformist Jewish men began to admit that Jewish women were undereducated, and that women had been exempted from the realm of the abstract, even as they condescended to, and in some cases, clamped down on women's efforts at self-education.

Neither traditionalist nor reformist men would probably have worried so much about what the conversionists were saying had they not had such a driving desire to become modern. To the extent that becoming modern meant anglicizing, it meant adopting as much as they could of Victorian Christian culture. One custom they did adopt was to restrict their recognizably Jewish activities to the domestic realm of the home and synagogue. Because they highlighted the home as the space of religiosity and cultural transmission, they ensured that Jewish women's roles as religious educators became increasingly important. Yet because these educators were themselves undereducated, children were not being taught Judaism, family life was suffering. The religious health of the Anglo-Jewish community was in danger.

It was into this context of condescension and persuasion from without, and condescension, circumscription, and censorship from within, that Anglo-Jewish women began to break through their exemption from intellectual life and publish books. In fictional terms, they had to respond to conversionists' and Jewish men's rewriting of Shakespeare and Scott so as to depict the modern Jewish community's crisis as a father/daughter plot. The next chapter argues that these women were particularly well suited by their heritage to respond in kind. And when they published, the genre of primary concern to them was romance.

Portrait of Marion Hartog by her daughter, Hélène
Darmesteter, 1900, from "Death of Marion Hartog,"
Jewish Chronicle, November 1, 1907. Courtesy of the
Jewish Studies Library, University College London.

THREE
MARION AND CELIA MOSS:
TRANSFORMATIONS OF "THE JEWESS"

Both to defend themselves and their religion against conversionist exposés, as well as to critique Anglo-Jewish men for defining them as the primary religious educators without providing them with the necessary knowledge, Anglo-Jewish women began to write. From the 1830s through the 1860s and 1870s Jewish women themselves called for increased female education, primarily on the grounds that, as mothers, they needed Jewish knowledge to pass on to their children.[1] Grace Aguilar, the most famous and highly praised of these writers, popular with Christians and Jews throughout the world, argued strenuously for the vernacularization of the Bible precisely so that it would be accessible to Jewish women. Abigail Lindon was the first English Jew to produce a Hebrew/English, English/Hebrew dictionary to the same purpose. Anna Maria Goldsmid argued for publication of sermons in English so that women, as "mothers and instructors," could become educated enough in their own homes to teach their children;[2] she also started the West Metropolitan School for Girls. Marion Moss started her school and her *Jewish Sabbath Journal*, the first Jewish women's periodical in modern history, and wrote sermons and tales and recommendations for synagogue reform, so as to make the tradition more accessible to women. As she says, "We would have seats provided in the synagogue for old and young, rich and poor, of both sexes. We would have all taught to understand the Scriptures, in the language of the inspired writers."[3] Miriam Mendes Belisario published her "Sabbath-Evenings at Home, or Familiar Conversations on the

Jewish Religion, its Spirit and Observances," ostensibly to help women teach their children in the domestic sphere.[4] And Celia Levetus published her tale, "The Two Pictures," in the American Jewish periodical the *Occident*, which its editor characterized as "a domestic story, illustrative of the pernicious effect that results from want of proper attention to the education of females."[5]

Two of the Anglo-Jewish women who most passionately took up the cause of female education were Marion and Celia Moss. While their work is not representative of all early Anglo-Jewish women's writing, the problems on which it focuses—female education, reform, emancipation—do reflect concerns that all Anglo-Jewish women writers felt and to which they all had different responses. Moreover, the Mosses' writing resembles that of the other early and mid-Victorian Jewish women writers in that all of these writers felt they must stake out a position for or against the form of the most significant text about Jewish women to have emerged in the dominant context in the early Victorian period—the romantic father/daughter plot of Walter Scott's *Ivanhoe*.[6] Even when they approached these problems and this genre from different perspectives, their dialogue helped create a community of writers who knew each other's work and responded to each other's symbol systems. In this way, fiction like that of the Mosses was crucial to the formation of the Anglo-Jewish subculture.

The Mosses' position was in favor of historical romance, with some revisions. In prefaces to their early historical romances, Marion and Celia Moss explicitly acknowledge a debt to Scott. Having had few Jewish literary role models, they assimilated the form from the dominant culture that most prominently featured Jewish women. But they do not merely assimilate the historical romance form—they alter it, so as to make it serve their Jewish—and Jewish women's—ends. They use the romance of the Jewish home to engage in a dialogue with two groups simultaneously—with non-Jews, on the subject of "the removal of Jewish disabilities," and with Jewish men, on the subject of the removal of Jewish women's disabilities. In their fictions, they see the Jewish home as the microcosm for these struggles for Jewish emancipation in the Christian world and women's emancipation in the Jewish world. By assimilating the romance form of English Christian novels after *Ivanhoe*, the Mosses legitimate their writings among non-Jewish readers, and promote toleration for Jews. However, in contrast to the Jewish daughters of conversionist fiction, their Jewish daughters are going to confront their fathers with their oppression face to face, and, without converting, break out of their traditionalist confines.

Two of twelve children born to Joseph and Amelia Moss of Portsea, Marion and Celia Moss grew up poor. Their great-grandfather was one of the founders of the Jewish community in Portsmouth, established in 1747; their grandmother, Sarah Davids, was the first Jewish child born there. They seemed to have been raised in a secularizing household, for their father Joseph read romantic poetry to them while they sewed, including Byron's *Childe Harold*, Moore's *Lalla Rookh*, and Scott's *Lady of the Lake*. They were not like Miriam Schreiber of the conversionist novel *The Jewish Maiden*, to be wooed away by the first philo-Semite presenting them with Byron. The two of them often amused the family from early on by telling fairy tales. When Joseph found them writing these stories down, however, "he became alarmed, having all the prejudice of the day against the idea of girls leaving the beaten track, and he threatened to take away their books and burn them. In fear of this, they learnt by heart most of their favourite poems."[7] But Joseph fell into an illness that kept him bedridden and unable to earn enough to support the family for two years. So in 1839, at ages sixteen and eighteen, without their parents' knowledge but with the encouragement of George Staunton, MP, Marion and Celia Moss published a collection of poems by subscription entitled *Early Efforts*, which sold well enough to enable them to help their family and to encourage them to keep writing. They moved to London and became teachers, and soon published their collections of historical romances, *The Romance of Jewish History* (1840), and after that succeeded well enough to deserve a second edition, *Tales of Jewish History* (1843). Celia married and moved to Birmingham, and Marion continued to publish poems in periodicals. In 1855, Marion, married since 1845 to the French Jew Alphonse Hartog, established the first Jewish women's periodical in history, the *Jewish Sabbath Journal*, which was at first supported but later attacked by the editor of the *Jewish Chronicle*. In the wake of the editor's attack, eleven numbers having been produced, the *Sabbath Journal* foundered for lack of funds (see chap. 2 for details). Except for a poem here and there, Marion rarely published again in her lifetime. Instead, until her death in 1907, she concentrated on developing her school and raising her children, many of whom became famous.[8] Meanwhile Celia published another volume of the historical romances she had written in the 1840s titled *The King's Physician and Other Tales* (1865).[9] Perhaps because she moved away from London, she died with less fanfare than her sister.

The Mosses dedicated their important first collection of tales, *The Romance of Jewish History* (1840), to Edward Bulwer Lytton. Bulwer Lytton had been an admirer since *Early Efforts* was published. Perhaps because their own father was ambivalent about their writing careers, they sought and found an alternative father figure in the novelist of "dark and stormy nights." If so, this was a rather bizarre choice. In *Leila,* published two years before, Bulwer Lytton had made the wicked Jewish father Almamen stab his spiritual Jewish daughter Leila as she was about to be baptized a Christian, reviving the ritual murder accusation.[10] Perhaps dedicating a romance of Jewish history to a conversionist could be seen as part of the Mosses' strategy to promote Christian toleration. More likely, the Mosses' need to be recognized as legitimate led them to find a literary "father" whose approval would guarantee them a reading. But, at the same time, their need to be recognized as legitimate in this non-Jewish sphere led them to place their hopes in a Christian whose sympathies were far from clear. The appeal to a conversionist "father" must have signalled to many Jewish men how far outside the accepted bounds of their subculture the writing of romances really was.

The Mosses were not the only Anglo-Jewish women writers to appeal to a patriarch to legitimate their writings. Maria Polack personifies her readership as a stern Jewish male tutor, and positions herself as a humble pupil to be chastised by this generalized Jewish father.[11] Grace Aguilar seems to have enjoyed a close relationship to her consumptive father, who promoted her education,[12] so that perhaps she felt less in need of justifying her intellectual endeavors by referring to his permission. In prefaces to her domestic tales, such as *Home Influence,* she addresses herself to Christian mothers rather than a Jewish father. Still, in her works on doctrinal Jewish subjects, she either submits them to the editorship of a rabbi (as in the case of *Spirit of Judaism*) or appeals to her Jewish male audience for a sympathetic reading (as in *Jewish Faith*). In her diaries, Judith Montefiore constantly invokes her husband's importance and zeal to legitimate her activities and writings—she depicts herself as her husband's moral support, smoothing the way for his achievements. A. M. Goldsmid, who in other respects is among the most independent of the group of writers, justifies her assertion that mothers need to take the main responsibility for their children's education this way: "My father, who has acted, both in public and private, on the opinion that religious education can be best conducted at home, shares with me this hope."[13] Only Charlotte Montefiore, who published her polemic *A Few Words to the Jews. By One of Themselves* anonymously, never seemed to bolster her claims to be heard by referring to a father or father figure. Perhaps her anonymity and social position were sufficient enough protections. The Mosses' tendency to invoke an idealized father in the preface seems ironic when compared with the tyrannical, neglectful, or condescending fathers that appear over and over in the fictions themselves. Under cover of fiction, the writers seemed to feel they could criticize Jewish patriarchy, while when they appeared as themselves, in essays, they seemed to feel such criticism inappropriate, unsafe, and contrary to the separation of spheres. For proof that such criticism could in fact be dangerous, one need look no further than Abraham Benisch's angry editorial response to Marion Hartog's criticism of him in the *Jewish Sabbath Journal.*

In their dedication to *The Romance of Jewish History,* the Mosses argue for historical romance as a Jewish women's genre. They argue that Jews must respond to conversionists and anti-Semites, who have portrayed Jewish women badly. Jewish men are not likely to take on the task, however, since fiction is a genre for which Jewish men have not spoken: "Our men of genius have neglected the lighter branches of literature, directing their attention almost exclusively to theology, metaphysics, and philosophy."[14] Jewish men think fiction trivial, part of the women's sphere, but this is not the only reason the men neglect the genre. The Mosses add that Jewish men also neglect the form out of a fear of anti-Semitism, for "even those who have desired to tread the more flowery paths of romance, have been prevented from appearing before the public, from a feeling that however much they might excel, the prejudice existing against us as a nation, might reflect an odium on their work, and consign it immediately to oblivion." Interestingly, according to the Mosses' assessment, Jewish men feel they have more to fear from publishing a romance novel than from publishing theological, philosophical, or metaphysical works—works that announce themselves as Jewish more directly than many romances might. Perhaps their fear is that non-Jews will perceive their religious works as typically Jewish forms, and therefore unthreatening, while they will perceive the romance as an attempt to appropriate a genre to

109

which they have no claim, and to compete for undue public attention. If in one sense the "flowery paths of romance" appear trivial to the men, in another, they seem to be quite dangerous. For both of these reasons, the Mosses perceive that men are unlikely to respond to the conversionist novels in kind, and set themselves to the task.

The Mosses do not share the men's fear of anti-Semitism. True, as they remark in their dedication, they believe they are "subjecting [themselves] to a severe ordeal by appearing in [their] present characters" as romance writers, and that "at the present moment the attention of the whole civilized world is directed to our nation" to be "our judges"— apparently, referring to the various Jewish emancipation movements going on throughout Europe.[15] Still, they believe they "shall not be judged unfairly." In their writing, they "follow the plan of the 'Romance of History' " in order, "by blending fiction with historical fact, to direct the attention of the reader to a branch of history too long neglected."[16] If Jewish men fear that their attempts at romance will inspire outbreaks of anti-Semitism, these Jewish women feel that their romances will reduce anti-Semitism by creating understanding and sympathy among their non-Jewish readers. As they explain, "we must revert to the circumstances which have induced us to publish the present work; namely, the fact that the English people generally, although mixing with the Jews in their daily duties, are as unacquainted with their history, religion, and customs, as if they still dwelt in their own land, and were known to them but by name." Whereas continental reformers often found causes for anti-Semitism within themselves and their own self-education, these Anglo-Jewish women share the tendency of Anglo-Jewish men to see anti-Semitism as a fault of the anti-Semites.

In sound Anglo-Jewish fashion, the Mosses attempt to persuade the anti-Semites to abandon their error. Their method of persuasion is not to show the Christian readership pictures of their Jewish contemporaries, however, at least not immediately; it is "to pourtray the Jews as they were while yet an independent people—to mark the most interesting events that took place after Judea became a kingdom—the decline of her splendour, and her final fall." Eventually they plan "to trace the destinies of her children after they were scattered through every nation, and bring down the history to the present year." In other words, they plan to acquaint the non-Jewish reader with the history, religion, and customs of the Jewish people, from the glories of Jonathan's self-sacrifice and the Maccabees' national liberation struggle to the degradation of the martyrs of Worms.

But while they want to dwell on the particulars of Jewish historical experience, they "do not intend this production to be considered in the light of a history." In fact, throughout the text, they mention the history books from which they are taking their descriptions, as if to show that the romantic coloring, rather than the accuracy of the historiography, is the innovation for which they are claiming their readers' attention. Moreover, they explicitly suggest that readers should not take their work as either complete or historically accurate in all its details and plots, for "our wish is to call the attention of the reader to the records of our people—to awaken curiosity—not to satisfy it." By entertaining non-Jewish readers, not with histories of Judaism, but with romance narratives set at crucial moments in Jewish history, they hope to inspire their public with "curiosity" about Jews. In the end, by romancing the Jewish past, they hope to inspire their public with sympathy for the Jewish cause in the present day. "Blending fiction with historical fact" is not so much appropriating a non-Jewish form, in their view, as it is assimilating that form to promote the liberal cause of toleration.

While promoting toleration for Jews is the Mosses' goal with regard to their non-Jewish audience, promoting moral reform within the community is their explicit goal with regard to their Jewish audience. The Jewish men's fear of anti-Semitism is misguided, in the Mosses' opinion, for "the time is now arrived, or is rapidly approaching, when such narrow-mindedness, the growth of a barbarous and priest-ridden age, will disappear. Our yoke is lightened, and will be more so every day." In the context of Victorian liberalization, the Mosses sought to encourage a shift in the Jewish male character away from a narrow-mindedness that was men's inheritance from centuries of persecution. Much of the Mosses' fiction is devoted to imagining a new type of Jewish man, one who is neither ritualistic nor tyrannical nor cringing, one who is neither "cramped" nor stooped with fear.[17] The implication, although in the preface they do not state it, is that there is also a need for a shift in the Jewish female character, and indeed, nearly every one of their tales centers on the drama of a Jewish female coming into conflict with her father over her independence. Jewish women need to become more autonomous and more educated. The Mosses' silence on this issue in the prefaces suggests that they felt it would not be seen as a legitimate justification for their foray into print.

Indeed, the Mosses justify their entrance into print using rhetoric that would place them well within the bounds of Victorian Jewish men's domestic ideology. Their stories are attempts to educate Jewish children, the activity allotted them by Jewish men who were assimilating Victorian domestic ideology, as discussed in chapter 2. In the preface from her 1865 collection *The King's Physician,* Celia Levetus recounts that in the 1840s she felt the particular need, not only to educate non-Jewish readers, but to educate Jewish youth who were ignorant of Jewish history: "It was considered by the writer that Jewish History, after the dispersion, was too little known or studied by the rising generation, and she wished, by selecting a few striking incidents and well-authenticated traditions, to awaken a desire to know more of records fuller of instances of fervent piety, courage, endurance, and constancy under suffering, than those of any other people." Here it is not the non-Jews who need to be awakened to Jewish history, but young Jews who need to have their attention focused on the moral attributes (rather than the particular rituals) of their diaspora ancestors.[18] This reformist vision of the Jewish woman writer as a teacher of ethics to youth would have fit in well with the Anglo-Jewish men's idea of women's moral mission.

In the tales themselves, the Mosses fulfill the aims they express within their prefaces in regard to their Christian audiences. At the same time, they leave some aims to be derived by the reader from the tales themselves, an explicit statement of which might open them to criticism from the authorities in both the Christian and Jewish communities. They do adopt the historical romance genre and the father/daughter plot of their non-Jewish models. Like the conversionist novels, the Mosses' tales depict spiritual Jewish daughters who are in conflict with their tyrannical Jewish fathers, and who leave their father's house for a romantic suitor. But if the Mosses' and the conversionists' tales have a similar form, they have a different meaning. From the setting to every major character and relationship to every major turn in the plot, the Mosses alter what they have assimilated and depict a complex Jewish community that eludes the stereotypes of most conversionists. If the non-Jewish novels of Jewish identity are part of a larger non-Jewish cultural shift in perspective toward Jews from coercion to persuasion, the Jewish novels of Jewish identity are responses from a marginalized subculture to the criticisms and temptations posed by both the mainstream culture and their own communities. By using the non-Jewish plot and form, these writers are able to legitimate their fictions within a non-Jewish context; but they alter the dominant form even as they assimilate it, tailoring it to defend

Jewish women against the charge of conversionism, defend the Jewish reform movement from the charge of Protestantism, and argue for Christian toleration. The Mosses take conversionist plots like Bulwer Lytton's and subject them to a series of transformations, a move they do not announce explicitly in their prefaces.

In addressing their Jewish audience, they likewise fulfill their expressed aim to be moral educators of the young, providing exciting stories of the Jewish dispersion. But just as the Mosses are able to transgress the boundaries of conversionist fiction in their tales, so also they use the veil of fiction to step outside of their communally prescribed role of moral historian and criticize the new domestic ideology being adopted by Jewish men. If in their prefaces, they felt they had to invoke a non-Jewish patriarch (George Staunton or Bulwer Lytton) to legitimate their writings, in the tales, they are able implicitly to depict Jewish patriarchs who are hardly appealing, transgress the demand that they "murmur not," and argue for an expansion of women's education and their political equality within the Jewish community. In addition, it quickly becomes clear from their tales that these women are not simply interested in a vague moral reform within the community; rather, they desire to encourage the new movement for religious reform that was slowly making its way from Germany to England. Under cover of romance, the Mosses engaged in a great deal of polemic to which it would have been unsafe to give voice when speaking directly to their public.

One example of many from the Mosses' work is Marion Moss's "The Twin Brothers of Nearda, A Tale of the Babylonian Jews" in *Tales of Jewish History* (1843). Moses Ben Yussuf is a Babylonian Jewish merchant and slave owner in the outlying village of Nearda. "A lineal descendant of the guilty but unfortunate Zedekiah, the king whose weakness and idolatry had plunged his people into ruin," Ben Yussuf "preferred retaining [his] rich possessions and pursuing [his] mercantile pursuits in the land of [the Jews'] captivity" to returning to Judea with Ezra, the leader who brought the Babylonian Jews back from exile to Jerusalem.[19] His materialism prevents his becoming a political Zionist, much to the Mosses' disapproval. In their poems in *Early Efforts,* the Mosses constantly expressed a yearning for return to Zion that Ben Yussuf scorns. Ben Yussuf is instead constantly at the synagogue, praying and embroiled in its politics. This materialist's outward observances, however, obscure a lack of true piety.

Ben Yussuf has a daughter, Paula, whom he treats with "oriental" opulence—her apartment is clearly drawn from a Beckford-inspired notion of the East, with its silk pillows, gilt embroidery, etc. The Mosses orientalize their Jewish female characters as much as non-Jews of the "La Belle Juive" tradition ever did.[20] Ben Yussuf's wife having died in childbirth, Paula's father "worships" her. He believes she "had more knowledge, perhaps, of the realities of life, at fourteen, than most Eastern women acquire in a lifetime. Her mind, gifted by nature, and enriched by education, had arrived at maturity at an age when most are yet in the childhood of intellect" (1:224). Still, although he recognizes her intellectual superiority, he also does not allow her to leave her room. "Many wondered, that the child of the cold and heartless being, whose name was a byword of selfishness, could be so gentle and loving" (1:225)—and so self-controlled. Paula is constantly hiding her true feelings from her father, fearing his anger. The setup of the absent mother, the tyrannical materialistic father, and the more intelligent spiritual "Eastern" and self-sacrificing daughter is virtually the same as that in the novels of Jewish identity by Christians.

The tale begins with Asinai and Anilai, orphaned twin Jewish brothers, who have been brought up by their gentle uncle. Just before his death when they are twelve years old he is forced to sell them into Moses Ben Yussuf's service as slaves. This is only one example of the father figure who in these tales is constantly abandoning or breaking faith with his children. If their uncle destroys their trust by his absence, the twins' master, Moses Ben Yussuf, manages to destroy their trust with his all-too-menacing presence: he whips them, puts them in chains, underfeeds them. One night, after Asinai's refusal to leave his brother to go on an errand, Ben Yussuf scourges both brothers, then tells his daughter what he has done. Appalled, for she is attracted to Anilai, Paula sneaks out of her luxurious imprisonment to see the slaves, finds them vowing to quit her father's service, and faints. When she awakes, she finds herself in the slaves' hut. She reveals her love for Anilai, who returns it; she gives the brothers money, and they escape. Ben Yussuf is enraged, and vows to recapture them, but the young men elude capture and become outlaws. Paula's first act of disobedience to her father stems from her attraction to a marginalized man. Romance involves acting on her own desires, which are in conflict with her father's. It means expressing her individual feelings rather than controlling them. It means not fitting into the traditional patriarchal power structure of the Jewish family.

Meanwhile Ben Yussuf becomes embroiled in synagogue problems and in trying to send money to Jerusalem for the rebuilding efforts there. If he is not a Zionist in the sense that he is ready to move there, he still lends monetary support, like the Jews of England in the Mosses' day, or the Jews of the United States in the late twentieth century. Just as Scott's Rebecca seems like a nineteenth-century Jewish woman in her ethical monotheism and her charitable acts, so Ben Yussuf is a modern diaspora Jewish figure displaced onto a fictionalized past era. A reformist caricature of a traditionalist Jew, Moses spends his public time working for Jewish concerns while in private he lords it over his daughter and his domestics. There is a split between his public and his private self, which becomes increasingly absolute as the tale proceeds. Even Paula begins to "distrust" him. Although, like the Victorian daughter of Jeptha, she attempts to obey and cheer her father, when alone she sings laments by the river asking how it is possible to "sing the songs of Zion in a strange land" and weeping over Babylonian Jews' "servitude" (1:118).[21] Whereas her father refused the chance to return to Jerusalem, she longs for it. It is difficult to tell whether the servitude she laments is that experienced at the hands of the Babylonians or at the hands of her father.

While at the river, she is surprised by a man, who argues that God did not ordain slavery.[22] It is as if the man were speaking to her secret longings, and she readily agrees. The man reveals himself to be Asinai and professes love and offers her escape from her father. The romantic hero has appeared in response to Paula's desire to rebel against her dutiful role. But this is the wrong romantic hero; the scene is clearly written so as to enable the reader to see that Paula is capable of making her own choice. She is not simply going to escape from her father; she is going to move toward a particular ideal. She refuses Asinai, for it is not he but his brother Anilai who represents that ideal. The trajectory of the tale is clear: Paula will have to make the choice to forgo her filial duty to her father in order to join her lover, Anilai, who has become an "outlaw," compared by the narrator to Robin Hood or Rob Roy. Paula will increasingly "distrust" her father, who will increasingly deserve her distrust. She will cease to find mirth in his gifts and in her domestic duties (principally caring for the garden) and will flee to make her own individual choice. Recognizing Ben Yussuf's materialism and hypocrisy, Paula will embrace idealism, in that "her hopes of happiness were set on things beyond the power of gold to purchase." Moses will not make her choice easy, attempting to marry her off to Abishai, son of the Nasi (leader) of the Sanhedrin in Jerusalem, in order to secure his own prominence, showing "that debasing selfism that degrades man below the brute creation" (231). Moses will continue to be "a cold, callous, selfish man, calculating to the utmost, even the returns his affections . . . would bear" (244). Like Shylock or Schreiber, he will understand his feelings about his daughter in mercantile terms.

A young dutiful but spiritual woman struggles with her father's materialism and eventually leaves him for another man. The mother is dead and there is no son. The plot is repeated over and over again in the Mosses' fiction.[23] It sounds virtually the same as that of *The Jewish Maiden,* and not accidentally. Jewish women had almost no Jewish models of fiction writing to draw from.[24] Despite Marion Moss's contention in "Malah, the Prophet's Daughter," that the Jews' "imaginative and inflammable natures gave a colouring of romance to the most common events of every day life," the romance form she is adopting had no Jewish antecedents.[25] The Mosses modeled their tales on those of Walter Scott, Latch Ritchie (*The Romance of French History*), and Henry Neal (*The Romance of English History*).[26] This assimilation of genre and plot itself is an emblem for Victorian Jews' attempts to anglicize and become assimilated into dominant Victorian society. The attempt was supported, not only by such liberal Christian Englishmen as Bulwer Lytton and Lord Palmerston, but by a subscription that included Moses Montefiore and many of the most influential Jews in the community. Because they seemed to promise successful acculturation without conversion, these novels were ardently desired by the Jewish elite as entry tickets into dominant Victorian cultural life.

But if this plot is virtually the same as *The Jewish Maiden,* it is not exactly the same. There are four principal differences—the setting, the father, the daughter, and the suitor. First, the setting. The romances of history that served as the Mosses' models were set in England or France, while the Mosses' tales could be set anywhere or at anytime that Jews lived. Except for Benjamin Disraeli's *Alroy,* written in 1831, in English literary history there had never been a tale about Jews set in "Jewish space"—a space in which Jewish communal life influences the action. By contrast, Shylock is singularly uninfluenced by any Jewish community, as are Isaac and Rebecca. Shylock says, "I represent the law," but there is never any evidence of a halachic community operating in the play. Already in the setting, then, one begins to sense that in the Mosses' efforts to assimilate there is also an effort to represent Jews as having a distinct collective identity regulated through distinct institutions and distinct communal decision-making procedures. There is an effort to set Jews in the context of historically appropriate locations and milieus. This change of setting suggests an important general point. The Mosses' fictions do not merely mimic their models, they enter into a dialogue with them. If the historical romance is the emblem of Jewish attempts to assimilate, it is also instrumental in the Victorian Jews' attempt to alter dominant perceptions of them, and to define themselves to themselves. It is a polemical practice and an exercise in self-definition as well as an experiment in literary adaptation.[27]

Of all the principal characters in the father/daughter plot, it appears that the Mosses typically alter the character of the father least of all. Like Shylock, Isaac, and Solomon Schreiber of *Jewish Maiden,* Moses Ben Yussuf seems to have trouble telling the difference between his ducats and his daughter. Yet for the Mosses the conflict between father and daughter finally centers less on his materialism than on the issue of his authority and her obedience. When Paula refuses to go to Jerusalem to marry Abishai, Moses threatens to "enforce obedience," and if she does not behave well to her betrothed, Moses says, "I will have thee scourged, even as I would the meanest slave who disobeyed my will" (1:242). The Jewish patriarch is revealed as a thinly veiled slave master. When he forces Paula to play the harp for Abishai, she says, "Give me air, for I am suffocating" (1:250), the classic nineteenth-century symptom of a woman suffering from patriarchal oppression. In tale after tale by the Mosses, the daughter finds herself painfully rejecting the basis on which her father legitimates his demands—traditional patriarchal Judaism's gender roles. In tale after tale, the daughter finds herself distrusting her father and losing confidence in him. In Celia Moss's "The Slave," for instance, Isaac, the father of Judah and Rachel, strikes his son unconscious and imprisons him in a "worse than Egyptian bondage" for Judah's disobedience and breaks "the confidence that had subsisted between" himself and Rachel, who will no longer obey him.[28] In "The Pharisee, or, Judea Capta," Eve's father Eli tries to force her to marry Elias against her will. She says she has learned "to fear, but not to love" her stern father, for "man may struggle, may brave wrath, may break the chains that bind him, but woman must obey and endure, though her heart break under the trial." Although she pays lip service to the need for this obedience, she says "there is an earnest desire in my soul to feel and know that a father's affection is to me more than a name."[29] Secretly she plights her troth to Julius, her reformist cousin, breaking her bond of obedience to her father.

Over and over in these tales one finds a father, who, if he does not break his daughter's confidence through his strict demands that she obey the letter of his law, breaks faith with her either through neglect, or through his powerlessness to help her in time of need. Thus Jacob, Judith's old father in "The Storming of the Rock," is powerless to save her from the Philistines, although she prays to him for aid, "Father, father! . . . let not these rude men touch me. I cannot bear their looks."[30] Thus while Malah the prophet's daughter is being sexually assaulted by Sadoc the courtier, her father is absent. Later, when Malah is abducted, her father is in prison for having prophesied against the king. He is not a tyrant, but due to his important job in the world he is absent from home when his daughter needs him most. His daughter cannot depend upon him. In the same vein, virtually every tale in Celia Levetus's collection *The King's Physician* is about a daughter who has been left behind by her father's death and who is now in search of a new father—one whom she can choose, because he is not bound to her by an accident of birth.[31] If the conditions of proper daughterhood are being negotiated here, so are the conditions of proper fatherhood; Levetus's heroines seek a fatherhood that will be more than a name. If M. G. Lewis provides only one option for a Jewish father—that he be a materialist tyrant—these tales offer a more complex critique. The Jewish father can be a traditionalist tyrant, a weak man cringing in the face of anti-Semitism and powerless to defend his daughter against Philistines, or an absent man abandoning her for his work.

But for all the complexity this multiplicity of paternal errors introduces into the tales, the most significant of these father types is still the traditionalist tyrant, precisely because in that type one can trace a direct assimilation of the Christian writers' Jewish father—and one can detect the Mosses' alteration of it to fit a context relevant to Victorian Jews. Compare the conflict between Moses and Paula over her obedience and his enforcing presence to the conflict found in *Ivanhoe,* for example. In that plot, there is never any question of the daughter's obedience, although Rebecca does approach many matters differently from her father. She will undo his avaricious deals in secret, but she will not disobey him to his face. In *The Jewish Maiden,* Miriam Schreiber hates her father, but will not disobey him until after his death. The spiritual daughter's inability to rebel against her materialistic father makes sense because the conversionists need the father figure to remain intact: they need his evil to be invincible, so as to justify as an act of salvation the hegemonic persuasion focused on his daughter. But in the Jews' own texts the father can be rebelled against, because he is not being invoked as the demon in a hegemonic discourse.

In the non-Jewish texts the father's traditionalism is a part of his materialism; his love for material things—principally, gold—results in a love for external ritual forms, "dead letters" with no connection to the needs of the inner spirit. In the Jews' texts, by contrast, the father's materialism is a part of his traditionalism, a result of his devotion to external ritual forms rather than spontaneous expressions of love for God. The difference between the conversionist father/daughter conflict and the Mosses' version rests on which term, traditionalism or materialism, is deemed the cause and which is deemed the effect. It is a subtle difference, but crucial nonetheless. For if in the conversionists' texts the father represents materialism and the daughter spirituality, in the Jews' own texts the daughter represents the voice of individual conscience while the father represents the voice of the law; she is the voice of liberty while he is the voice that demands obedience to the letter of tradition and will enforce it if necessary. That is, the father represents traditionalism, and the daughter represents reform.[32] The Mosses have translated the father/daughter plot into terms that make sense within the Jewish communal context, in which reformers and traditionalists argued with one another on the question of how much freedom to permit the conscience of the individual.

In the Mosses' reformist endeavor, this means that the daughter will be honored over the father. For since Marion Moss is controlling the plot, Paula's experience of suffocation at her father's hands will not last forever; the romance form ultimately means that individual choice will be honored over duty to traditional affiliations.[33] Just at the moment when Paula's father threatens her with enslavement, romance intervenes in the form of the suitor: she is rescued by Anilai and whisked away to the brothers' hideout. Later Paula sends her father into a rage by saying, "Ask me to make any sacrifice which conscience does not disapprove, and thou shalt find me ever a willing and obedient child" (2:24). The terms of Jewish romantic obedience to the law rest in the individual "conscience." When fathers are good (generally only in stories directed to a Jewish-only audience), it is because they respect the daughter's conscience, and grant her the right to make her own choices, as in Marion Hartog's "Milcah: A Tale of the Spanish Jews in the Fifteenth Century." When Milcah's betrothed, Jacob Ben Asaph, caves in to Inquisition pressure and apostasizes, Milcah has to decide whether or not to honor the engagement. Enoch, the good father, "had not said to his child, 'Thou shalt not wed with the lover of thy youth.' . . . for they who are compelled to fulfil one duty, while their heart yearneth after one that is away, make but poor worshippers. . . . Therefore 'Thou shalt make thine own choice.' "[34] The father speaks in the form of the law ("Thou shalt"), but his commandment is that the daughter should take the law into her own hands. The romance form itself is aligned with the good father's recognition of the daughter's individuality—that is, with the victory of reform over tradition. The father's reformist commandment produces a better form of worship. The Mosses have altered the plot they have assimilated so as to reflect the tensions that exist between various factions of the Anglo-Jewish community in its movement into the modern world.

The Mosses' other two major alterations in the family romance, besides the setting and the father, concern the shape of change they hope to see in the newly emancipated Jewish community. The first concerns their transformation of the Jewish female heroine. To be sure, the typical Moss heroine is just as self-sacrificing and controlled as most Victorian heroines. Some things must remain the same, it appears, if the Mosses' assimilation of the dominant plot is to remain recognizable. Like the Victorian version of Jeptha's daughter, cheering her self-recriminating father after he has foolishly forced her into permanent exile, many Moss heroines would literally rather die than express their anger or sense of abandonment.[35] In "Gertrude; or, Clouds and Sunshine," the title character has grown up in luxury, but must learn to adjust when she loses her father and the family's wealth to a shipwreck on the way to America. Although devastated, she is able to ask, "while I have [my mother] to love me, what more can I desire?"[36] Still, when she and her mother move in with her grandparents—a traditionalist and devout grandfather and a grandmother gone quietly senile—her equanimity is challenged. Her mother, who is "Patient, enduring, and self-denying" (63), "save when employed completing my education, toiled incessantly at a kind of embroidery in which she excelled, to support herself and me" (62–63). When her mother finally dies of overexertion, cheering Gertrude to the last, Gertrude must face her own ordeal, supporting her grandparents with her work, and waiting for Earnest, her fiancee, to find a way to support her, although he has lost his career to an accident with a scalpel. At one point, when he must leave her to find work in England, she thinks, "It was well for me at that moment that I had

been so long schooled in suffering and self-denial, that after a moment's silence I could say, 'Do what you think best, dearest Earnest,
and I will be contented' " (73). The extremity of this and other portraits of the self-denying woman in the Mosses' work recalls Nina
Auerbach's ironic assertion that women writers often punish their
female characters for desire more severely than male writers do:
"women novelists have tended to cast a lugubrious and punitive
glower over the lives of their heroines. . . . women writers tend to
deny the flexibility, scope, and joy that are a vital dimension of all
human life." The Victorian women writers' paradigm of women in
particular, Auerbach remarks, "was endowed with an often mon-
strously outsize nobility that led to her extinction."[37]

Still, if the Jewish female heroine fits this dutiful self-sacrificing
description perfectly, she does not at all resemble her Jewish female
counterpart in the conversionist novels in terms of education. Chapter
1 argued that a fundamental feature of conversionist fiction is the
representation of the Jewish woman as undereducated, especially in
"secular" culture. Thus Miriam Schreiber is first introduced to Byron
by the Christian man who will become her husband. It was not that
Jewish women disagreed that female education was lacking in the
Jewish community. On the contrary, it should already be clear, they
were the primary promoters of increased female education in the
community. But the acts and texts with which they advocated for this
cause are all directed exclusively at Jewish audiences; and in this
context the women feel they can afford to air the community's dirty
laundry.[38] In those fictions directed at two audiences simultaneously,
the women feel the need to keep up a polemical front. Moses Ben
Yussuf tells Paula that he has "lavished on thee health, time, and
money . . . to educate thee, a female child, as if thou hadst been a son
who could transmit my name from generation to generation" (1:241).
Over and over again, the Mosses give us female characters who have
been trained as well as sons. Malah, the prophet's daughter, is herself a
prophet. Tales of women who are storytellers, message givers, or well-
trained martyrs resisting conversion abound, clearly in opposition to
the conversionist polemics describing female undereducation and the
vulnerability it creates.[39]

In addition, the Mosses imagine female characters who consistently
take power into their own hands at crucial moments. In Celia Moss's
"The Slave," Jehoida, a supporter of Saul, falls out of favor upon Saul's
death and David's ascension to the throne. Jehoida is imprisoned and

his impoverished wife is forced to sell their daughter Abia into slavery for seven years to Absalom's daughter Tamar.[40] A lutist, singer, and poet, Abia lightens Tamar's anguish over having been raped by her brother Amnon. Later, she cross-dresses as a male minstrel in order to deliver a message from Tamar to King David warning him of Absalom's plot against his life. Still later, she repeats her adventure, with David's permission, for "when a woman's heart is resolved, but few men can resist their passionate pleading."[41] Like many Moss heroines, Abia spends the greater portion of her life outdoors rather than inside the domestic sphere. In other words, Abia takes a traditionally "male" role in the stories, which according to the domestic ideology examined in the preceding chapter, would make her liable for the censoring hand of the father. But oftentimes these heroines escape the expected punishment. In another tale, Berenice who loves Judas the Maccabee, dares to speak first to him of love just before he goes off to battle. "I trust he will not love me less, because for his sake I cast aside all forms and ceremonies, and dare to offer that, which in other circumstances should be humbly sued for." Her suit of love sounds very much like a reformer casting aside forms and ceremonies, as if the projects of religious reform and reform of gender codes were aligned. And Judas does not despise her love, but rather questions the timing of it, saying in the present crisis he must "tear each gentler feeling from my heart, and live or die but for my country." Berenice, however, recognizing that this attempt to separate the personal from the political will exclude her from involvement in either realm, argues back: "And am not I a Jewish maiden? Am not I an Asmonean? And thinkest thou my woman's heart could not bear—aye, firmly bear—as much as thine? Try me—I will not shrink, I will not falter; but cast aside the weakness of my sex." By placing "Jewish maiden" in parallel with "Asmonean" (the name for the governing Jewish dynastic line of the Maccabees), Berenice suggests that she ought to be allowed to participate as much in the political life of the community as in the domestic sphere, casting aside the "weakness of her sex" as she had cast aside all forms and ceremonies. Public and private collapses here into a singular assertion of heroic female identity. Judas responds by looking on her with "love and admiration," and they are married, with Mattathias's permission, at midnight before the battle.[42] The depiction of intelligent, courageous, powerful women in the Mosses' fiction simultaneously refutes the conversionist charges that Jewish women are malleable and undereducated, and argues for a more expansive role for Jewish women within the community. It simultaneously argues for emancipation from external philo-Semitic conversionism, and from internal patriarchal condescension.

If in their portrait of the father the Mosses represent their understanding of tradition, and in the portrait of the daughter they represent the new female-centered reform, in the portrait of the suitor, they represent their vision of the new Jewish man. In "The Twin Brothers," the man Paula will leave her father for is not a Christian or a Babylonian, but a Jew. This already represents a major break with the romances the Mosses inherited as sources. For in seeking to criticize Jewish patriarchy the Mosses are not seeking to vitiate the Jewish community altogether.[43] If some Jewish men (principally, fathers) are constantly breaking faith with Jewish women (principally, their daughters), not all Jewish men are doing so. As the concept of romance replaces the concept of arranged marriages, the hopes of Jewish women are transferred from their father to their suitor. And not just any suitor, either, but one who can represent an ideal alternative to the father who disappointed them. Marion Moss's ideal suitor in "The Twin Brothers," Anilai, is a former slave, a marginalized Jew whose band is comprised of all of "the discontented of the towns and villages in the vicinity" (1:131). Starting out as an "outlaw"—as one outside of the traditional law—gives Anilai the advantage of not having been introduced into the traditionalist hypocrisy of religion and money into which Paula's father has become immersed.

Anilai and Asinai are self-made men, who have "raised them[selves] from the degradation and miseries of slavery, to a position which rendered them feared and admired" (2:45)—they are individualists out of necessity. And indeed, Anilai becomes a gentleman in the end, and he and Paula are wed. Moreover, besides raising himself to be a middle-class gentleman, Anilai is a religious reformer, for "he prayed as he had prayed when a child—not in prescribed sentences. That was no prayer of form. The words of homage come warm from the heart" (2:5). Drawing on inspiration from the prophets, as reformers did, Anilai believes that spontaneous devotion from individuals is more genuine than prayers said by rote in communally prescribed and received traditional forms. Finally, like a good middle-class Victorian reformer, Anilai is conscious of the dilemmas of fitting into the diaspora Babylonian society, for through his merits, he is offered the governorship of an entire section of the country. When the prince making this offer proposes to give him Parthian wives in order to cement their friendship, he replies: "the God of my people is a jealous God; he brooketh not that . . . the young men of Israel wed with the daughters of the stranger. . . . But His law teacheth his children . . . to reverence their governors and rulers; and by His Holy Name I swear . . . to administer the laws impartially, and to be in all respects a true and loyal subject" (2:89–90). Anyone who knows the history of the Victorian Jews' attempts to have the words "on the true faith of a Christian" removed from the oath of abjuration so that they could enter Parliament will immediately recognize the fantasy operating here.[44] Anilai, a middle-class, reformist Jew, manages to convince the governors of his country to admit him to a high level office *without* an oath of abjuration. A middle-class reformer and emancipationist—he is the Mosses' ideal of the early Victorian Jewish man. Marion Moss agrees with the conversionists that some alternative to the oppressive Jewish father must be found. But where the conversionists offer a charismatic Christian figure such as Glanville, Moss finds her alternative figure *within* a more broadly construed Jewish community, providing a portrait of variety within the community that eludes most non-Jewish writers. Marion Moss has assimilated the father/daughter plot of Shakespeare, Scott, and Lewis, but has rewritten it so as to take place within a complex Jewish context. She has altered the inherited plot so as to include the introduction of the sons.

This typical plot of the Mosses' historical romances of the 1830s and 1840s may appear from a late-twentieth-century feminist perspective to have several limitations. In setting the materialistic and traditionalist father against the spiritual and reformist daughter, the Moss sisters have provided a critique of Jewish women's position in the Jewish home, but do not appear to have provided a model for a truly independent woman who could make her own choices. Paula must depend on Anilai to save her and protect her, a damsel in distress being rescued by her knight. She leaves her father's house only to enter the house of another man. Indeed, women who attempt to step beyond this paradigm, unless, like Berenice, in a righteous crisis, are often condemned as "demons." In Celia Moss's "The Slave," for example, Absalom's Syrian bride Yemima tries to enter into affairs of state, and inspires this comment from the narrator: "Most beautiful is the nature of woman when her soft hand smooths the couch of sickness, or her gentle voice speaks comfort to the wretched. In all the relations of society she can soften man's rugged heart, and wake him to good and kindly feelings; but when she forgets her proper sphere, and mingles with the ambitious, the blood-thirsty, the selfish and cold-hearted, the fallen angel becomes a demon. Thus it was with the wife of Absalom."[45] Such a programmatic statement of dominant Victorian gender spheres is somewhat belied by all of the female heroines who enter affairs of state and receive admiration for doing so. Still, the necessity of mouthing these cultural codes in order to assimilate limits the feminist possibilities of these writers. It is difficult to create a politicized women's community when one is focusing on maintaining the domestic sphere.

These protofeminists were certainly aware of such limitations, however. Marion Moss sends a cautionary note to Anglo-Jewish women when in a coda to "Twin Brothers" she has Anilai, perfectly content fifteen years into his marriage, begin lusting after a Parthian woman, who brings about his downfall. Both Marion and Celia Moss were all too aware of the limitations of their vision for Jewish women's independence, since that independence was dependent on a man, who himself was subject to the desire to assimilate. On the other hand, within these limitations, the Mosses go far to mitigate the loss of their female characters' independence. The two men's houses are not identical. The women leave a traditionalist tyrant's house for a gentle reformer's. Inasmuch as they could not yet imagine, in the 1840s, the scenario of the New Woman that would develop in the 1860s and 1870s, the Mosses still tried to reduce the damage to women's independence implicit in this transfer of houses.

Principally, they lessened the damage through the limitations they placed on the suitor. For the suitor had to have more qualifications than being a middle-class reformer to marry one of their heroines. The Mosses tended to ensure that he had some experience of disempowerment that would allow him to sympathize with the "slavery" of Jewish women. Having himself escaped from slavery, Anilai does not subject his wife to slavery—that is, until he forgets his origins and tries to become a Parthian. Often suitors in the tales have physical disabilities. Ernest, a medical man, the suitor of Gertrude, cuts himself with a scalpel on their wedding day, and must have his arm amputated. His career is ruined, as is their wedding, and it is only when Gertrude wins a lottery that they are able to marry, she having control of both the money and the arrangement of their affairs.[46] Asher, the suitor in "The Priest's Adopted," is a pale thin hunchback, "weak and deformed," who is spurned or shrunken from or joked at and so "retir[es] altogether from notice, ch[ooses] the remotest corner, the least noticed spots."[47] It is this feminized man with his beautiful

singing voice who speaks truth to power and criticizes Nebuchadnez-
zar's imperialism to his face at a festival, reminding the king of "the
misery of the vanquished, the groans of the captives, . . . the ruins of
nations . . . , the curses heaped upon the lawless and grasping ambition, [and] the justice of an avenging God" (39), causing the king to
slip into "a state of madness" (41) and become "helpless and speech-
less" (41). And it is this feminized man, although deformed, who wins
Ada's affection, after her first husband, the corrupt Ezra, practices
polygamy, beats his wives, and sells Ada into slavery. The hunchback
emancipationist turns out to be the proper suitor.

Perhaps the most fascinating and thoroughgoing portrait of a disabled reformist suitor appears in Celia Moss's "The Pharisee, or, Judea
Capta." Eli, a strict Pharisee who believes "there was . . . no such thing
as love" (2:227), and who "look[s] on a woman as a piece of furniture"
(2:207), has his marriage to Dora arranged by his father. The romantic
Mosses give a scathing critique of arranged marriage in Eli's treatment
of Dora, for he gives her money, jewels, and slaves, but not love, and
"love was as necessary to the heart of Dora, as sunshine to the flower.
She drooped beneath coldness and neglect" (2:207). However, Dora,
"like most Eastern women," "murmured not" (2:207),[48] for she realizes
that Eli is too busy with worrying over the Jews' oppression at the
hands of the Romans and their drift from the halacha into decadence
in imitation of their Hellenistic neighbors to pay too much attention
to her trivial sentimental desires. The Mosses criticize the split between public and private, inner and outer, for as the plot bears out,
Eli's unromantic view of marriage and his traditionalist attempt to
wrap himself in "the outward observances of religion" (2:208) leads to
his own downfall.

Dora has the ill luck to bear Eli a daughter first, and he refuses to
look at the infant, named Eve. When next she has a son, he rejoices,
but only to find that his son, Benoni, "was cursed . . . for the cruelty
[Dora's] husband had shown the firstborn" (2:208). For Eli's cruelty to
Eve, that is, Benoni is cursed with muteness. The father's oppressive
and traditionalist sexism leads to a feminizing of the son, the taking
away of his use of language, the male Jew's source of power. This
discovery turns Eli's heart away from Dora completely, and he sends
her back to her mother, or as in the language of the Mishnah, he "puts
her away." She is absent from the narrative for fourteen years. He
turns away from Benoni as well, whom he believes to be unfit to
receive and transmit the law. Eli is furious at Benoni because he "has

never called me father" (3:52), and he adopts a foster son, Elias, who later turns out to be a Roman spy, and who proves to be the family's undoing.

While Eli is tutoring Elias in the law, Benoni is sent to study and live in the women's quarters, raised and taught with his sister Eve by an intellectual slave woman, Kesiah, whose granddaughter Hindlah also lives with them. Retrospectively, Benoni explains his own feminization less as a result of his father's treatment than as his own choice: "I sought not companions of mine own sex, lest in their rude mirth they should mock my misfortune" (3:159). While Eli observes strictly the separation of himself from women, refusing even to look at his daughter, his son grows up living among women. And while Eli is a traditionalist, Benoni, without the benefit of his father's strict religious education, turns out to be a reformer, for when he and Eve bury their dead mother-substitute Kesiah, they perform a reformist ritual: "although the rites of their faith were not all performed, never were prayers more pure and fervent breathed over dust" (3:62). In the romance novel, sincerity counts for more than ritual exactitude. It is the disabled Benoni who will become the suitor of the Jewish woman in this tale. It is the man who suffers the curse of his father's traditionalist sexism who becomes a reformist hero.

Given the dynamics of the father/daughter/suitor plot, Benoni the suitor ought to be marrying Eve, the oppressed daughter. Since this marriage would constitute incest, however, Celia Moss provides an alternative for both children. Eve ends up with Julius, a Hellenized Jew who reads Sophocles to her, who promises to be "father, mother, brother" (2:237) to her, and who is hated by Eli for educating his daughter in Greek. As Eli castigates him, "Thou hast forsaken by degrees the faith of Jehovah. Thy very name was borrowed from the Romans. Thy birth was in the land of the oppressor" (2:240). Julius, however, disputes that an acculturated and reformist Jew is necessarily a traitor, for in defense of his own father's reformist ways he tells Eli: "if he has not thy austerity in the practice of form and ceremony, he performs more essentially the duties of a Hebrew by feeding the hungry and clothing the naked. The sons of Israel, in the remotest lands, have cause to bless his bounty" (2:240). Like a member of the Board of Deputies of British Jews, that Victorian Jewish association par excellence, dispensing aid to foreign Jews, arguing on behalf of English Jews to Parliament, and helping to organize local charities, Julius's father is an acculturated Jew whose Jewishness consists in his ethical actions rather than in his ritual acts.[49] Still, although he appears a viable alternative to Eli's strict Pharisaism, Julius is not yet ready to be married to Eve as far as Celia Moss is concerned. Before he can fulfill all of the conditions for being a suitor, Julius must be wounded in the doomed war against Titus and Vespasian, and must choose death rather than becoming Titus's slave. Only after this ordeal, and his escape due to a Roman man's friendship-—only after he is wounded and enslaved—is Julius deemed fit to become Eve's husband. He must suffer physical pain and emotional longing; he must know what it means to be oppressed.

Benoni also must undergo an ordeal before he can marry Kesiah's granddaughter, Hindlah. Hindlah is Eve's other half, for she says Eve is her "more than sister" (2:245). She is beautiful whereas Eve is intellectual. The two of them together constitute an ideal of a Jewish woman, as the traitor Elias perhaps understands when he plans to marry one and have an affair with the other. Benoni, then, has fallen in love with his sister's other half. But his disability ensures that he is constantly unable to express his feelings to Hindlah. "Often, oh! how often he longed for language to tell her how dear she was to him" (3:66). Again, Benoni's "heart swelled almost to bursting, but he was powerless even to utter the rage he felt" (3:96). His disempowerment from the use of the male Jew's proudest gift, the use of language, frustrates him, but humbles him, too. Finally, in a burst of love and rage, Benoni "burst the string that had bound his tongue for so many years and swears his love to Hindlah" (103), but his power to speak comes only after it is too late, for she has already bound herself to Elias in order to save Benoni and Eve from death. Once during the narrative, when Elias is about to kill Eve, the gentle and peaceful Benoni claims a violent masculinity—he takes a bow and arrow and shoots Elias's eye out, saving his sister from ruin. In romance fashion, the feminized man is able to invoke violent masculine power in order to protect the woman he loves. But this violent expression is not characteristic of him, and it is only after years of suffering as a Roman slave, after he is altered, withered, aged, and saddened, that Benoni is finally made happy when Elias dies: he and Hindlah are married and have a child, a son to carry on the alternative patriarchal tradition. He is able, after years of suffering, to make with Hindlah a "beautiful scene of domestic happiness" (3:186). In the meantime, his father, too, has undergone a complete transformation. Eli comes to see Elias's treachery, repents of his cold Pharisaism, blesses his children, asks forgiveness of Julius, and, with many apologies, is reunited with Dora.

This pattern of the suitor's suffering suggests that while these writers see an alternative Jewish male authority as the only escape from their female characters' conflicts with their fathers, they construct these alternative authorities in such a way as to place a greater measure of power in the hands of the female protagonists. These alternative men intervene at crises in the father/daughter relationship to help the women disobey their fathers and follow their own consciences. They are "enablers." And they are reformers as well. In the Mosses' hands, the romance genre is deeply allied with religious reform, the literary and the religious practice each valuing the individual's experience over prescribed forms. Yet, although the Mosses feel they must invoke another male hero as the means of enabling the heroine to make her own choice, they reveal a deep resentment of this restriction on their Jewish heroines' freedom, which they play out on the bodies of their alternative male characters. If the fathers, whose traditionalism is unbearable, have to be killed off or completely transformed, the alternative men, the supporters of religious and national reformation, need to undergo a gender reformation that can only take place through their marginalization, suffering, and physical deformation—through a gradual recognition of their own feminization vis-à-vis traditional Judaism's standards and the dominant culture's coercive power. The reformers who become suitors in these tales present a masculinity that is qualitatively different from the aggressive and charismatic masculinity characteristic of either the fathers or the Christian suitors in conversionist or Jewish men's novels of Jewish identity.

From these transformations it ought to be clear that these Anglo-Jewish women writers do not simply assimilate the historical romance form they inherit from the non-Jewish novelists of Jewish identity. They use the form to engage in a dialogue simultaneously with two audiences, the dominant Christian and the Jewish. In engaging with the dominant readership, they attempt to use the form to elicit sympathy for the removal of Jewish disabilities, and to respond to conversionist charges that Jewish women were oppressed, undereducated, and malleable. In engaging with the Jewish community, they use the form to claim power for themselves by extending the power of individual choice to women, by arguing for women's ability to write and to be educated, and by creating an alternate reality in which women will have the ability to control whether and whom they will marry and on what terms.[50] By confronting both the external and the internal world, these romances are attempting to theorize the Victorian Jewish community's dual movement into the modern world.

As the work of theorists, the Mosses' romances bear comparison to the work of many other Anglo-Jewish women writers flourishing during the period, work that taken together defined a generation of Anglo-Jewish responses to emancipation and reform—work that has now been all but forgotten. It was a woman, Grace Aguilar, who was the first Jew to produce a widely read anonymous secular history of the Jews of England, a history that, although well received at the time, has not been reprinted in this century.[51] It was she who in *The Spirit of Judaism* was the first to call for a translation of the Bible into the English vernacular, on the model of Moses Mendelssohn's translation of the Bible into German, a suggestion that was subsequently taken up by Abraham Benisch in England and Isaac Leeser in America without acknowledging her.[52] Charlotte Montefiore's *A Few Words* is a remarkable series of essays on religious reform, Jewish materialism, the split in the community between rich and poor, the laborer's Sabbath, the passover, the feast of weeks, and the Jewish woman, along with an allegory about acquiring moral tenets. Her *Caleb Asher* is a scathing critique of conversionists' methods. Her *Cheap Jewish Library,* which she funded and edited anonymously, provided didactic Jewish tales for working-class Jewish families. In her own time her works were reprinted and hotly debated. Two of her works have been lost. Anna Maria Goldsmid's preface to her translation of Götthold Salomon's sermons could be called the first act of the English reform movement. But David Woolf Marks, the first rabbi of the reform synagogue in Burton Street, borrowed the terms of Goldsmid's preface to justify his reforms without acknowledging her.[53] It was she who called most critically for the English Jews to send aid to persecuted Jews in Rumania. Judith Montefiore was the role model of many Jewish women, keeping diaries of her travels in aid of Jews in the Levant, and writing the first modern Jewish cookbook in English.[54] Yet she is frequently remembered only as Moses' wife. It was women who set up the most successful literary libraries, *The Cheap Jewish Library* and the "Little Miriam" series, and started the literary periodical *The Jewish Sabbath Journal,* when Haim Guedalla's earlier attempt, *Sabbath Leaves,* lasted just five issues. These women provided many of the most important texts and institutions for reflecting on Anglo-Jewish experience in the early and mid-Victorian periods.

They had a measurable effect on each other and on their community, especially on Victorian Jewish women's self-perception. Grace Aguilar and Charlotte Montefiore corresponded and Aguilar published in Montefiore's *Cheap Jewish Library*.[55] Marion Hartog wrote poems in honor of Judith Montefiore and Grace Aguilar, and she corresponded with many young female writers in the provinces and in London.[56] True, as Linda Gordon Kuzmack argues, a Jewish women's movement as such did not really begin in England and America until after 1880. But there were still many separate writings by individual Jewish women in the period between the start of the agitation for the removal of disabilities in England in 1830 and the mass immigrations of the 1880s, and there were many separate acts that, taken together, represent a new movement of Jewish women into the arenas of literature and politics.[57] If there was as yet no coordinated Jewish women's movement, there were individual Jewish women who were active, not only through their writings, but also through the pressure they brought to bear on powerful men, and through the educational and charitable societies they founded.[58] If they did not produce a unified movement with self-sustaining political institutions, their actions nevertheless influenced their female contemporaries. Marion Hartog's *Jewish Sabbath Journal* certainly influenced the group of "Jewish ladies of Liverpool" who "form[ed] an association for the promotion of cheap Jewish literature, having in the first instance immediate reference to the *Sabbath Journal*."[59] Aguilar's mother Sara collected many tributes upon her daughter's early death, some of them showing that her influence spread across the Atlantic. A Mrs. R. Hyneman wrote:

> Thou wert a stranger unto us; thy name
> Alone was wafted o'er the Atlantic wave,
> But true hearts mourn'd thy loss when tidings came
> That thou wert in the cold and silent grave,
>   Aye, true hearts grieved for thee.

The Female Hebrew Benevolent Society of Philadelphia paid its tribute on its twenty-eighth anniversary, November 3, 1847, just after Aguilar's death: "Where so many 'Women of Israel' are assembled, it would seem ungrateful not to pay a small tribute to the memory of the benefactress of her sex and nation—the pious, the wise, the excellent, the beloved Grace Aguilar, to whose talents and piety we are indebted for the best religious books of modern times." The Ladies of the Society for the Religious Instruction of Jewish Youth of Charleston called Aguilar's death "a national calamity."[60] But perhaps the best proof of these writers' power to inspire other women, at least from their own class, is the testimonial Grace Aguilar received from a group of middle-class Jewish women just before her trip to the Continent in 1847. This moving tribute, presented by several hundred of "the most influential ladies of our community . . . in acknowledgment of the great service which that gifted authoress has rendered to her co-religionists, and to the females in particular, by her numerous and clever writings" (JC, April 16, 1847), praised her as follows:

> Until you arose, it has, in modern times, never been the case, that a woman in Israel should stand forth the public advocate of the faith of Israel. . . . You have taught us to know and to appreciate our own dignity, to feel and to prove that no female character can be more worthy than the Hebrew mother—none more pure than that of the Jewish maiden—none more pious than that of the women in Israel. You have vindicated our social and spiritual equality with our brethren in faith; you have by your own excellent example triumphantly refuted the aspersion that the Jewish religion unmoved the heart of the Jewish woman.[61]

If Jewish women writers have not been recognized by most later historians as having effected changes in Anglo-Jewish life in the modern period, they were recognized by their contemporaries, both as early feminists and as promoters of Jewish reform.

The emergence of a disparate group of women writers debating the issues of female education, Jewish emancipation, and religious reform separates the English Jews from the German, French, and American Jews, none of whom produced many women writers in this period. Many scholars of the Anglo-Jewish enlightenment have claimed that English Jews, in contrast to their coreligionists on the Continent or across the ocean, had no theory of what constituted emancipation or reform. Rather, their method was more practical—they tested laws by running for office, and anglicized without really articulating the reasons why.[62] But the truth is that the English Jews had a set of highly articulated theories. It was just that these theories were articulated by women—in polemics, in prefaces to their fictions, and especially in romances set in the Jewish home. The fictions were considered trivial by many Jewish men at the time and since, and in the biased transmission of history their theories have been left behind. These women are the unacknowledged Mendelssohns of England.

Engraving of Grace Aguilar. Courtesy of the Jewish
Museum, London.

FOUR
GRACE AGUILAR: "THE MORAL GOVERNESS OF THE HEBREW FAMILY"

THE VEIL AND THE SPIRIT

The Mosses articulated an important response to conversionists and Jewish men in their historical romances. They were championed by luminaries in the Jewish community like the Mocattas and the Montefiores, and in the Christian world like Edward Bulwer Lytton. Their work sold well, going through several editions, and was discussed by contemporaries in the pages of Jewish and Christian periodicals. But when they died, it passed with them into obscurity. Obscurity was the fate of work by Charlotte Montefiore, Anna Maria Goldsmid, and Maria Polack as well, even though their texts were in some cases highly touted and highly controversial when first published. Of all the early Anglo-Jewish women writers, only Grace Aguilar's work was reprinted after her death. In anthologies of Jewish women's work even today, only her writings from this period continue to be excerpted.[1] Why? How did her work uniquely exemplify the contradictions and dilemmas of the early Victorian Jewish subculture?

Aguilar was recognized by Christians and Jews alike as the writer who best defined the Anglo-Jewish response to the challenge to enter the modern world. Besides being reprinted widely, her works were advertised in the end pages of Dickens's *Bleak House,* suggesting that she was fairly well integrated into the mainstream literary culture. She achieved such fame partly because she was able to construct an identity for Jews as English citizens based on different principles than those articulated by "tolerant" liberal Christians. She criticized "toleration's" requirement that all the nation's citizens be converted to a fundamental sameness—that is, to Christianity. But paradoxically, in setting out to convince Christian liberals to quit their tactics of toleration, their pity and projection, Aguilar agreed to a trade-off: Jews would in turn restrict their expressions of differentness to the domestic sphere. This trade-off accounted in good measure for her work's appeal to a wide audience.

While Aguilar was negotiating the terms of Jews' increasing participation in the Victorian world, she was also negotiating terms for women's increasing participation in the Jewish world. For Aguilar, gender and ethnicity were intertwined categories of identity, sometimes supporting one another, at other times at odds. In regard to gender, too, Aguilar produced a trade-off: if Jewish men would provide women with education, women would in turn restrict their sphere of influence to the home. Because she balanced demands with concessions, both in relation to men and the dominant culture, she became the most lauded Jewish woman writing in Victorian England.

Aguilar undoubtedly gained a wealth of stories as well as a particular stance toward them from her Sephardic upbringing.[2] The eldest of three children (with two younger brothers), she was born in 1816 in Hackney. Her ancestors had fled during the Inquisition from Lisbon to Amsterdam and from there to England. Her father, Emmanuel, came from a merchant family that lived in a town called Aguilar near Cordova; her mother, Sarah Dias Fernandez, came from Portugal via Jamaica. Her family had a history of literary activity and community service. Her maternal great-grandfather wrote religious polemics (eventually published by the same Isaac Leeser of Philadelphia who would later publish her *Spirit of Judaism*). For a time, until he became ill in 1828, her father was the Parnas, or lay leader, of the Spanish and Portuguese Congregation in London. Perhaps because her family was so involved in Sephardic affairs, she received what Lask Abrahams calls "the oral traditions of Spain and Portugal"—the expulsion, the Inquisition, the traditions of crypto-Judaism. And like the Oral Law, which had its Judah HaNasi to redact it and pass it down, these traditions would need a teller.

Families like Aguilar's who had fled the Inquisition often had a matriarchal structure: the oral traditions of the crypto-Jews were passed down from mother to daughter in the domestic space because the traditionally male Judaic public spaces (such as the synagogue and yeshiva) had been closed down.[3] Sarah Aguilar seems to have fulfilled the matriarchal role of storyteller, giving her daughter a great deal of material for her popular novels about mothers and daughters, *Home Influence; A Tale for Mothers and Daughters* and *A Mother's Recompense*. Rather than focusing on the conflict between father and daughter, as did the conversionists, Jewish men, and the Ashkenazic Mosses, the crypto-Jewish culture focused on the transmission of tradition by mothers to their children.[4] Aguilar's father seems to have accommodated the maternal role of storytelling, becoming in his illness Aguilar's amanuensis until his death in 1844. In this, he was certainly different from the Ashkenazic Joseph Moss, who threatened to burn his daughters' books. The crypto-Jewish tradition supported female storytellers.

Crypto-Judaism was a secret, domestic Judaism, hidden from the outside world as if by a veil. For example, in Aguilar's Inquisition romance, the *Vale of Cedars,* the Jewish family is quite literally hidden from Christian view in a secret labyrinth behind a "vale"—or valley—of cedars. Aguilar defamiliarizes her descriptions of Jewish customs and ritual by describing them as if from an outsider's perspective and not in great detail.[5] In contrast to conversionists, who typically described Jewish rituals with an ethnographic "thick description," Aguilar's description is thin and hazy.[6] Zatlin argues that Aguilar employs this distancing method so as to focus less on differences of form between Judaism and Christianity and more on similarities in spirit. While this emphasis on spirit over forms was a standard strategy of emancipationists, Aguilar reached it through an unusual path, through the traditions of secrecy from her crypto-Jewish heritage. To put it another way, Aguilar invokes the lessons her ancestors learned from hiding during the Inquisition in order to express the dilemmas of passing in a liberal state.

Aguilar received much of this mother-daughter teaching in provincial Devon, where her family moved for her father's health in 1828. Here and in her subsequent provincial home in Brighton, she kept numerous diaries and notebooks. These manuscripts were collected by Rachel Beth Zion Lask Abrahams and bequeathed to the Jewish Museum in London early in this century. The Museum loaned them to the Manuscript Library of University College London in 1990, where for

137

the first time they could be viewed by scholars. They include her first novels, written by hand for a Christian friend, "The Friends, a Domestic Tale" (1834), and "Adah, a Simple Story" (1838), as well as a series of books of poetry, tales, journals of excursions, such abstruse writings as her "Notes on Chonchology" (the science of conch shells), and sermons. In addition, the collection includes numerous tributes to her upon her death (collected by her mother), a physician's account of her final illness, and seven of her published works.

It was in Devon that Aguilar first began to write poems, culminating in her first book, *The Magic Wreath,* published anonymously in 1835 when she was nineteen. This book met with praise in the non-Jewish press, which encouraged Aguilar to write poems for such non-Jewish publications as *Keepsake, La Belle Assemblée,* and *Chambers' Miscellany.* She also began to publish poems in Jewish periodicals, such as the *Hebrew Review and Magazine of Rabbinical Literature, Voice of Jacob,* the *Occident,* and the *Jewish Chronicle.* In the twelve years between the publication of *Magic Wreath* and her death in 1847 Aguilar wrote twelve books, only six of which were published while she was alive. *Israel Defended* (Brighton 1838), her translation from French of a polemical work by Orobio de Castro, was her contribution to the emancipation debate. *The Spirit of Judaism,* her meditation on the humanistic spirit that underlay the formal rituals of Judaism, was written as an aid in her brothers' education. Isaac Leeser agreed to publish it in 1840, but it was lost in transit to America and had to be rewritten. It appeared in print in 1842, with Leeser's editorial comments and refutations, and nonetheless achieved an enormous success. It was reviewed in the *Voice of Jacob* (April 1, 1842), which praised its "many beauties" as "fervid, eloquent, and truthful," while criticizing Aguilar for entering into "the province of schoolmen." This faint praise did not, however, prevent the book from being reprinted well into the 1880s. *The Spirit of Judaism* was followed, in 1844, with *Women of Israel,* an account of the women of the Bible and the Talmud, which, more than any other of her works, achieved lasting popularity. It was given as a prize to Jewish students and to Christian Sunday school students up through the 1950s. Also in 1844, Aguilar published *Records of Israel,* a compilation of several tales that combined aspects of historical romance with domestic fiction. By this time she was known to her Christian public as an authentic spokesperson for Judaism. She followed *Records* with "The Perez Family," the first modern-day tale of domestic Jewish life in Anglo-Jewish history, published in Charlotte Montefiore's *Cheap Jewish Library* to a Jews-only audience. In 1846, she published *The Jewish Faith,* a series of letters from an older woman to a younger on resisting conversion. And in 1847, she published the first history of English Jews by a Jew in *Chambers' Miscellany.*

In November, 1847, suffering from a combination of measles and consumption, Aguilar left on a trip to Frankfurt both for her health and to visit her ailing brother. Just before she left she received a tribute from approximately three hundred middle-class Anglo-Jewish women, reprinted in chapter 3, in honor of her efforts on behalf of Jewish emancipation and women's education. While in Frankfurt, her illness worsened until she died on November 16, 1847. Her tombstone in the Frankfurt Jewish cemetery reads, "Give her of the fruit of her hands; and let her own works praise her from the gates." These words, taken from the famous passage on the Ideal Woman ("Eshet Chayil") in Proverbs 31, constantly quoted by reformers, were a fit epitaph to this prolific reformer's life.

Her other six books were published posthumously by her mother, who also wrote a memoir of her daughter and collected Aguilar's short stories into a single volume. These books included *Home Influence; A Tale for Mothers and Daughters,* written in 1836 but published by her mother just after her death in 1847. This novel about domestic Christian life, published by a non-Jewish press for a primarily Christian readership, went through twenty-four editions by 1869. Its sequel, *A Mother's Recompense,* was published in 1851 and also went through many editions. *Woman's Friendship* (1850) was another domestic novel about Christian characters that went through several editions. *The Vale of Cedars; or, The Martyr,* Aguilar's popular Jewish historical romance, was written between 1831 and 1835 and published in 1850. According to Lask Abrahams, it achieved "a wide circulation, not only in England, but also in many countries abroad and was translated into Hebrew." By 1916, when it was last printed, it had gone through twenty-nine printings. A Scottish historical romance written in imitation of Walter Scott's Waverly novels, *Days of Bruce* (1852), was perhaps the most popular of all her books; like *Vale of Cedars,* it was written early in her career but only published after her death. *Home Scenes and Heart Studies* (1852) is a compilation of her short fiction, including "The Perez Family," the tales from *Records of Israel,* and other miscellaneous stories and midrashim. Finally, *Sabbath Thoughts and Sacred Communings,* the first collection of sermons to be published by a Jewish woman, appeared in 1853.

The subsequent publication history of her works shows that she was continuously in print until the middle of the twentieth century. Her *Works* were republished in 1871 to great acclaim in the *Jewish Chronicle.* In the 1930s, a children's book based on her life called *Young Champion* appeared.[7] And excerpts from *Women of Israel* and *Spirit of Judaism* continue to be anthologized in collections of Jewish women's writing. Her fictional works, however, have suffered a different fate. Beginning with Cecil Roth's review in "The Evolution of Anglo-Jewish Literature" in 1937, critics have systematically neglected, rejected, or trivialized Aguilar's fiction, while taking seriously her theological and biographical efforts.

If one looks at the path of her writing career, not in order of publication, but in order of composition, one can see that the work that has been best remembered came from the middle period of her brief career. Her career begins with a sustained engagement with historical romance ("Adah," *Vale of Cedars, Days of Bruce*)—the first period; moves through translation (*Israel Defended*), theology (*Spirit of Judaism*), and midrashic biography (*Women of Israel*)—the middle period; and ends with a sustained series of moral and domestic fictions (*Records of Israel, Woman's Friendship, Home Influence, Mother's Recompense,* "The Perez Family")—the final period. It is intriguing that critics and historians have fastened on to the middle period, when from this chronological perspective domestic fiction appears to have been Aguilar's final destination, the genre in which her version of domestic ideology found its most lasting home. Without undermining the importance of the contributions of her middle period, this chapter aims to analyze both the first and final periods of her career more carefully than has been done up to now, by reading both the historical romances and the domestic fictions against similar work by her Christian and Anglo-Jewish female peers. By recontextualizing her work so that the conditions of its composition become apparent—by denying the critical commonplace that Aguilar was a writer "sui generis"—the chapter is able to answer a number of questions that have eluded earlier critiques: Why did Aguilar's writing career develop between the poles of historical romance and domestic fiction? How and why did her career path differ from those taken by her contemporaries? What was her relationship to the themes that so concerned her contemporaries—female education, reform, emancipation, and romance? And how did Aguilar's choices position her to be remembered beyond all other early Anglo-Jewish women writers?

If as a Sephardic woman in the crypto-Jewish tradition Grace Aguilar received a mandate to pass down her oral traditions, as a Jewish woman in liberal England she discovered that her ability to carry out this task had been limited by the sparse educational opportunities afforded her. In *Spirit of Judaism,* she expanded on the power and importance of maternal storytelling for the continuation of Judaism. Describing the barriers to public education for Jewish children, she moves to a call for mothers to be instructors: "Debarred from the public exercise of devotion on his Sabbath; never hearing public prayers in a language he can understand;—having no public minister on whom he can call for that instruction [there was a dearth of teachers in the community] he may not have received at home; never hearing the law expounded, or the Bible in any way explained: to his mother alone the Hebrew child must look, on his mother alone depend for the spirit of religion."[8] She also admits, however, that "It may be, that doubts of her own capability of executing [this] task . . . may naturally exist" (123). As mothers, women were expected to transmit the cultural traditions, but as women, they were expected to have little or no voice, subjectivity, and knowledge.[9] Aguilar herself, though an avid reader, felt that she lacked crucial knowledge of Hebrew, of the Talmud, and of rabbinic tradition.

To mediate this conflict, Aguilar goes on to provide a detailed instruction manual for mother-instructors—as if she herself were the mother to the "daughters of Israel," providing the crypto-Jewish mother/daughter teaching. She encourages women to teach both girls and boys Hebrew and the prophets, and, most importantly, to relate Jewish history in the form of "interesting tales" during "those many leisure hours that the child looks up so clingingly and fondly to his mother for amusement. Vividly and interestingly might these narratives be opened to the young and eager mind, till almost insensibly he feels it a privilege to belong to a nation so peculiarly blessed" (130). In this moment, women's storytelling—especially if it includes "simple, domestic, highly moral tales"—becomes a defense against conversion, and a primary means of infusing Jewish identity.[10] Aguilar goes on to defend in advance this pedagogical procedure from critics who felt "tales" were a trivial waste of time, by focusing on the relation between the telling of tales and the training of the heart: "Tales read for recreation and enjoyment might be made of service in the promotion of piety. There are many who deem the perusal of such works but mere waste of time and intellect, creating evils even worse, in filling the mind with romance and folly. Nay, so far is this mistaken prejudice extended, that all books but those of instruction either in history, geography, arts, or sciences are excluded from the child's library. The infant mind is crammed, its intellect exhausted, while the moral training and the guidance of the *feelings* are left to their own discretion" (154). While Ashkenazic reformers such as Anna Maria Goldsmid and David Woolf Marks commonly called for maternal instruction in the community, the emphasis here on "tales" as the mode of instruction was particular to the matrilineal Sephardic oral tradition. Isaac Leeser's editorial objection that "in permitting such works to be placed in the hands of children, especially in our novel, romance, and story-writing age, great care must absolutely be exercised in the selection" (154) illustrates the "mistaken prejudice" that existed outside the Sephardic oral tradition from which Aguilar drew.

As Leeser suggests, tales can take many forms, and the question was in what form these traditions would be passed down. Both the English and American Sephardim had been settled in their liberal countries since the seventeenth century, whereas most of the Ashkenazim had arrived much more recently, starting in the 1750s. Although these Sephardim recalled the Inquisition, their distance from it enabled them also to recall the Golden Age of Spain, which produced such Jewish worthies as Maimonides and Jehudah HaLevi. They could be proud of their history, which they told often in heroic terms, as if they were the unharrassed nobility of the Jews. They could identify with their romantic history rather than with what many of them increasingly saw as a severe religious practice,[11] and could look back with pride as well to their ancestors who, stopping off in Amsterdam on their way to both England and America, had developed the earliest philosophy of liberalism in Europe.[12] Thus it seems to have been generally the case in liberalizing English-speaking countries like England and America in the 1830s and 1840s that Sephardic women were more prone to support the historical romance genre than any other genre. Through their publications, and through Rabbi Isaac Leeser's Philadelphia periodical the *Occident,* English and American Jewish women knew about and influenced each other.[13] By contrast, the Ashkenazim, at least those with memories of persecution fresh in their minds, were less likely to romanticize their past, and more likely to have a recent memory of traditional religious observance.[14] In this way, it could be said that English and American Sephardim tended toward a philosophically liberal, reformist, and romantic stance.[15] In the Sephardic community, indeed, liberalism, religious reform, and romance seemed internally connected by virtue of the fact that each of them gave priority to individual freedom and desire over communal dictates.

If from her Sephardic heritage Aguilar received a matriarchal oral tradition, a tendency to wrap a "veil" around the particulars of Jewish life, a liberal and romantic stance, and habits of literary endeavor and community service, she received quite a different influence from the surrounding Christian culture. When she was twelve, the family moved to Devonshire for Emmanuel's health, and it was there she had her first major contact with Protestants, making friends among them, and attending church on occasion. Having no access to Hebrew, she read Protestant sermons and the King James Bible. Her earliest attempts at fiction—the first attempts by a Jewish woman in modern history to place a Jewish woman at the center of the narrative—were two manuscript novels entitled "The Friends, a Domestic Tale" (1834), and "Adah, A Simple Story" (1838). Both are dedicated to female Christian friends. Indeed, "The Friends" concerns two young girls, Ellen, a Jew, and Constance, a Christian. It was in these tales that she first articulated the desire to portray Jewish women in contact with the Christian world but not overcome by it. From the beginning of her writing career, she already rejected conversion as the answer to the dilemmas posed for Jews by modernity. As she puts it in the earlier tale, written when she was eighteen: "One . . . feature . . . has never yet appeared in any other story it is the introduction of a young Jewess in the familiar way in which I have brought her forward—when one of that race has been introduced in any book it has been merely to give an exagerated [sic] feature of their habits customs and observances living entirely among themselves and never mixing among Christians in any familiar intercourse. . . . The minds of their readers must remain with the impression that they are a bigotted illiberal race."[16] But Jews are neither "unfamiliar" nor "illiberal," according to Aguilar. In fact, by all the standard indicators, they are the epitome of liberal virtue. "As members of a community," she says, "[Jews] are industrious, orderly, temperate, and contented; as citizens, they are faithful, earnest, and active."[17] It is just that being liberal does not entail desiring to be Christian. Christians who do not perceive Jews' liberalness are the ones who are bigotted and illiberal. They are the ones who cannot imagine that Jews can "mingl[e] . . . in [Christian] society" and "yet retain [their] own faith." Aguilar complains of the conversionist tales in which "a Jewess is introduced and by a series of misfortunes is thrown upon the mercy of Christians [she] at last either dies in their faith or is converted to it by marriage."[18] As she says in the preface to her second tale, "Adah," "The modern tales in which [Jews are] introduced, are written by Christians, who know nothing of, and are consequently prejudiced against them."[19] According to Aguilar, Christian bigotry and illiberalness are based on ignorance of Jews and breed a lack of imaginative sympathy for Jews, which impedes true toleration.

Her own tale is set up to counteract the assumption that Jewish contact with Christians must end in persecution or conversion.

> I have endeavoured to show in the character of Ellen, [she writes], that tho [sic] she lived from the time she could think in the midst of Christians mingling alone in their society she would yet retain her own faith . . . with the pure and holy conviction of the truth of her religion and she with the consent of her Parents even staying with Christians living under their roof yet keeping her own faith in all its primitive beliefs and adhering to its forms. We see the young girls of opposite faiths clinging to and loving each other in all the primitive warmth of Friendship which nothing could shake nothing could dispel—then we see them in the action of prayer and tho the form is different the prayers of both . . . at the same moment ascend together on high and are listened to with equal complacency by the merciful God to whom they are addressed.[20]

Jewish women can share intimacy with Christians and even with Christian theology without losing their Jewishness because they retain their difference in form. Aguilar's emphasis here that the difference in form masks a sameness of spirit would become the basis for all her later theological efforts to identify and inculcate the "spirit of Judaism." Her focus on this spirit instead of on peculiar forms would bring accusations from many Jewish quarters that she was a "Jewish Protestant,"[21] and that this period in her life rendered her an unauthentic Jew. This was particularly the case when she published a sermon in *Sabbath Thoughts and Sacred Communings* advocating prayer with Christians. Veiling the difference in forms was interpreted by some Jews as abandoning Judaism altogether.

But if the accusations that Aguilar's views were outside the bounds of Judaism were arguable, it was certainly the case that Aguilar's positive early provincial Christian contacts prepared her for later efforts on behalf of Jewish emancipation. If many Jews from the London community were wary of publishing in the non-Jewish press, Aguilar sought opportunities of adding her name to mainstream and even explicitly Christian Victorian periodicals. Besides those already mentioned, she published the occasional poem in conversionist periodicals, and when the *Voice of Jacob* rejected a piece, in the evangelical *Ladies' Magazine.* In these periodicals, and in such polemical works as her translation of Orobio's *Israel Defended,* she spread her message of toleration—soothing her audience's fears that the "Christian state" (in Carlyle's phrase) would be defiled with assurances that Jews were after all not different in spirit from Christians. In addition, she was friends with such prominent Christian literati as Felicia Hemans (to whose work hers was compared), Mrs. Samuel Carter Hall, Mary Howitt, and Southey's second wife Caroline Bowles.

This emphasis on spirit, which was the major legacy from her Christian contacts, would combine with the crypto-Jewish emphasis on veiling ritual forms from public view to produce a domesticated Judaism. Aguilar proposed a bargain: if "tolerant" Christians would agree to quit their philo-Semitic persuasion, Jews would in turn restrict their expressions of differentness to the domestic sphere. Not accidentally, her "spiritual" home-based Judaism looked a great deal like the Judaism of the religious reformers. If there was a difference between Aguilar's version of reform and Jewish men's, it was that hers was motivated by an acute awareness that she had been excluded from many of the primary texts of her own tradition because of her gender. When Aguilar attended Christian sermons in Brighton and read Christian biblical exegesis, it was not only because she loved her Christian friends or was drawn to Christianity's "spirituality"; it was because she had no access to the Hebrew language in which Jewish exegesis and sermons were made available. She laments in *Women of Israel* that many Jewish women would make the Bible their daily guide in life but "they know not how, from the sad scarcity of religious books amongst us, in modern tongues."[22] Indeed, she regrets that her attempt in that book to provide a comprehensive history of Jewish women must be incomplete because she has been "debarred" as a woman from knowledge. When giving her review of women in the Talmud, she cites several sources of knowledge: a male friend conversant in Bible and Talmud, *The Hebrew Review and Magazine of Rabbinical Literature,* and "one or two other casual notices in divine history."[23] These "have . . . enabled us to form an opinion: but the Talmud itself should be its foundation; and from that we, as a female, are unhappily debarred" (2:290). In her view, this debarment has left the Jewish woman seeking knowledge little recourse other than to read Christian texts. Her awareness of her exclusion from Jewish tradition is what motivates both her departure from it, and her attempts to provide increased female education in the community. "The religious as well as the moral duties of the law are . . . equally incumbent on *women* as well as men" (1:180), she argues in *Women of Israel*. Women must have enough education to participate in the religious life of the community. Contact with the Christian community taught Aguilar what Jewish women were missing.

But by attempting to supplement her education with texts written by and for Christians, Aguilar inevitably opened her authenticity as a Jew, and that of the Jewish women she spoke for, to question. She hoped to avert this problem with overt declarations of her loyalty, with explicit refutations of conversionist claims that Judaism oppressed women, and with increased Jewish female education. When a reviewer of *Spirit of Judaism* from the London Society for the Promotion of Christianity Amongst the Jews criticized her for not having read Christian works she replied by publishing a letter in the *Voice of Jacob*. She says, on the contrary, she has read them, and that "the conclusion at which she has arrived in favor of Judaism, does not arise from ignorance of other creeds, but from a conviction of the truth of the Mosaic dispensation."[24] Furthermore, the *Women of Israel* was written, she says, to protest the conversionists' charge "that the law of Moses sank the Hebrew female to the lowest state of degradation, placed her on a level with slaves or heathens, and denied her all mental and spiritual enjoyment" (1:9). By writing biographies of the women of biblical, Talmudic, and modern times, Aguilar could refute the idea "that Jewish women can have no comfort in adversity, but that as Christians they will find all they need; that in the one Faith they must feel themselves degraded, as in the other exalted and secure" (1:177–78). By refuting conversionist claims of Judaism's oppression of women with specific, knowledgeable instances to the contrary, she could subtly prove that she was an "authentic" Jew.

Aguilar hoped to help future generations of women avert the authenticity issue by writing the *Women of Israel,* in which she undertook to rectify Jewish women's exclusion from Jewish history, literature, theology, and culture. In this groundbreaking book, she

Advertisement for Grace Aguilar's *Women of Israel*, reproduced from the end
pages of *Home Scenes and Heart Studies* (London: George Routledge and
Sons, Ltd., 1894). Photo: Michael Dunn.

sought to provide the very education whose absence the conversionists pointed to as evidence of Judaism's neglect, and whose absence Jewish men pointed to as evidence that women were "the weakness in our camp." Essentially, she expanded her interpretation of the require- ments of the crypto-Jewish maternal storytelling tradition to include, not just the "oral traditions of Spain and Portugal," but the written and oral traditions relating to all women in Jewish history. By reinter- preting biblical tales using the conventions of the Jewish male literary genre of midrash, she hoped to instruct Jewish women in the princi- ples of her domestic ideology, which she identified as the ideology of the Torah itself. She interprets biblical heroines as positive or negative exemplars of Victorian respectability, grace, sympathy, and domestic- ity, and thus provides role models for her Victorian Jewish women readers. For instance, Moses' mother Jochebed provides an example of a "mother-instructor":

> We would here conjure the [mothers of Israel] to follow the example of the mother of Moses, and make their sons the receivers, and in turn the promulgators, of that holy law which is their glorious inheritance. Their faith, in England, may not be tried as that of Jochebed—they may not be called upon to expose their innocent babes to the dangers of the river, to save them from the cruelties of man—but they are called upon to provide a suit of defence for riper years. They must so instruct, so guide, the first ten or twelve years of boyhood, that even then they may leave their maternal homes as Israelites rejoicing in their faith.[25]

Exodus tells of Jochebed's providing no training to Moses, only of her nursing Moses for the daughter of Pharaoh.[26] Yet Aguilar expands on Jochebed's story so that she will exemplify a mother-instructor, train- ing her children in the secret home space away from Pharaoh's eyes to be the future leaders of the Jewish people. Other biographies in the series attempt to show that God cared for women as much as men in the legal, civil, religious, and social systems of the Bible without treating them exactly the same as men; that women can inquire di- rectly from God through prayer just as men can; that women, once having been prophets and judges, ought to have their opinions re- spected while at the same time recognizing their subordination to men; that women ought not to gossip; that they are "weaker in frame" and "less mighty in mental powers" (1:152) than men; and so on.[27]

Except to argue that God is gender-deaf when listening to prayers,

Aguilar is not attempting to argue that Judaism has provided for exactly the same roles and responsibilities for women and men. Rather, God has provided for separate men's and women's spheres, and therefore women's struggle for "equal rights" is futile. If Marion and Celia Moss, with their transgressive heroines, seek to expand women's roles into the public life of the community, Aguilar is interested in maintaining a strict separation between the public and the domestic. Abram and Sarai share "equality," she says, and yet Sarai "knew perfectly her own station, and never attempted to push herself forward in unseemly counsel" (1:49). Women "in the sight of God, in their *spiritual* privileges, in their peculiar gifts and endowments, in the power of performing their duties in their own sphere, in their *responsibility*," are "on a perfect equality with man," she insists. "But I would conjure them to seek humility, simply from its magic power of keeping woman in her own beautiful sphere, without one wish, one ambitious whisper, to exchange it for another" (1:43).

Although Aguilar clearly supports Victorian domestic ideology, the version she advocates is not precisely that of the dominant culture. Her crypto-Jewish tradition inflects her version in a marked manner. That is, Victorian domestic ideology can be reached through a number of different paths, and it is not as monolithic a cultural formation as is sometimes supposed. Typical Victorian domestic ideology is founded on the separation of the public sphere from a sphere conceived of as private. As Nancy Armstrong, Michel Foucault, D. A. Miller, and others have shown, Victorian privacy means precisely that one is not free from being watched by others, but is constantly being policed, if only by the authoritative "eyes" of a culture one has internalized. In this scenario, "technologies of power" such as conduct manuals and novels set the patterns by which individuals and families are to regulate their "private" behavior—which has, at least potentially, to be perpetually open to view. The home is the place in which the family performs its essential similarity to every other family, its bourgeois respectability and decency.[28]

Aguilar certainly advocates respectability and decency. But by contrast, she imagines the home as a place in which the Jewish family can, in safety, perform its difference from surrounding families—its Jewish ritual, its subcultural particularity. The "oral traditions of Spain and Portugal" passed down to her by her mother first suggested the necessity of transferring the responsibility for religious practice and cultural transmission from synagogue to home, from father-space to mother-space, from public to secret. They suggested the necessity of creating a matriarchal extended family space shut off from the prying eyes of outsiders. Hiding Jewish ritual in the home would help ensure that outsiders would not comprehend the full extent of Jews' differentness: if Christians were allowed to view the secret rituals, they might lose sight of the similarities in spirit for the strangeness of the forms. English Jews might not be able to pass as English and as a result might suffer social or political ostracism.

But if this departure from dominant Victorian domestic ideology starts out as a necessary strategy for surviving persecution, it is eventually transvalued into a positive cultural opportunity. The English Jews' secret space is not only where they escape from the dominant "technologies of power"; it is also a positive place in which the Jewish subculture can flourish. Because the home hides Jews' practice of their formal differences, it enables them to broadcast the elements of their essential sameness to Christians. It enables them to appear like Christian liberals in public—assimilating Christian literature, dress, music, and other social forms. The secret space thus enables their successful integration through assimilation. At the same time, it enables them to continue to perform their cultural particularity behind their "veil," ensuring generational continuity and the maintenance of tradition, if only in a shrunken sphere.

This Sephardic domestic ideology produces a number of paradoxes that frustrate attempts to evaluate it either as feminist or antifeminist. Aguilar's support for women's full communal participation and education seems to contradict her support for women's domesticity and subordination. In *Women of Israel,* an enormously ambitious text, she makes an extremely intelligent argument that women need to seal off their ambition and intellect from the view of men. The ardent support for a separation of spheres evidenced here and throughout Aguilar's domestic fiction seems to limit her utility as a feminist foremother; on the other hand, compared to the absence of Jewish women's self-representation that preceded *The Women of Israel,* this attempt to narrate a Jewish history that is centrally focused on the experience of women constitutes a major break with the androcentric Jewish past.

Whether Aguilar was a feminist or an antifeminist is but one of the conundrums her writing poses. Was she a Jewish Protestant on the verge of conversion, a reformer, or, as later critics have sometimes claimed, a traditionalist? Was she the spokeswoman for her people, or an ignorant fraud? Did she fill her station as a crypto-Jewish woman passing down the Sephardic oral tradition, or did she defile that station by writing the traditions down and placing them in the public sphere? Did she speak to Jews, or to Christians? Reviewers, critics, and historians have long disagreed on these questions. Christians and Jews, women and men, traditionalists and reformers—all had a stake in defining her. Perhaps because her works can be interpreted in all of these lights, her texts went through as many as thirty editions. While Jewish women thought her early death was a "national calamity,"[29] while some Jewish men questioned the value of her labors on behalf of orthodox Judaism, some Christians, such as Camilla Toulmine of *La Belle Assemblée,* felt that Aguilar's works "teach professing Christians Christian charity."[30] From the moment she began to publish until today, the only opinion almost every reader of Aguilar has been able to agree upon is that she was a writer sui generis.

SUI GENERIS

The first critic to give Grace Aguilar this label was Jacob Franklin, editor of the orthodox periodical the *Voice of Jacob,* who in "looking around in order to assign Miss Aguilar a rank among Israel's women," found himself "at a loss to discover a suitable position. We must place her by herself. She is single among Israel's women—she was a person *sui generis.*"[31] Ever since, this label has cropped up repeatedly in Aguilar criticism, from the tributes Aguilar received after her death to the children's story written about her in the early twentieth century, even up to Philip M. Weinberger's 1970 dissertation.[32] In some ways, of course, this characterization makes sense. For sheer variety of production, fictional and nonfictional, for sheer popularity and widespread influence, no Anglo-Jewish writer could compare to Aguilar. Her readership was largely Christian, even for her writings of explicitly Jewish content—another point of uniqueness, shared perhaps only by novelist Benjamin Farjeon later in the century. Whatever Jews themselves may have thought, Christians understood her to be the legitimate spokeswoman for her people. And certainly no Anglo-Jewish writer was written about, praised, and eulogized as much as Aguilar. On her death she received tributes from most major literary periodicals in England, and also from Germany, France, Philadelphia, New York, North Carolina, and Jamaica. Few Jewish writers of any period have inspired such an outpouring. In some ways, the label sui generis seems perfectly appropriate to her.

And yet, to invoke that title is to discourage comparison between Aguilar and other Jewish women writers who shared her context. Philip Weinberger's dissertation is a good example of what can happen when this context is eliminated. He compares Aguilar to the medieval philosopher Maimonides rather than to her contemporaries, using Maimonides' thirteen articles of faith to "prove" that she was an orthodox Jewish writer. But though Aguilar fulfills Maimonides' articles, she is by no means orthodox (when asked to take sides between the traditionalists and the reformers, she officially struck a neutral position).[33] In context, Weinberger would have seen that Aguilar's attitude toward the Oral Law and the rabbis as fallible human beings rather than as vessels of the unbroken chain of tradition from Sinai marks her as a reformer, as do many of her claims for expansion of women's roles, and her emphasis on the Bible's reasonableness. Had he compared her attitudes on these issues with those of, say, Judith Montefiore or Maria Polack, both traditionalists, he would no doubt have changed his position.[34]

Weinberger attempts to prove Aguilar's Jewish authenticity in response to a tradition that looked upon Aguilar's work as Christianized. Jewish women were particularly vulnerable to the charge of unauthenticity, since they were denied access to the language of their sacred texts, and were prohibited from education. Denied education, they were then faulted for not knowing enough. Isaac Leeser perhaps started this particular discussion when he edited *Spirit of Judaism* and publicly disagreed with Aguilar's conclusions in the edition. He contributed to the discussion further in his obituary of Aguilar, where he remarked that "some differences of opinion prevail in respect to the value of her labours in behalf of orthodox Judaism." At the same time, he agrees with the sui generis designation, declaring that "there has not arisen a single Jewish female in modern times who has done so much for the illustration and adornment of her faith as Grace Aguilar," and that "the blank occasioned by the removal of this gifted Jewish Authoress, is not likely to be supplied for some time to come by any of our Jewish sisters."[35] This double movement—of calling the value of Aguilar's work into question while elevating it to a level of uniqueness—continues throughout her reception history. When Aguilar's *Works* were reissued in 1871, the *Jewish Chronicle*'s reviewer repeated the movement subtly. "Miss

Aguilar," he begins, "though a Jewess—a Jewess who dearly prized and loved her faith—did not write for Jews only. Her views were of a more catholic character. She was essentially an English authoress. . . . It is needless to remark that highly as she was appreciated among the community of which she was so distinguished a member, she was quite as highly prized—perhaps more so—by the general public." This Jewess with a "catholic character" is nevertheless highly lauded for her "purity of thought and feeling," her "chaste . . . cultured and elegant" prose, her "graceful" and "sympathetic" mind and her "heart." She is praised for seeking to "accomplish the aim of using, in the best possible manner, the genius with which [she] had been endowed; but always in a womanly way."[36] She is unique as a woman, unauthentic as a Jew. She is not compared to any of the Anglo-Jewish women writers; rather, her "school of writing was that of the celebrated women who adorned literature in the early part of this century—Maria Edgeworth and Jane Porter." This comparison, with a later one to Charlotte Brontë, is rather a backhanded compliment, however. It applies to "her romances, but not to her historical sketches [i.e., the *Women of Israel*]. In these [sketches] she touched her subject with a dignity worthy of it. She rose to the height of its importance, and appropriately accomplished the task she had set herself." The reviewer leaves the impression that her romances had less dignity and were on a lower height. When she is compared to women, it is to Christian women, the value of whose work in romances is then minimized. The tokenizing of Aguilar as sui generis enables the almost immediate erasure of the burgeoning Anglo-Jewish women's intellectual community from historical memory. Women of the succeeding generation, such as Amy Levy, the Jewish feminist poet and novelist of the 1880s and 1890s, and Lily Montagu, Aguilar's obvious successor as a theologian of liberal Judaism, show no trace of knowledge of Aguilar or any other early Anglo-Jewish woman writer.[37]

Once this erasure is accomplished, and Aguilar is singled out, the influence of Aguilar's work is further diminished in two ways. First, critics have almost all contended that Aguilar's work is "promising, but unfinished." Her youth is blamed for many faults which make her, finally, a second-rate writer, a historical curiosity, not someone to be canonized. Franklin, of the *Voice of Jacob,* wrote that "full as the deceased was of performance, she was still fuller of promise." The *Athenaeum*'s obituary echoed this assessment almost word for word when it said: "Graceful as were her works, they were yet more full of promise than of performance."[38] Seventy years later, Rachel Beth Zion Lask Abrahams, in her "centenary tribute" to Aguilar, repeated the truism: "To say that she was by no means a major writer is not to decry her contribution to the development of Anglo-Jewish life. Gifted with great facility in the art of expressing herself, she was yet without that equipment and solid learning which could have measured up to her indomitable spirit, her phenomenal industry, and her unquestioning loyalty to her people."[39] It might be just as true to say that she was aware of her deficiencies in traditional knowledge, understood the source of them—the prohibition of Jewish female education—and did her best to supply herself. The content of much of her prose consists precisely of her calls for this situation to be rectified. To blame her for lacking equipment is to blame her for being a product of the very situation her work seeks to alleviate.

The second means of diminishing the influence of her work is a bit more subtle. Almost immediately upon her death at thirty-one, critics created a myth about her life: Aguilar's writing, the myth said, was an attempt to be a "mother" or a "governess" to the entire Jewish "family." It went on to acknowledge that she was very accomplished and powerful at her self-imposed task, but that the great strain of her selfless efforts weakened her body and ultimately led to her death. This myth served several purposes. It helped explain, in terms acceptable to the prevailing domestic ideology, the central paradox of Aguilar's life—that this champion of the domestic, of motherhood, and of wifehood, herself chose not to marry or bear children; it helped heighten the sense of her uniqueness (and thus diminish the possibility of comparing her to others); and it helped to undermine her use as a role model to other women. How was such a myth created, and how did it come to be almost universally accepted?

Jacob Franklin of the *Voice of Jacob* writes in his "Memoir of the Late Grace Aguilar" that "Depth and delicacy of feeling, nicety of observation, charitableness and gentleness of sentiment, form the principle characteristics of her writings. Hers was not the vigor of the oak." Franklin confuses the delicate characteristics of her writing with the vulnerability of her body. "Naturally of a delicate frame, her body was little calculated to resist the powerfully injurious influences, with which an over-sensitive and inquisitive mind worked upon it."[40] The suggestion is that measles and consumption did not kill Aguilar; her mind did. In their representative tribute, the Ladies of the Society for

the Religious Instruction of Jewish Youth of Charleston, South Carolina, recognized Aguilar's "power"—comparing her to young David
slinging stones at Goliath—while echoing Franklin's assertion of the
cost of that power to her body:

> At the announcement of her departure, the whole house of Israel
> rises up to honor the memory of our spiritual kinswoman; whose soul
> seemed divinely commissioned to execute Truth's righteous embassy.—
> The sling of the son of Jesse was not wielded with more power and effect
> against the scorner of his people, than was the pen of this champion of
> our faith against that giant Prejudice whose shadow blackens the
> earth. . . . Her devotional offering was more costly than the oblation of
> the temple builder—a life consecrated to sacred culture; until ceaseless
> labour laid its fragile framework in ruins! The sinews of her mind
> shrank not even while she wrestled with the angel of death.

Having thus propounded the myth that her writing killed her, the
tribute goes on to reassert her uniqueness as a consolation, doing so in
terms that will already seem familiar: "Where shall that other be found
who can properly fill the station of this moral governess of the Hebrew
family?"[41] The expected reply is that no other shall be found who is
willing to sacrifice her life for the moral improvement of the "children"
in her care. Aguilar presented a problem to memorializers, who wanted
to idealize her ideologically sound writing but needed to find a way of
discouraging others from imitating her ideologically unsound life.[42] By
suggesting that her literary efforts quite literally led to her death, the
tribute warns other women of the dire consequences of following in her
path. By invoking the image of the governess (one cannot help but call
to mind Amy Levy's later assertion that governessing is "drudgery"),[43]
the tribute places Aguilar's efforts more properly into their gendered
domestic sphere than it had by invoking the image of young David with
his sling. It contains Aguilar in a familiar space, not the space of the
single ambitious literary intellectual, but the space of the other-
directed caregiver. Aguilar's childlessness and marriagelessness are explained as results of her devotion to community service, rather than by
some other reason, such as that she simply preferred the company of
women to that of men, or that she preferred her independence to a
conventional wife's domestic obedience to her husband.[44] The myth
helps fend off the notion—which most likely would have attached itself
to Aguilar's career otherwise—that she was an independent minded

"old maiden aunt," as Amy Levy would jokingly refer to herself in the 1880s.[45] Instead, she is looking after her communal children's morals rather than her own advancement. The myth surrounding her death thus acknowledged her power, more or less contained that power in an ideologically defensible form, and warned other women against attempting to appropriate it for themselves.

And yet—these two images remain in tension—the image of the upright self-effacing caregiver does not quite rub out the image of the female emancipationist cross-dressing as a fearless boy so as to gain the power of the sling against oppression. If in the one case the image is of a servant to the community, in the other, the image is of the young founder of the Messianic line, unique in that he is the highest servant of God.[46]

SELFLESS AMBITION

In places, Aguilar's writings seem to anticipate and validate the myth of the author as selfless governess or "mother instructor." In so doing, she reveals the dangers for women writers of being perceived as self-promoting. Aguilar was acutely aware that if women's attempts at educating the public were perceived to be at all personally fulfilling, and not simply exercises in caregiving, these efforts were likely to be criticized as selfish or unwomanly. For, under the terms of her own domestic ideology, to be a proper woman meant that one did not act on behalf of oneself, but rather acted on behalf of others without regard for oneself. In *Woman's Friendship,* for example, the heroine's mother is a writer who dies from overexertion in the act of creating art that will benefit others. What is at stake in this other-directed writing appears most clearly, perhaps, in her story entitled "The Authoress" from *Home Scenes and Heart Studies.* Aguilar depicts a woman who gains fame by writing, and who nevertheless attends to her domestic duties without losing a sense of her place in the gendered separation of spheres. In the story, Clara Stanley, a writer of genius, has fallen in love with one Sir Dudley Granville, who returns the feeling but leaves her for fear that she will not be able to unite her intellectual pursuits with her domestic duties. His own mother had been a bluestocking—in the narrator's words, "one of those shallow pretenders of literature which throw such odium upon all its female professors. From his earliest childhood Dudley had been accustomed to regard literature and authorship as synonymous with domestic discord, conjugal disputes, and a complete neglect of all duties, social or domestic."[47] But if his mother, whose intellectual ambition obstructed her domestic service, was a pretender with "superficial knowledge and overbearing conceit," Clara Stanley is a "real genius" with "true literary aspirings" (229). Dudley cannot differentiate between Clara's genius and his mother's fraudulence, leaves Clara, and marries another woman unhappily. Women's literary work will leave them alone indeed.[48]

But this is not the end of the story. What are Clara's "true literary aspirings"? It is difficult to know, for it is almost as if Clara has nothing to do with her own success. Aguilar does not reveal the content of Clara's writing, nor anything about her writing process, only the results. As soon as Clara publishes, she becomes an enormous success. She does not take much pleasure in her success, however. As in the myth that would follow Aguilar after her death, Clara is not interested in the "notoriety which the constant success of her literary efforts had flung around her." She is, rather, "desirous for retirement and domestic ties. . . . She did not disdain or undervalue fame; but all of expressed admiration, all public homage, was so very much more pain than pleasure that she shrunk from it; longing yet more for some kindly heart on which to rest her own. . . . It was not for love, in the world's adaptation of the word, she needed; it was . . . one friend to love her for herself, for the qualities of *heart,* not for the labours and capabilities of *mind*" (237). The domestic space to which she desires to retire is the space of the heart, and the heart, rather than the mind, is here defined as Clara's "self." Aguilar's definition of the domestic as the space of woman's "self" makes sense when one considers her statement, in *Women of Israel,* that "women's sphere in the law of God, without doubt, is HOME" (1:165). Her belief in a separation of spheres in which the domestic is assigned to women renders difficult the prospect of a woman's going public. By placing her writing in public view, which is to say, by focusing attention on her mind, literary fame takes Clara away from herself and causes her pain, just as one would expect from the myth of Aguilar's life. But this report of pain in her notoriety only raises a more basic question: for what reason, then, does Clara write?

Perhaps what is painful is not so much the gaining fame as the having to admit that she desires such fame on behalf of her mental efforts. For years later, when Dudley returns, Clara is no longer shy about the pleasure she takes in her literary successes—for she now claims these successes are direct results of efforts, not of her mind, but of her heart. "Will you tell me, Miss Stanley," Dudley asks, "how you can possibly contrive to unite so perfectly the literary with the domestic characters? I have watched, but cannot find you fail in either—how is this?" Clara replies, "Simply, Sir Dudley, because, in my opinion, it is impossible to divide them. . . . [I]t is not possible to be more than usually gifted without being domestic. The appeal to the heart [in domestic fiction] must come from the heart; and the quick sensibility of the imaginative woman must make her *feel* for others, and *act* for them, more particularly for the loved of home" (242).[49] If ten years earlier, Clara felt that writing had overexposed her mind to public view, now she has learned to defend her writing as an exposition of the domestic heart to the sympathetic reader perusing the volume in her own domestic chamber. Clara's writing is as domestic as a mother's care for her young. She draws a parallel between the selfless sympathy required to create fictional characters and the selfless sympathy required to be the Victorian domestic ideology's ideal of Mother. In other words, Clara's care for the characters she creates stands in for her care for the husband and children she never had. Aguilar is able to defend her writing as other-directed domestic labor, and therefore short-circuits in advance any attempt to identify her efforts with a public-minded desire for fame, or her unmarried state with a desire for independence. Proponents of the myth that Aguilar was the "moral governess of the Hebrew family" may find their prooftext here.

Upon hearing her defense, Granville repents of the seven years he has spent away from her, assures her that her "resources of mind as well as of heart" can make him happy, and proposes to her. She consents to the marriage, but only on the condition that he allow her to remain a writer, for, at thirty-one years of age, she says she is set in her ways, and besides, she says, she feels her writing "accomplishes good." Thus the end of this story seems both to validate and criticize the myth created for her upon her death. A literary woman's life does not have to end in her being alone, in overexertion, and in death, as long as she "accomplishes good" for and administers "sympathy" to other people rather than simply ministering to her own ambition. She does not have to sacrifice everything; she merely has to sacrifice the desire to receive any acknowledgment of her intellectual (as opposed to emotional) gifts.

Still, beyond a doubt, Aguilar *was* ambitious for self-advancement and notoriety. Although she tends to suppress these ambitions in print, she does not suppress them in her manuscript novels and in her journals, in the process revealing what is so dangerous for a Victorian Jewish woman about self-promotion. She tells her friend in the preface to "Adah," "You have smiled, when I said I was ambitious." When solicited to write a tale for the *Cheap Jewish Library,* she wrote to Charlotte Montefiore: "I still indulge the hope, however fallacious, of one day seeing my writings more known than they are now."[50] And she is even more forthright about her ambition for literary fame in a journal presumably written for her eyes alone, when she goes on an excursion to a friend's estate. There she meets a Mrs. F. S. who "completely fascinated" her. She goes on to speculate on the motive for her fascination: "Perhaps . . . this feeling was greatly heightened by having previously learned . . . that she already knew and was attracted towards me as the author of the *Spirit of Judaism*—and that as such she was quite convinced she should like me—To be known and loved thro' my writings has been the yearning and the prayer of my secret heart from the earliest period in which I could wish or hope."[51] That she only expresses this literary ambition in her "secret heart" suggests that women's intellectual ambition was a taboo she felt she was breaking. Indeed, if in "The Authoress" and *Woman's Friendship* she helped to create her own myth, it was to ensure that her writings would be lauded by the community as a righteous woman's attempts to "accomplish good" rather than spurned as an ambitious woman's attempts at gaining fame. To a large degree, this myth succeeded in keeping questions of her ambition at bay. For the ambition to sacrifice oneself for the sake of others was a kind of female ambition encouraged by Victorian Jewish domestic ideology. Examples across the women's work abound: Marion Hartog's *Jewish Sabbath Journal* was shut down in large part because she manifested her literary ambition too publicly; Charlotte Montefiore published anonymously throughout her life to avoid the accusation; and Judith Montefiore presented her writings as adjuncts to her husband's good deeds.

Aguilar's genuine commitment to assigning women to the sphere of the domestic was in conflict with her genuine desire to have her ideas on the separation of spheres known and acknowledged by the public. When she eschewed public notoriety, then, she probably did so at least as much out of policy as passion. Someone as thoroughly familiar with the intricacies of domestic ideology as she was must have feared that her reputation would be tainted, her work would lay un-read or forgotten, if the slightest hint of self-interest accrued to it. Aguilar was able to fend off obscurity better than other writers in part because she was able to hide her "secret heart" from public view. Because she publicly denied her desire for publicity, because she adver-tised her writing as mother/daughter teaching, she was able to publish in her own name without attributing her ideas to her father or her husband. In this regard, she did resemble Victorian Christian domestic ideologists such as Felicia Hemans or Sarah Stickney Ellis.[52] But this dynamic suggests there are other reasons for Aguilar's being sui generis than critics have previously suspected. She was not singular because she was the only Anglo-Jewish woman writer, or the only good one, but because she was the only Anglo-Jewish woman writer who explicitly embraced the restrictions on women's public notoriety, and simultaneously took full credit for her work.

Ironically, however, although this strategy has enabled her work to remain in print longer than any of her contemporaries' and to be seen as *the* early Anglo-Jewish woman's literary outpouring, the strategy has done her work's breadth, ingenuity, originality, and historical significance a disservice. Over time the idea that Aguilar was sui generis has sealed her writings off from the context in which they resonate most—the context of other early Anglo-Jewish women writ-ers. By scaring women away from literature and ensuring that her work would have no successors, the myth that Aguilar was a governess who sacrificed her life in her selfless exertions on behalf of her Hebrew family has rendered her work nearly illegible. The question of her authenticity as a Jew, the value of her labors on behalf of reform Judaism, the extent to which she was a champion of women—without comparisons, none of these questions can be investigated in any sophis-ticated way.

REWARDS AND PUNISHMENTS

Like Marion Hartog (née Moss), Aguilar was brought up middle-class in the provinces, started publishing at a young age, was a strong advocate of reform, or Liberal Judaism, and ran a boarding school in London. With all of these similarities, one might have expected their literary careers to take a similar path. But Aguilar's flourished while Hartog's came to an early end. Two major differences stand out when comparing these writers. The first is that Aguilar's Sephardic heritage left her with a maternal "oral tradition" to which Marion Hartog as an Ashkenazic Jew could not lay claim. This heritage was the basis for Aguilar's idealization of the maternal and the domestic. The second difference is directly grounded in the first: Aguilar learned to speak the language of domestic ideology so well that she never expressed her ambition in public, while both Hartog's public statements and her fictions suggested that women ought to transgress the limits of the domestic space. These differences had enormous consequences for the kind of fiction the writers produced as well as for how it was received. Even when the two writers were working in the same genre, the historical romance, the differences were marked. Hartog taps into an English female novelistic tradition that uses romance to imagine a more feminist world.[53] Aguilar ultimately takes a stance against romance because it leads to such dangerous feminist imagining.

Indeed, even within her own romances, Aguilar does all she can to diminish the genre's liberatory impulse. In Hartog's version of the historical romance (chap. 3), the father/daughter conflict is resolved when the daughter leaves the father for a reformist Jew, rather than, as in conversionist romances, for a Christian suitor. In Aguilar's Jewish historical romances—principally, *The Vale of Cedars; or, the Martyr* and the short story entitled "The Escape"—Aguilar's Jewish daughters do not come into conflict with their fathers, even when they fall in love with Christian suitors, because they sacrifice their desires at their fathers' first word for the sake of the community's safety and integrity. The absence of father/daughter struggle in Aguilar means that the daughters do not gain the same degree of independence from their fathers. And because they marry men of their fathers' choosing, they do not gain parity with their husbands as they do in Hartog's tales, either.

Like Hartog, Aguilar was aware of the conversionist romances targeting Jewish women. She also complained about the conversionist tendencies of Christian liberal fiction attempting to depict contemporary Jewish women. In her dedication to her third novel-length tale, "Adah, a Simple Story," written in manuscript in Brighton in April 1838 when she was twenty-two, Aguilar makes explicit her desire to write a tale that would compete with non-Jews' perceptions of Jewish women as seen in most tales of modern Jewish life following the publication of *Ivanhoe*.[54] Addressing her "dear Friend," apparently a Christian woman named Miss F., she introduces

> a Tale, whose Heroine is one of that race, by some Christians so despised and scorned.
>
> "I know but one Author," you once said, "whose portrait of a Jewess pleased me, and that was Sir Walter Scott. The modern tales in which that race is introduced, are written by Christians, who know nothing of, and are consequently prejudiced against them."
>
> From the hour that observation was made Adah has been present to my imagination. . . . My wish in the following very simple story, was to pourtray a Jewess, with thoughts, and feelings peculiar to her faith and sex, the which are not in general granted that race, in Tales of the present day.

Like the Mosses, Aguilar sees the historical romance of Scott as the most significant text about Jews to be produced in the dominant culture. But Aguilar believes that *Ivanhoe* invokes sympathy only on behalf of historical Jews. On the other hand, in this short manifesto for Anglo-Jewish women's writing, Aguilar argues just as the Mosses did that the tales set in the modern day that have followed *Ivanhoe,* tales that rewrote *Ivanhoe* so as to convert Rebecca in the end, misrepresent Jews: "If the Jewess be a Heroine of olden times—she is permitted to retain her religion—for the [ ] of history on her misfortunes, which form the interest of such narratives, but if she be introduced in modern and domestic life, and the virtues of a ~~Christian~~ religious person are lavished on her she invariably becomes a Christian as if the charges of the illiberal were just, and . . . virtues, and good principles could not exist with Judaism."[55] According to Aguilar, this misrepresentation of Jewish women as vulnerable to conversionist persuasion undermines these philo-Semites' efforts on behalf of toleration. She asks: "While such is the general tenour of tales, in which the Jewish nation is introduced, how can prejudice be removed? how can the Christians, who never have an opportunity of associating with Israel, obtain more liberal notions [?]." For Aguilar, liberalness is synonymous with toleration, and according to her, toleration ought not to require Jewish women's conversion. On these grounds, she doubts whether the type of "toleration" depicted in Christian romance—whether historical or present-day—is useful to Jewish emancipation efforts.

But what kind of romance will a Jew produce? What assumptions

162

will ground a Jewish romance that will produce "liberal notions" among Christians? She identifies these by calling attention to their absence: "Why will they [i.e., Christians] not sometimes permit them [i.e., Jews] to have the same feelings, virtues, sentiments, as other people: why should their very domestic affections and domestic lives, be exposed to the Christian world in distorted coulours [?]." If liberalness leads to toleration, it does not lead to toleration of Jewish difference, for Jews must be seen to have "the same feelings, virtues, sentiments" as other people. In other words, by writing in the genres of historical or contemporary romance, Jews need to assert that they can be, as she had written just above, "Christian religious" in the modern world. Her strikeout of the word "Christian" and its replacement with the word "religious" throws light on Aguilar's early conception of "goodness." Her description of the modern Jewish ethos as a crossed-out "Christian" ethos—a secularized Christian morality—lends some justification to the claims of those conversionists and traditionalist Jews alike who saw Aguilar as a "Jewish Protestant." The major assumption of Aguilar's Jewish romance would be that Jews and Christians were "the same."

But her commitment to arguing that Jewish spiritual principles are the same as those of Christians does not have to be understood in conversionist terms. Aguilar goes on to say that she has "not touched on the forms, and ceremonies, it is only the Spirit of Judaism I wished to vindicate; to prove, that even as [with] Christians it can . . . support us under every briar, by bidding us look up for thoughts and comfort where alone they can be found." By splitting Judaism into two parts, a spiritual and a formal part, Aguilar is able to isolate the spirit so as to argue humanistically that Jews and Christians share the same virtues. This splitting was to be her strategy in all her later theological and polemical works as well, although in those works she would attempt to reconcile ritualism with spirituality, stipulating that ritual not be just a "strict but lifeless adherence to mere ceremonial things and neglect of the spirit."[56] But as the attempt to reconcile form and spirit suggests, this splitting does not have to be understood in "Protestant" terms, for the formal part does not drop away; it is only reformed to be more intelligible to present-day Jews by the standards of "reason." This was the standard strategy of Jewish reformers, or supporters of Liberal Judaism, who by invoking such a split were able to transform Judaism from a total ideology to a domestic and religious ideology resembling that of their Christian neighbors. Several years after "Adah," a novel about the "spirit of Judaism," Aguilar published her important apologetic work *The Spirit of Judaism*, which is an argument for Jewish reform and a defense of the ethical teachings of Judaism against the philo-Semites' portrait of Jews' empty, materialistic, rigid formalism. She often and clearly responded to charges that she was near to conversion with a stout refusal, and many of her books are explicitly about Jewish characters refusing conversion. If she believes that Jews and Christians share the same principles, she nevertheless believes that Jews deserve their own reformed set of rituals and cultural life. And she sets out to suggest this duality of spirit and reformed ritual, both here and in her own romances.

Thus, just like Marion and Celia Moss in *The Romance of Jewish History,* Aguilar begins her career by attempting to refute *Ivanhoe* and the conversionists, and by attempting to argue for reform. Although she criticizes the historical romance form for distancing readers from the plight of actual Jews, she nevertheless begins her career, like the Mosses, by writing historical romances. *The Vale of Cedars* actually predates *Romance of Jewish History* in composition, although it was not published until after Aguilar's death. Written between 1831 and 1835, when Aguilar was between the ages of fifteen and nineteen, the novel is filled with secret passageways, combines historical figures such as Isabella and Ferdinand with fictional characters, and brings a Sephardic woman into a doomed romantic liaison with a Christian Englishman. It can only be classified as a Jewish historical romance.[57] But despite its similarity in motive, genre, and theme to the Mosses' tales, it reads quite differently. Unlike the typical Moss heroine, Aguilar's Jewish female heroine, Marie, does fall in love with a Protestant man, one Arthur Stanley, a Protestant Englishman who happens to be passing through Catholic Spain, and who is deeply in love with her. In this, Aguilar's text is much closer to M. G. Lewis's "tolerant" philo-Semitic text than to the Mosses' tales. By having the Englishman meet the Jewess in Spain, however, Aguilar places the Protestant in an endangered minority position and thus elicits sympathy for the Jews' own minority position from her Protestant audience. Having the Englishman fall in love with Marie reflects Aguilar's desire that Jews should be acceptable to Christians. Having Marie fall in love with an Englishman reflects Aguilar's desire that English Christians should know that Jews are patriots. Marie's and Arthur's love reveals that, in spite of superficial differences of form, each recognizes in the other a kindred spirit.

But Marie's falling in love with a Christian suitor does not make her identical to the heroines of conversionist romances. Unlike Miriam Schreiber of M. G. Lewis's conversionist text *The Jewish Maiden* or Rebecca of Thackeray's *Rebecca and Rowena,* Marie does not leave her father's house, convert, and marry her Christian suitor. Rather, she resists a temptation that would take her away from her community and, she feels, the will of God, and marries a Jewish suitor chosen by her father, telling Stanley she can never see him again. Jewish communal integrity carries greater weight for her than individual romantic fulfillment. By having Marie resist the pull of conversion, Aguilar undermines the "tolerant" premise that Jewish women are malleable and amenable to persuasion. They are, rather, well educated and steadfast. She assimilates the structure of the conversionist romance plot, only to alter its vision of Jewish women and its "illiberal" conclusion. Her transformation of the genre is an emblem for what Victorian Jews were trying to do in general: to adopt, as far as possible, the habits and customs of their Christian neighbors while maintaining a thriving subculture with a distinct collective identity.

When her husband is murdered by Torquemada's men, and Stanley is charged with the crime, Marie is forced to make some difficult choices. To save her beloved Englishman from death, she must reveal her own Jewishness, which will mean confinement, torture, forced conversion, and quite possibly her own death. The secret Jews have hitherto hidden themselves behind a "Vale of Cedars," a valley that "veils" them from public discovery while they perform their daily rituals. For Marie, coming out from behind the "Vale of Cedars," coming out as a Jew, could be dangerous not only to herself but to the entire community. Nevertheless, Marie is so loyal to the Englishman that she is willing to undergo the risk for the sake of his security. This willingness to martyr herself (and potentially her community) for the sake of the Englishman is Aguilar's clear response to those antiemancipationists like Thomas Carlyle who argued that Jews' loyalty to Zion would detract from their loyalty to England.

Because of Catholic tactics of coercion, on which Aguilar trades heavily to gain sympathy from her largely Protestant audience, Marie's revelation of her identity leads the inquisitor to demand her imprisonment as a relapsed Jew. But by appealing to Isabella just at the moment when the queen's daughter is hugging her, at the moment when she is most maternal, Marie is able to find common ground with her as a woman rather than difference as a Jew appealing to a Christian monarch.[58] Isabella allows Marie to escape the palace, escape forced conversion and torture, and return to her vale. But the strain of her revelation has taken its toll on her health, and having asked Stanley to care for the queen's daughter, she repairs back behind the Vale of Cedars. She dies in the secret space of her crypto-Jewish home, having practiced the sacred death rites within the enfolded arms of her community. The lesson seems to be that, in Spain, Jewishness can only be exhibited safely when concealed in the domestic sphere. For when Jewishness is revealed publicly, brutality ensues.

But if this domestication of Judaism is the lesson for Jews living under the brutal conditions of the Spanish Inquisition, surely there is a different lesson for Jews living under the tolerant conditions of English liberalism—or is there? To some extent Aguilar does point out a difference between brutality and persuasion, coercion and toleration, practiced by the two countries. When depicting Marie's retreat behind the "Vale of Cedars" in full view of her largely English Protestant audience, she relies on liberals' pity for Jewish suffering. She produces a similar paradox here as in "The Authoress": there, the domestic ideologist attempts to call for women to remain domestic in a public medium. Here, the paradox takes place not only in the realm of gender, but in the realm of ethnicity: in a mainstream literary medium, the reformer attempts to call for Jews to perform their peculiar cultural practices behind a veil of secrecy. To publicize one's intention to hide would have been foolhardy in a less liberal atmosphere than that of England.

And yet it is not so clear that Aguilar drew such a solid distinction between brutality and persuasion. Aguilar subtly equated living under liberalism with living under the Inquisition, for in both cases, a form of punishment resulted if Judaism were not restricted to the home.[59] True, in Spain, torture, expropriation of property, and even death inevitably followed the revelation of Jewishness; while in England, the punishments were only misunderstanding, bigotry, and social ostracism. Yet these punishments were painful enough to convince Aguilar that Jews should maintain a version of their "vale" once in England, as the discussion of her tale "The Perez Family" below will demonstrate. Ultimately, Aguilar depicts the choice between crypto-Judaism and assimilation as one of degree.

Perhaps this refusal to dissociate completely English toleration from Spanish coercion explains her reluctance to take English Christians to task. Unlike the Mosses, Ashkenazim whose family had been in England for generations and who felt comfortable in criticizing England, Aguilar's maternal oral tradition of the Inquisition suggested that it would be better to appease than to criticize. The Mosses explicitly longed for a return to Zion and criticized English anti-Semitism. Hartog's *Jewish Sabbath Journal* often printed references to Christians as "the stranger" and castigated "the nations" for imagining Jews as "stricken with darkness, and our mental vision obscured by the veil of blindness, because we cannot discern truth in their errors."[60] For the Mosses, Judaism was a national cause; for Aguilar, a domestic practice. She believes that Anglo-Jewish men can gain office not, as in the Mosses' tales, while forthrightly practicing their ritual and cultural life, but while emphasizing their spiritual similarity to the dominant culture and keeping their formal differences behind their vale, just as women must hide their ambitions behind the veil in their secret heart.[61] For her, women and Jews must agree to similar bargains if they hope to be accepted: just as women must hide their criticisms of patriarchy, so Jews must hide their criticisms of the dominant culture.[62]

Although Aguilar's heroine refuses to convert to consummate her love for the Englishman, she willingly undergoes martyrdom on his behalf. While in this and other instances Aguilar soothes her Christian audience with expressions of patriotism, she also soothes her Jewish male audience with expressions of support for domestic ideology. Just as her heroine does not gain the same degree of independence from her father as in the Mosses' tales, neither does she gain the same degree of parity with her husband as the Mosses' heroines. Recall the women in *Romance of Jewish History* who cross-dress as male minstrels to deliver important messages and then are rewarded for their courage by marriage to a Jewish reformist suitor. Hartog's "unveiled" heroines never think of Christian men. Recall the sufferings of their suitor, who might be enslaved or have his arm cut off or be a hunchback before he can win the heroine's hand. In the Mosses' tales, the heroine gains power through her independence of her father, and the suitor loses power through his suffering, so that a kind of parity is reached. In Aguilar's romances, however, the husband and wife do not share parity—they occupy separate, hierarchically arranged, spheres. Marie's husband Julien occupies the public sphere as the king's adviser, while Marie tends the home. What would happen if the woman were to transgress the boundaries of her sphere in an Aguilar tale? What if, as in a Moss tale, she were to claim a masculine identity to carry out some important mission?

167

As it happens, Aguilar directly answered this question in her short story "The Escape," which first appeared in *Records of Israel* in 1844 (one year following the Mosses' second collection of historical romances, perhaps written in direct response).[63] This "Tale of 1755" is again set during the Inquisition, but this time in Portugal in the year in which a massive earthquake shook the city. Aguilar subtly acknowledges the crypto-Jewish matrilineal storytelling tradition by giving her heroine, Almah, her mother Sarah's maiden name Diaz. The tale opens with a wedding ceremony. In this case, the wedding ceremony in a church at Montes gives way to another, secret ceremony between Almah Diaz and Alvar Rodriguez, the beneficent, seemingly Catholic, merchant. Almah's entrance to the crypto-Jewish ceremony is marked by her putting on a "veil," which was "thrown around her, so as to completely envelope her face and form" (164) and proceeding behind a secret door hidden behind a tapestry where the bridal canopy awaits her. The ceremony is described in defamiliarizing language, assuming a Christian audience.[64] Appealing to the "God of the nameless and the homeless" (164), Alvar breaks the glass, and the couple is married.

Having explained to the assumed Christian reader that Almah and Alvar are Jews, and that they are "binding themselves to preserve and propagate a persecuted faith" (167), Aguilar proceeds to illustrate the dangers for them of being revealed as Jews. These include being betrayed by one of the entrusted circle of friends, having their property confiscated, being imprisoned, tortured, forced to convert, forced to inform, and burned at the stake. One Señor Leyva is particularly distrusted by Alvar's "Moorish secretary, in other words, an Israelite of Barbary extraction," Hassan Ben Ahmed. After several years have passed, and the couple has a son, the black Jewish secretary is proved right: Leyva turns out to be an Inquisition informer, and Alvar is accused of relapsed Judaism. He is taken to a secret prison, whose labyrinthine corridors are hidden beneath a church. His entire circle, indeed, the entire crypto-Jewish community, is in danger. It is in this extremity that Almah begins to take on roles to which readers of *Romance of Jewish History* might be more accustomed than Aguilar aficionados.

Almah's first act is to renounce, possibly permanently, her maternal role, parting from her child, and sending him with Hassan to England, "where the veil of secrecy could be removed" (172). Almah's renunciation of the maternal is almost unheard of in Aguilar's universe, whose other heroines (such as Rachel Perez in "The Perez Family"—see fig., later in this chapter) would rather die than separate from their children. Then, unbeknownst to the reader, Almah cuts her hair short, dresses up to look like Hassan (the reader is led to think she is Hassan mysteriously returned from England), and bribes her way into the Inquisition secretary's office to offer herself (as Hassan the Moor) as an informer against Alvar Rodriguez.[65] The masked Hassan wins the secretary's trust, and becomes a clerk of the Holy Office. This Hassan is filled with "activity and zeal," and gains goodwill quickly, enough to be admitted to the trial of Alvar, watch him be tortured and hear his refusal to reveal his Judaism. Not long afterward, Almah/Hassan, who has become extremely active, making friends with a well-placed gardener, securing resources, and planning, helps Alvar escape out the window of his cell with a ladder, and attempts to take him to a secret subterranean passage leading to freedom.

To this point, "The Escape" seems similar to a Moss tale. Filled with an important communal and personal purpose, the heroine transgresses the domestic sphere, cross-dresses, and takes on the active role of a man. Almah's husband suffers persecution like a Moss suitor. Perhaps, a Moss reader might suppose, this couple will also achieve parity. But the further course of the tale establishes the differences between Aguilar and the Mosses quite clearly. Whereas Moss heroines are usually rewarded for their courageous exploits with recognition and some power, Aguilar's heroine meets a far different fate.[66] For while Aguilar is intrigued by the extremity of Almah's behavior, ultimately she does not support it. In the section of *Women of Israel* concerned with biblical laws relating to women, Aguilar has this to say of cross-dressing: "The express prohibition relating to woman's adopting, on any pretence whatever, the garments of the male, is another beautiful ordinance marking her natural sphere, and proving that any departure from it was not acceptable to the Lord. It was not only the act itself which is so forcibly brought forward . . . , but the thoughts and feelings included in such an act, the temptation to depart from the retirement, the modesty, the purity of that home station which woman should so quietly fulfil" (1:198). By making the spheres more fluid than nature and God have ordained, Almah has violated a basic law of domestic ideology, which Aguilar identifies with the Torah itself. In this view, even the pretence that Almah is attempting to release her husband from bondage, attempting to restore the patriarch to his rightful sphere, does not justify her transgression. In fact, if Alvar was already feminized by being imprisoned, divested of property, and tortured, he is only further feminized by being the passive recipient of his wife's action, especially if she acts while dressed as a man. The transgression of spheres feeds on itself.

The result: rather than being rewarded, Almah must pay. Alvar and Almah are caught before they can reach the secret passage to freedom. Shame and remorse for her adventure immediately overwhelm her, prompting her to cry, "O God, my husband—I have murdered him!" and to sink lifeless to the earth. She recovers consciousness long enough to talk back to the Inquisitors, who provide her with "proper feminine attire," and to be sentenced to death. She spends her last day in self-recrimination: "One image was ever present, seeming to mock her very misery to madness. Her effort had failed; had she not so wildly sought her husband's escape—had she but waited—they might have released him; and now, what was she but his murderess?" (178) No thoughts on her own impending doom are recorded—all her selfless thoughts are focused on her husband. On All Saint's Day, the day chosen for the auto-da-fé, she and Alvar exchange words, and she begs him for forgiveness. He gains strength from her submissiveness, and with "impassioned tones of natural eloquence" (179) castigates his executioners in prophetic ire and proudly claims his and Almah's Jewishness.

From the moment Alvar gains his voice to the end of the story, Almah never utters another word, except to echo, in "the sweet tones from woman's lips," his utterance of the Shema, the prayer conventionally uttered by Jews going to their deaths. When, just before their execution, a providential earthquake begins to shake Lisbon, and in the confusion Alvar escapes and carries Almah away, the narrator reports nothing of her feelings. By the time he has reached the outskirts of the city, she has become "his precious burden" (181); he is guided by "a merciful Providence," and the experience of the apocalypse is only his. When the sea begins to heave and flood the city, she wakes and gazes with him, but does not speak. And when the city bursts into flames, it is Alvar who "traces the full extent of destruction" (184) and who feels the "conviction that the God of his fathers was present with him, and would save him and Almah" (184). Alvar has only suffered, not transgressed—his reward is to be restored to manhood, his limbs never tiring as he carries his "burden" over mile after mile of rubble. Almah, on the other hand, has transgressed as well as suffered. Her punishment is biblical: she must lose the very capacities that in her immodesty she had claimed for herself; she must suffer the complete loss of consciousness, speech, and agency. That is, she reverts to being a proper woman. In the same way, one might say that Lisbon's punishment is also biblical: like Sodom and Gomorrah, it is destroyed for having created institutions that have forced Jewish women and men to transgress their "natural" roles.

When Almah and Alvar finally reach England, land of liberty, their property and family are reunited, Almah is restored to motherhood, and the "veil of secrecy" is removed. England's liberal government is like God, "merciful," and "grant[ing] to the exile and wanderer a home" (185). In this sacred land, the pair are now known as "Alvar and his Almah." With his possession of her, the spheres have been fully restored. The tale ends with the narrator noting that the couple celebrates this return to "biblical" ways with a yearly gift of clothing to "a limited number of male and female poor" (185). Critics have puzzled over the oddness of this ending, but given the tale's focus on clothing it seems perfectly appropriate. If one imagines that before Almah and Alvar distribute the garments, they separate them clearly by gender, their ritual comes to seem like an annual act of *teshuvah*—repentance—for Almah's cross-dressing transgression. The lesson of the spheres is to remain with them year by year to the end of their days.

For Almah, as for Aguilar, the commitment to secure the future of the Jewish family and carry on the matrilineal crypto-Jewish tradition comes into conflict with the commitment not to mix spheres. But although this conflict permeated Aguilar's work, its explicitness did not mar her work's reception. Just the opposite. Marion Hartog's career was ruined and her name forgotten precisely because she attempted to resist the demand that she be self-effacing in her public statements and that her heroines retire to their station. Grace Aguilar did not resist but spoke the contradictions of her culture, and for that reason she has been remembered.

THE RICH, THE MIDDLE CLASS, AND THE "CHEAP"

Had Aguilar remained within the confines of the romance, perhaps she would still have met with obscurity.[67] But Aguilar's prolific imagination, combined with her discomfort with the historical romance form, took her into a variety of genres. Branching out into sermons, philosophy, apologetics, midrashim, and histories, she discovered new genres, collaborated with many different kinds of women, and revealed the fault lines in the social and political structures of the Jewish community. She left behind a literary and historical legacy of immense worth. One particularly revealing avenue she explored after her departure from historical romance was domestic fiction. The move to domestic fiction revealed the pressure of writing for a Christian and a Jewish audience simultaneously; and by bringing her into contact with the Jewish upper class, it made more complex her representation of the class differences within the Jewish community.

By the middle 1840s when Aguilar wrote *Records of Israel,* she was already moving away from historical romance as a genre, because unlike the Mosses she began to think it antagonistic to reform. She was moving toward domestic "home scenes" and moral "heart studies." It was not that she was against historical fiction, but that she distinguished between historical romance and "religious" or moral history. In her preface to *Records,* she writes:

> The following tales have no pretensions whatever to what is termed historical romance. They are simply, what their name implies, "Records" of a people, of whose history so little is generally known, that the word *Jew* is associated only with biblical and ancient recollections, or as connected with characteristics, feelings, and spiritual incitements, wholly distinct from those which relate to man in general. . . . The author is aware . . . that, from the important incident on which the first tale is founded, a far superior *romance* might have been woven, but she preferred the simple illustration of religious feeling, to all the richer and more delusive glow of romantic incident and plot. She has only so used fiction, as to bring historical truth more clearly forward. . . . [T]he incidents, even as the actors, are fictitious, yet their original may be found many times repeated in the history of the Jews during their secret existence in Portugal and Spain.[68]

Although she insists that these are not romances, in fact, "The Escape" and the other "simple" historical tales in this collection are full of romantic adventures, even if they acknowledge the value of domesticity in the end. Aguilar's very struggle against the historical romances of Scott and the Mosses reveals the genre's cultural power. She recognized that it was the form with which Jewish women had to contend most powerfully in the dominant culture, because it was the form in which Jewish women most powerfully appeared. Still, she hoped to move away from it in order to write tales of modern domestic life that would more accurately reflect her own experience.

But the desire to write domestic fiction posed a difficult problem of audience for Aguilar. Since in her calls for reform, she was interpreting Judaism as a religion of the home, writing "home scenes" made it increasingly difficult for Aguilar to maintain the "veil" of secrecy about Jewish life. Writing domestic tales meant going, as it were, into the heart of Judaism itself, as Aguilar understood it—into the home's particular and secret rituals. How could she reveal these practices to Christians if her aim was to distance Christians from Jewish differences? How could she refrain from revealing these secret practices if her aim was to portray Jewish domesticity? The disadvantage of historical romances was that they distanced the Christian reader from the lives of actual Jews in Aguilar's own time. The disadvantage of domestic fictions was that they brought the Christian reader too close. The crypto-Jewish impulse to hide competed with the emancipationist impulse to reveal.

In response to this dilemma, Aguilar began to conceptualize her work as addressing two audiences. The splitting of audience occurs in two stages. The first stage is apparent in *Records of Israel,* where writing for a Christian and a Jewish audience strains both the genre and the voice of the speaker. On the one hand, she says in the preface to *Records* that her concern to reveal an accurate history and religion is to relieve Christians of misconceptions. These tales "are offered to the public generally, in the hope that some vulgar errors concerning Jewish feelings, faith, and character may, in some measure, be corrected." She speaks to the general public as a confident demystifier and emancipationist. When addressing Jews in the same preface, however, she speaks in a different voice. To her "Jewish public," she offers these tales, which she admits are "far less valuable in matter" than her earlier *Spirit of Judaism,* but which she hopes will "still humbly serve the cause . . . by raising from the dust of time and silence such records of our ancestors as cannot be wholly valueless to Israel."[69] This double address reveals a double consciousness and a double project. As an emancipationist, she speaks with authority and erudition, as a teacher to an admittedly ignorant but willing Christian audience. As a Jewish woman speaking to Jews, however, she speaks in a much humbler tone; rather than a teacher, she is a servant to the cause and she deprecates her own efforts as not "wholly valueless."[70] Because she is addressing two audiences, she must be two different personae as the

173

circumstances require, sometimes at the same moment. The strain of this double address is apparent throughout the tales. When, in "The Escape," she steps back from the *chupah* to explain that this man and woman are Jews undergoing a wedding ceremony, her Jewish audience is immediately distanced from the narrative, but her Christian audience might be distanced from it if she did *not* give the explanation. By giving the explanation, she prioritizes the attempt to gain toleration by Christians over the need to reflect Jewish experience back to Jews.

The difficulty of maintaining this double position resulted in an increasing tendency to separate her domestic stories into two groups: a group of "general" domestic tales that did not specifically address Jews or contain Jewish characters (e.g., *Home Influence, Woman's Friendship, Mother's Recompense*) and a group of "Jewish" writings that addressed a Jewish-only audience and centered on Jewish characters (primarily "The Perez Family," but also "The Fugitive"). In the preface to *Home Influence,* she felt constrained to assure "Christian mothers" that "as a simple domestic story, the characters in which are all Christians, believing in and practicing that religion, all *doctrinal* points have been most carefully avoided, the author seeking only to illustrate the spirit of true piety, and the virtues always designated as the Christian virtues thence proceeding."[71] She assumes, as Camilla Toulmine was to assume in her tribute to Aguilar, that a Jewish woman can write of "Christian virtues." She assumes that there is nothing intrinsic to her experience that has formed her to be a "Jewish writer." Since the spirit is the same for Jews and Christians, one is a Jewish writer only when discussing the particular customs and forms of Jews or Judaism.[72] "Doctrinal" differences do not enter into the everyday habits of domestic life, because in that world everyone, Jew or Christian, practices "Christian virtues," which might just as easily be called "Jewish virtues."

Still, if this were wholly true, there would be no need to write specifically Jewish domestic stories at all. Or, if one did write stories centered in the Jewish home, these could be read equally by Christian children as by Jewish children because the "Christian virtues" would still be recognizable and "doctrinal" differences would never have to come into play. That this was not totally the case was clear from Aguilar's increasing tendency to write Jewish domestic tales for Jews-only audiences. Aguilar does maintain some sense of a Jewish particularity. Her novella "The Perez Family" was the first story ever by a

Victorian Jew to focus on a contemporary Jewish family's domestic life. Given Aguilar's desire not to reveal Jewish domesticity to Christians—motivated by residual crypto-Jewish fear of the Inquisition as well as by a desire to maintain communal separateness and integrity—how did such a tale come to be written? How could Aguilar be sure her readership consisted only of Jews?

To realize a desire to write for Jews only would not have been possible had there not already existed publications for a Jews-only readership. For that reason, the story of the publication of "The Perez Family" can tell us a great deal about the Jewish readership, about the institutions and people who served it, and about Aguilar's relationship to the Jewish reading public. Aguilar produced this landmark tale for Charlotte Montefiore's *Cheap Jewish Library,* a series of didactic tales written for working-class Jewish families and sold anonymously by Montefiore for pennies. Charlotte Montefiore was a member of the Cousinhood, that circle of aristocratic Jewish families who held sway over the community's governance, and who were in contact with MPs on issues of emancipation. Unlike middle-class Sephardim, Sephardic aristocrats like Montefiore or her more famous aunt and uncle Judith and Moses Montefiore, did not generally engage in fiction writing. Having vast resources of money and influence at their disposal, they interpreted the oral tradition of Spain and Portugal to mean that they must secure social justice for persecuted Jews around the world rather than tell tales. Judith and Moses Montefiore were by far the most lionized members of the Anglo-Jewish community for their missions to Palestine, Syria, Rumania, and elsewhere on behalf of persecuted Jews.

Charlotte was similarly interested in helping Jews in need, but she focused on helping the increasing number of Jewish poor in England itself. Helping Christian and Jewish poor was an activity for which upper-class Jewish women were noted, and Montefiore was among the leading wealthy Jewish women active in this cause.[73] Indeed, Montefiore's efforts to organize the numerous Jewish charities predated the development of an official umbrella organization, the Jewish Board of Guardians (established 1859), by some fifteen years. In 1845, she published *Caleb Asher* (1845), a satire on the conversionists' bad faith attempt to target the poor. The satire is historically interesting and passionate in its defense of poor Jews, but reveals a lack of interest on her part in the details of aesthetics. In fact, her subsequent work reveals her belief that, to be valuable, fiction must subordinate any aesthetic ends to the end of usefulness—in this case, the end of training poor Jews in resisting conversion efforts. Usefulness is the standard by which all written work must be measured. Her justification of the *Cheap Jewish Library* reveals such a standard at work. The *Library* consisted of "moral and religious tales or . . . useful information." She wrote that "Amongst the many means that have been employed to inculcate religious truths and principles of morality, none have proved more efficient than the publication of tracts in the form of tales conveying instruction and entertainment."[74] Like Aguilar in *Women of Israel,* she hopes to use tales to a didactic purpose. Unlike Aguilar, who wrote mainly for her peers, middle-class women, Montefiore directs these tales to the working class and is concerned with the tales' "efficiency." When Aguilar came to work for her, she would have to confront their class difference and Montefiore's emphasis on the social uses of fiction.

Indeed, had Aguilar developed her interest in writing Jewish domestic fiction several years later, she might not have found a willing supporter in Montefiore. Montefiore's emphasis on efficiency only increased with her later work, and she found that tales were not the most efficient pedagogical sources after all. Her polemical work, *A Few Words to the Jews. By One of Themselves* (1851; second edition, 1855),[75] was published anonymously, and grew out of her awareness of "such points of religion as can hardly be treated in tales. I purpose writing little essays or discourses."[76] *A Few Words* is in fact a remarkable series of essays ("unparalleled in Anglo-Jewish literature,"[77] according to a contemporary reviewer) advocating religious reform, castigating Jewish materialism, derogating the split in the community between rich and poor, depicting the laborer's Sabbath, the passover, the feast of weeks, defining the character and tasks of the ideal Jewish woman, and providing an allegorical homily on acquiring virtues. As Montefiore explained to Rabbi Abraham de Sola, the man who acted as her agent so that she could publish the *Cheap Jewish Library* anonymously, in these essays utility is her great aim: "All the information I may have, all the energy and perseverance that has been bestowed upon me, I have long wished to consecrate to the religious good of our poor brethren. . . . I am prepared to find it a losing concern, in one sense of the word; but if it should be of real utility to but even a very few, I shall be amply repaid." As an aristocratic Jewish lady she is concerned to use her wealth and power for spiritual and charitable ends, and in fact the library did lose money. She goes on to encourage de Sola to found a Jewish literary periodical, saying that she "should be really delighted if in some little way I could promote the success of an undertaking likely to be productive of so extended an utility."[78]

Because they are more extreme expressions of tendencies latent in her earlier work, the essays in *A Few Words* offer insight into the differences that existed between these two Anglo-Sephardic women reformers. The primary difference is how they view fiction. Aguilar celebrates her crypto-Jewish heritage as a source for fiction; Montefiore denigrates that heritage as a shameful source of fiction. Fiction, according to Montefiore, was the life led by crypto-Jews during persecution:

> our best, or indeed our only chance of safety was to wear a mask. . . . We wore, so as not to attract attention, poor and faded garments in public, lived in mean-looking houses, and only when in the privacy of home could we assume the appearance and indulge in the luxury befitting our station. We adopted the ignoble callings that were thrown open to us, whilst we carried on beneath some disguise the vocation more suited to our tastes and talents. . . . We led, therefore, almost simultaneously, two lives, one false, one real; but they necessarily mingled, the impure sullying the pure, the fictitious degrading the true. (53)

Montefiore argues that fictionalizing was a crypto-Jewish necessity, but it certainly was not laudable. Compare this view of crypto-Jewish fictionality to Aguilar's, in such tales as "The Escape" with its hidden marriage ceremony or *The Vale of Cedars* with its hidden home, which depend on the donning of various masks for their novelistic effects. Like Montefiore, Aguilar analogizes fiction writing to crypto-Judaism. Unlike Montefiore, Aguilar sees the mask making of crypto-Jewish experience as a fictionalizing inheritance to be celebrated for its proof of Jews' loyalty and resourcefulness in the face of persecution. For Aguilar, the crypto-Jews' self-fictionalization is related to the masking in which English Jews engage when they restrict their observances to home and synagogue while assimilating English Christian fashions, modes of speech, and occupations. Fictionalizing in this sense is the key to emancipation and is to be celebrated in the form of written fiction. But again, when Montefiore is criticizing the rich for showiness, she argues that "we were not intended to be actors but real and earnest beings" (60), and urges the rich to "rouse ourselves from this artificial state, to wake up from these illusions, shake off these fictions" (57). The ideal Jewish woman likewise must not be "a pleasing

177

ornament, approved of and smiled at by the world"—meaning the non-Jewish world—but should be full of useful "energy, strength of purpose, and active zeal" (162) on behalf of poor Jews in need. For Montefiore fiction is false and allied with materialism and romance—that is, the pursuit of immoral and useless ends. Her didacticism and negative view of fiction would eventually force her out of tale writing altogether.

In fact she replaces fiction with a discourse of truth, for she hopes to be "a true disciple of Judaism" (18) who understands "the true God" (19) and who enlightens the community about its own materialism. She argues that Judaism has become a false religion, for "materialism, the great antagonist of Judaism, is still the crowned chief of our community, and we must dethrone the usurper" (29). Those who practice a "skin-deep sanctity" (29), a sanctity made of showy masks, have made Judaism "a creed composed of rites and ceremonies rather than a spiritual religion, an outward rather than an inner law" (27).[79] Like Aguilar she wants to reform the community by spiritualizing it. Like Aguilar, she asserts that Talmud is a production of fallible humans, that sermons should quote directly from the Bible and not quote "Rabbis without end" (154). But unlike Aguilar she believes that the rites and ceremonies have become fictions, false shows of true spirituality. "All ceremonies, all forms and rites, are to be looked upon only as means, not ends, of no value in themselves, save as they are moral helps, and as they awaken in us a stronger virtue, a deeper religious feeling" (31). This deeper religious feeling, reached through the instrumentally viewed rites, seemed to her to have been forgotten among all the new decorous reforms instituted in Victorian synagogues. Fiction must never become an end in itself, for its masks destroy the possibility of "sincere and conscientious" (17–18) spirituality.

Notice that Charlotte Montefiore reaches the same conclusion as Aguilar—that Judaism needs reforming. But whereas for Aguilar telling tales represents the means by which Jews can reform themselves, for Montefiore fiction is what needs reforming. In the early part of her career, she embraces some forms of fiction, as her *Caleb Asher* and *Cheap Jewish Library* bear out. But she insists that to be acceptable fiction has to be didactic, polemical—useful. This explains why she writes homiletic tales rather than treading in what the Moss sisters call "the flowery paths of romance,"[80] why she produces serious fables, sermons, satires, and exposés rather than crypto-Jewish escape fantasies.

As Aguilar began to define herself in opposition to historical romance, she was drawn to those aspects of Montefiore's didactic project
that emphasized women's work on behalf of others, and that attempted to doff crypto-Jewish masks to reveal the "truth" of Judaism
in domestic tales. Perhaps Montefiore's explicit aim of directing her
Library toward only Jews also appealed to Aguilar as a venue in which
she could depict the Jewish domestic scene without fear of her work
being seen or reviewed by Christians. Each tale in the library, of which
between 250 and 500 copies were printed, was distributed by hand
rather than through booksellers, so Aguilar could be assured of her
readership. True, Aguilar was more accustomed to appeal to Christians
than Jews. She wrote in response to de Sola's solicitation of a story for
the *Library* that "in a Christian country we should . . . enlarge on the
tenets of our faith, not perhaps so much for own people as to do away
with some of the mistaken notions regarding it adopted by other
creeds."[81] Yet, given the strain she had felt in writing domestic fiction
for Jews and Christians at once, perhaps she saw an opportunity at last
to lift the veil on Jewish domestic life.

A more serious obstacle to her publication in the *Library* was the
class make-up of the audience, for the *Library* was directed toward
working-class and poor Jews, what Montefiore called "the humble
classes of Israelites," and Aguilar was accustomed to writing for the
middle class.[82] Indeed, accepting the task of producing such a tale
would mean in some sense inhabiting the position of a wealthy
woman, for it was wealthy women who were primarily involved in
educating the poor. To be asked to write a tale for the *Library* was to be
extended an invitation to impersonate the upper class. The class difference between Aguilar and Montefiore came to the fore when, in a
response to Aguilar's letter expressing her hope to see her writings
"more known than they are now," Montefiore "sincerely congratu-
late[d] her upon having the means of raising . . . , by her talent, the
opinion that is entertained of Jewish intellectual abilities. It is quite a
satisfaction to think a Jew may become celebrated for something else
than their wealth and their talent on the stock exchange. For this
alone, it would be worth Miss Aguilar's while to devote her energy,
time, and talents to the cultivation of her intellectual powers."[83]
Montefiore recognized in Aguilar a fellow spirit, a woman cultivating
her intellectual powers to produce essays for the public good, a critic
of materialism, and an advocate of strength, morality, and energy
among women. Yet, her reference to "raising . . . by her talent," and

179

her allusion to the fact that Aguilar was not wealthy were rather frank acknowledgments of a distance between them. For Montefiore, this distance could be overcome if the two of them, as representatives of the upper and middle classes, joined together to help Jews lower down on the economic and intellectual scales. But Montefiore's invitation to this middle-class woman for a joint venture on behalf of the poor should not be understood as representative of the treatment Aguilar received from wealthy women. Many female members of the Jewish aristocracy did not praise perceived efforts of the middle class to raise themselves. Indeed, when Aguilar received her massive tribute from Anglo-Jewish women just before her death, there were no wealthy women in attendance: her major appeal was to the middle class.[84]

Produced in this context, "The Perez Family" was unlike any other fiction Aguilar had yet written. Not only was it the first Victorian Jewish domestic tale, but the circumstances of its publication—for a working-class Jews-only audience in a wealthy woman's publication— were completely unfamiliar to her. Her desire to depict Jewish "home scenes" must have been great to convince her to cross class lines and turn inward to the Jewish community where the wide audience she so hoped to secure would be unavailable. When she turned her mind to this audience, her innovation was to leave behind the historical romance and speak directly to her audience in what she conceived of as its own language, its own environment, its own concerns. She was not interested, however, in merely telling mimetic tales reflecting back reality to her readers; rather, she was attracted by the *Library*'s pedagogical imperative. She must not paint her readers' lives exactly, but must paint their lives in ideal form. Her characters must be drawn from actual types, but must serve as exemplary models of working-class Jewish faith.

To realize this aim, she tells the story of a working-class Jewish family in Liverpool whose materfamilias must undergo the trials of Job and withstand them. In this case, Job is a petit bourgeois woman named Rachel Perez, whose faith in God is tested when her house burns down, she loses the use of an arm in rescuing her daughter from the flames, her beloved husband dies and leaves them penniless, her profligate eldest son marries a Christian woman, and her devoted niece is forced to leave her to care for her dying father. Like Job, Rachel attempts to remain upright and pure in the face of adversity. She does this in a particularly Aguilarean way: as a mother-instructor, she gathers her family around her every Sabbath eve to give them a

Line drawing of Rachel Perez carrying Ruth from the flaming house, frontispiece to Grace Aguilar's *Home Scenes and Heart Studies* (London: George Routledge and Sons, Ltd., 1894). Photo: Michael Dunn.

discourse on a particular verse in the Torah, the most relevant one being, "Commit thy ways to the Lord, and also trust in him, and he will bring it to pass." Proving the truth of this verse, that mitzvot and faith will bring rewards, is the burden of the story, and indeed, Rachel's mitzvot and faith are ultimately rewarded. Her daughter, blinded by the fire, regains her sight, her wayward eldest son returns to the fold and marries her returned loving niece, her youngest son chooses to become a hazan, and she herself is filled with joy.

Besides the example of Rachel's steadfastness in adversity, each subplot in the story becomes an exemplary tale. Reuben's struggle, as the eldest son, to balance his desire to consort with "the stranger" and his love for family and religion is the type of all such struggles for emancipating Jews. Simeon, Reuben's brother, must struggle with his own "prejudice" against Christians. Sarah, Rachel's niece, struggles with the command to "honor thy father," for she must decide whether to continue serving her loving aunt or return to tend to her dying father, who has squandered all his resources, neglected her and her mother (until her mother's death), and quite possibly committed a crime. Leah, Rachel's eldest daughter, has to decide whether to go with friends to a circus, or sacrifice her immediate interests for the long-term goal of earning money for the family. Each character must sacrifice something for the sake of maintaining the family's viability and integrity. And each character ultimately chooses to do right.

All of these exemplary struggles take place in the Perez home, which, although it undergoes many changes, is always kept tidy. Whereas, according to Aguilar, other poor and working-class Jews allow their homes to become dirty or dingy, the Perez family who are working toward a better (i.e., middle-class) existence keep their surroundings neat, no matter how much their circumstances are diminished. When their middle-class home burns down, and they must move to a smaller, dirtier house in a "low neighborhood" (11),[85] they immediately set about transforming it into what they think of as a bourgeois home. But this product of domestic ideology is not precisely the same as a bourgeois Christian home. The Perez family's first act is to close off the front entrance so that none of their prying neighbors will be able to look in and gossip about them. They decorate the interior neatly and keep it clean. Then they plant a garden in the backyard, for although "both local and national disadvantages often unite to debar the Jews from agriculture" (11), they want to reaffirm their connection to their plot of land, as was customary in middle-class Christian homes. Aguilar uses what will later become a Zionist trope—Jews returning to the land—to justify the Perez family's rooting itself in its English Christian-like home. Again, this family appears to be the same as their Christian neighbors'—but the detailed practices that take place inside, hidden from view, are different. These descendants of crypto-Jews express their Judaism, not by Zionism, but by turning their home into a sealed-off vale of cedars, a middle-class paradise on the outside, a place of Jewish ritual and cultural life on the inside. Recreating "HOME," that crypto-Jewish space of maternal domestic power, means for Aguilar training the poor to aim to become bourgeois and to hide their Jewishness from prying eyes. This is her pedagogical imperative.[86]

In this enclosed domestic space, for this enclosed Jewish audience, Aguilar does what in her other tales of Jews she avoids: she describes their ritual practices in detail, particularly their practice of celebrating the Sabbath. All the children (except Reuben) return from their various occupations to spend Friday through Sunday with Rachel. They dress all in white. They decorate their home with flowers. They sacrifice a great deal of labor to repurchase a pair of candlesticks, a family heirloom they were forced to sell after the fire, and they forgo meals during the week to purchase oil or wax candles for Friday night. They learn Torah together, and do not speak of frivolous things on the Sabbath day, unlike their neighbors. It makes sense that Aguilar would focus on this ideal working-class-cum-middle-class family's Friday night observance since the Sabbath is the ritual most particularly associated with the home and with maternal activity. The halachic mother, after all, is positively commanded to light the candles, one of the few positive commandments halacha bestows on women. True, the entire ritual does not take place in the home: Rachel's sons do attend synagogue on Friday night, but while Aguilar records this fact, she never shows them praying there. By focusing on the home rather than the synagogue as the place of ritual activity, Aguilar attempts to transfer the center of religiosity and instruction from public to secret space.

There are several reasons for this focus on the domestic as the center of Jewishness. First, since women could not participate equally in the synagogue, and Aguilar was particularly concerned with female education, women's roles, and home instruction, she focused on the home as a source of women's power. Her crypto-Jewish heritage particularly prepared her to emphasize the maternal space as the space of transmission of Judaism from one generation to another. Her support

183

for religious reform prepared her to emphasize the dignity of the individual's commitment to Jewish learning in the home rather than the shame of bowing down before the wisdom of rabbis at the synagogue. When, after the dishes have been cleared on Friday night, Rachel is giving her sermon on the chosen biblical text at the dinner table, the narrator assures the reader that she is no rabbi:

> the widow opened the large Bible, and after fervently blessing God for His mercy in permitting them all to see the close of another week in health and peace, read aloud a chapter and psalm. . . . Rachel was no great scholar. Let it not be imagined amongst those who read this little tale, that she was unusually gifted. She was indeed so far gifted that she had a *trusting spirit and a most humble and child-like mind,* and of worldly ways was entirely ignorant; and it was these feelings which kept her so persevering in the path of duty, and, leading her to the footstool of her God, gave her the strength of wisdom that she needed; and to every mother in Israel these powers are given. (29, italics Aguilar's)

Unlike Clara Stanley, who is gifted, Rachel Perez is an idealized vision of an ordinary mother. She has no direct access to Hebrew (although her youngest son Joseph's employer has offered to teach him), but is able nonetheless to do a sophisticated philological study of the text simply by being open to the varied meanings of the English in different contexts. Whether this Bible is a Jewish translation or not is impossible to determine, but in either case, she is able to read it directly, without any mediating rabbinical commentary to interpret it for her. Her religious power as an individual reader is supposed to give solace to those reformist working-class women who cannot read Hebrew and will not attend synagogues.

The other reason for transferring the focus of Jewish life from synagogue to home has to do with the Perez family's class status, and the class status of Aguilar's supposed audience. Since, in Aguilar's day, many of the synagogues required payment for the honor of participating in the service or for the best seating, many working-class families could not afford or did not want to attend. Indeed, some groups of working-class Jews eventually opened their own visiting societies for the sick and prayer meeting places, called "friendly societies of Jewish working men," to avoid having to contend with class antagonism in the Sephardic synagogue in Bevis Marks or the Ashkenazic Great Synagogue in Duke's Place.[87] Until these were in place, the home—

particularly on Friday night—was the center of their Jewish life. Thus, by focusing her attention on domestic ritual, Aguilar attempts to draw a picture to which a Sephardic woman-centered working-class family could relate and on which it could model itself.

It seems, then, that with its manifold exempla, its didactic tone, its modern setting and multiple incidents, and its focus on working-class women's domestic religious observance, that "The Perez Family" is well-suited to fulfill the self-imposed mandate to educate and entertain of Montefiore's *Cheap Jewish Library*. Without locating some testimonials from working-class Jewish readers, it is impossible to determine whether the story actually achieved the aims of educating and entertaining working-class Jews in faith and domesticity. Ironically, however, although Aguilar's addition to the *Library* was intended for these voiceless members of the community, the story brought her most notice from the middle classes. After its publication in the *Library*, Montefiore's agent Abraham de Sola handed on the story to Isaac Leeser of the *Occident* in Philadelphia. Leeser then published it, to much praise, and it made its way back to the *Jewish Chronicle* in England, where it was received with great acclaim. What began as an unusual excursion for a middle-class woman into the realm of an upper-class undertaking—the education of the poor—became Aguilar's ticket to fame among Jews of her own class. None of her other efforts, except *Women of Israel,* brought her such unalloyed praise from middle-class Jews. If Isaac Leeser solicited and published her *Spirit of Judaism,* he also criticized its outreach to the Christian community. The *Voice of Jacob* published her poems, but wondered about her orthodoxy. The *Chronicle* reviewer liked *Home Influence,* but was disturbed that his point of reference for this "Tale for Mothers and Daughters" was a non-Jew, Maria Edgeworth. Only when, with Charlotte Montefiore's encouragement, Aguilar took a chance and wrote a domestic tale focusing on particular Jewish rituals, did men of her own class fully accept her as a Jewish writer.

LEGACY

By balancing a critique of Christian toleration with an appeal to Jews to maintain a veiled double life, Aguilar redefined the goals of liberalism and of Judaism at the same moment. At the same time, by balancing a critique of patriarchal condescension with an appeal to women to remain subordinate and domestic, Aguilar redefined the roles of men and women. For doing so, she was hailed by Christians and Jewish women and men alike as a cultural ambassador of good will.

First and foremost, her work as a writer and as an educator was celebrated by other Jewish women, and influenced their establishment of a set of women's institutions and a literary community in support of the expansion of women's roles. She was successful in getting "women moving," as bell hooks phrases it, even if she did not aim to establish a "women's movement." Her emphasis on women's domesticity would certainly have been an obstacle for women desiring to set up formal institutions of women's education and advocacy. She needs to be understood as a transitional figure. Yet she did nonetheless influence the self-perception of nineteenth-century Jewish women readers, many of whom were also writers. She provided a history and a literature centrally focused on women's lives.[88]

Her influence on Jewish women can only be evaluated fully when set inside this milieu of readers and writers. For Aguilar was not sui generis. She was not the only early Victorian Jewish woman writer, or the only good or interesting one, as one might have imagined by reading earlier histories of Anglo-Jewish literature.[89] Other women—who were more orthodox or more religiously radical than Aguilar was, who were more feminist or more traditionalist, who were richer or poorer, who were Ashkenazic rather than Sephardic—other women also produced work that is invaluable for a complex understanding of the gendered experience of Jewish modernity, particularly in England. To recover Aguilar's legacy requires more than simply excavating her work alone: it requires reconstituting a dynamic Anglo-Jewish literary subculture just in the act of coming to life.

To accomplish this reconstitution, it is not enough to explore Aguilar's complex interaction with Jewish women. Her polemical writings, especially *Women of Israel* and the *Spirit of Judaism,* were instrumental in influencing the direction that prominent Jewish male writers took. While Isaac Leeser disputed Aguilar's Jewish authenticity in his critique of *The Spirit of Judaism,* he nevertheless took up her suggestion of the necessity of an English translation of the Hebrew Bible for women's use, and produced the first such translation in the history of the English-speaking world. This feat was soon repeated by *Jewish Chronicle* editor Abraham Benisch, also in response to Aguilar's polemic.

Still, while Aguilar influenced and was influenced by Jewish women and men, it is important to keep in view that Jews represented the minority of her readership. All told, her books sold hundreds of thousands of copies. The republication of her *Works* some twenty-five years after her death was greeted with enthusiastic reviews in mainstream periodicals such as the *Athenaeum*. Her *Women of Israel* was given as a Sunday School prize in churches in England up through the 1950s. A branch of the New York Public Library was named after her. How her writings influenced Christian perceptions of Jews is difficult to determine, but her continuous popularity suggests that her vision of a type of "toleration" that emphasized coexistence rather than conversionism struck some sympathetic ears.

Whether she was writing to other Jewish women, to Jewish men, or to a sympathetic Christian audience, one can infer that her work was perceived to provide a model of toleration and education that challenged prevailing notions of conversionism and sexism without completely undermining liberalism or patriarchy. Her trade-offs enabled her work to appeal to groups on every side. Conversionists could see her as a "Jewish Protestant," while Jews could laud her as a moderate reformer with strong traditional leanings. In the 1860s, when women's rights debates grew strong, Aguilar's work could appeal both to feminists and to antifeminists. Feminists could support her work as a Jewish woman's groundbreaking act of self-representation and advocacy, a stage on the way to liberation, while antifeminists could support it as a model of modesty and domesticity.[90] Perhaps because she was willing to bargain, Aguilar was able to maintain a place in the memories of both English Jews and Christians that other Jewish women writers were not able to sustain after their deaths.

Once Aguilar's work is viewed in context, those aspects of it that truly defy comparison become visible. To begin with, the sheer volume and diversity of her efforts on behalf of Jews and Jewish women have no rival. Her revisionist strategy of rewriting the gender politics of Talmudic midrashim like "The Sun and the Moon," had to wait a century and a half before Jewish feminists claimed it as one of their most basic tools. Her history of English Jews laid the groundwork for Piccioto, Roth, Lipman, and all the Anglo-Jewish historians who followed her. Her "Perez Family" pulled back the veil on Anglo-Jewish domesticity and set the scene for subsequent writers (such as Amy Levy in *Reuben Sachs*) to depict English Jews' intricate life within and without the tribal limits according to the conventions of realism. Her

Women of Israel, truly a landmark in the history of Jewish women's biography and midrash, did more to legitimize thinking about and celebrating Jewish women than any other single writing of the time. Her sermons and theological writings were the first stirrings of a Liberal Jewish women's theological tradition that would culminate in Lily Montagu's theology later in the century.

Moreover, because she covered the entire range of Jewish women's writing—from historical romance to domestic fiction, from translation to sermons, from philosophy to apologetics, from lyrics to epic poems—her work functions as an encyclopedia with which to identify Anglo-Jewish women writers' major issues and genres. It indicates the forms and fault lines to which scholars must attend in any reconstruction of the Victorian Jewish subculture. If Aguilar's work is bounded by its middle-class positioning, its crypto-Jewish heritage, and its reformism, this does not mean her work is "lacking equipment"; rather, these boundary conditions are what enable its peculiar and abiding power. Calling attention to the existence of a diverse women's literary community ought not to diminish Aguilar's specific contribution. On the contrary, her specific contribution is to expand the frame of reference, to populate the Victorian discursive field with "Women of Israel," by comparison with whose work hers can resonate all the more. Placing her texts in a comparative framework enables scholars more vividly to reconstruct the complex subculture of the period of Anglo-Jewish emancipation and reform from which her life and writings emerged and to which they spoke.

Yet for all of these achievements, her most significant still remains the effect she had on Jewish women's self-perception. As evidenced by the numerous tributes to Aguilar by Jewish women on her death, by the poems written in memory of her, and by the numerous letters to Jewish periodicals signed "A Woman of Israel," her work provided Anglo- and American Jewish women with a proud identity at a time when they were being severely criticized and pressured by Christians and by Jewish men. Moreover, unlike any of her contemporaries, her work continued to inspire investigations into the content and quality of Jewish women's lives. In 1869, Mrs. Isaac Cohen established a prize for the student at the Jews' Free School who could write the best essay on "an applied biblical subject." The topic chosen for 1872, the year following the republication of Aguilar's *Works,* was "the Women of Israel according to the Bible, broken down into four parts: the education of Hebrew Women; their relation to their parents, their husbands, and their children; their social position; and instances of remarkable Hebrew Women, with descriptions of their work and age."[91] Mrs. Isaac Cohen's essay topic reproduced Aguilar's concerns precisely. There could hardly be a better testimony to Grace Aguilar's legacy.

Epilogue:
Anna Maria Goldsmid
and the Limits of History

The Women of Israel in the foregoing pages lived and wrote in reference to particular pressures. They had to respond to conversionists depicting them as malleable and vulnerable, as too spiritual for the heartless rituals of their dead letter religion. They had to respond to Jewish men who accused them of being undereducated (while refusing to educate them) and of being seduced by the insincere persuasion of the romantic dominant culture. Finally, they found themselves responding to one another's representations of Jewish women, as, collectively, they tried to define Jewish women's privileges, duties and needs. Their definitions differed depending on a number of complexly related factors, including how long their family had resided in England, whether they were Ashkenazic or Sephardic, whether they were middle or upper class, and whether they were traditionalist or reformist. Yet, although these women did not for the most part act as a group, although they found themselves divided from one another along many lines, in retrospect it is apparent that they formed a loose community of writers in dialogue about the necessity for women's education. Moreover, while arguing for women's intellectual emancipation in the Jewish world, many of them were arguing for Jews' emancipation in the Victorian world. They did so, by and large, under the constraint that they must at all times represent their project in the language of Victorian Jewish domestic ideology, which restricted women's activity to the sphere of the home and to charitable work among the poor. Working within these constraints, they were still able to find many different ways of exploiting domestic ideology's demand that they be "mother-instructors": they discovered a way to speak in a public voice as if they were merely dispensing maternal wisdom within the confines of the home. And they discovered a genre, the romance, in which they could imagine a release for their heroines from the constraints they themselves experienced.

Their contributions to Jews', women's, and Victorian literary history are many. Virtually unknown today, early Anglo-Jewish women writers produced the English Jews' most significant attempts at self-definition during the period of emancipation and religious reform (1830–80). Moreover, they were the preeminent Jewish women writers in the world during the first two-thirds of the nineteenth century. They produced the first Jewish novel, the first Jewish women's periodical in modern history, the first history of Jews in England written by a Jew, and the first modern Jewish conduct manual and cookbook in English, among other achievements. Their writings were extraordinarily popular with both Jewish and general audiences, sometimes running to more than thirty editions (as many as Dickens). These audiences met with writers who consistently revealed the complexity of a number of dominant cultural Victorian trends, such as trends in liberalism, domestic ideology, women's education, the feminization of religion, and the development of the novel by women.[1] In literary terms, they were able to make the historical romance genre, a form generally used by conservatives like Scott, serve progressive ends. They produced very popular examples of domestic fiction. They overturned the standard representations of Jewish women as malleable and undereducated. And they discovered a way to rewrite Jewish male literary genres like midrash Aggadah from their perspective.

Although the term must be qualified, there were elements of this perspective that were feminist. These women were transitional foremothers who came to prominence by decking themselves submissively in the mother's mantle, but who nevertheless managed to create a woman-centered vision of Jewish history and Jewish practice. Their works would have served as a starting point for more of their forthrightly feminist descendants had they not been systematically suppressed and forgotten. Grace Aguilar, Celia and Marion Moss, and Judith and Charlotte Montefiore were only the most important of the many Anglo-Jewish women writers, who included Maria Polack, Emma Lyons, Constance and Anna Rothschild, "Little Miriam," R. H. A., and Abigail Lindon. These writers together laid the groundwork for the development of a more formally and consciously structured coalition of English and American Jewish women writers that developed later in the century. In England, Amy Levy, Julia Frankau, Mrs. Alfred Sidgwick, and Lily Montagu stepped into the cultural space opened by these early and mid-Victorian Jewish women writers, while in the United States it was, among others, Rebecca Gratz, Rebekah Kohut, Henrietta Szold, and Emma Lazarus who took the next step.[2]

Anglo-Jewish women did all this despite the many obstacles they faced from a philo-Semitic liberal culture and from Jewish men, obstacles that sometimes threatened to define them out of their subjectivity. A final biographical sketch of the life and work of Anna Maria Goldsmid, a contemporary of Aguilar's and also her successor, can serve to suggest the ways in which these women resisted others' definitions, as well as the ways in which early Victorian Jewish women's goals would be carried into the next generation. Among Anglo-Jewish women, Goldsmid was the exception to every rule, the breaker of every barrier. Her life seems to suggest that in a liberal culture hegemonic institutions and ideologies do not always manage to prevent, punish, or "contain" every behavior that transgresses societal expectations.

"If Grace Aguilar had been spared to add an eighth part to her volume on 'the Women of Israel' we cannot doubt that Anna Maria Goldsmid would have been enrolled among them."[3] So writes the editor of the *Jewish Chronicle* on the death, in 1889, of one of the most active women in Victorian Jewish history. In posthumously enrolling Goldsmid in Aguilar's magnum opus, the editor both acknowledges that Aguilar's massive effort has opened a cultural space for the recognition and remembrance of important Jewish women, and at the same time suggests that Aguilar was not the only, and not necessarily the most powerful, Anglo-Jewish woman of her day. Indeed, if anyone could challenge the critical consensus that Grace Aguilar was a Jewish woman sui generis, it was Anna Maria Goldsmid, translator, lecturer, reformer, pamphleteer on behalf of persecuted Jews abroad, founder of girls' schools, and advocate of teacher's colleges. Both Aguilar and Goldsmid were reformers, both advocated women's education, both advocated Jewish emancipation. But these women's differences in class and religio-cultural heritage influenced the positions they took on these issues and the form in which they expressed their positions.

Goldsmid was born in 1805 into a family of wealthy Ashkenazim who consistently broke the established rules in the community and nevertheless remained prominent members of it. Her father, Isaac Lyon Goldsmid, was one of the first emancipationists, acting on his own to contact MPs when he felt that the Board of Deputies was moving too slowly to lobby for reforms. Her brother, Francis Henry, was the first English Jew called to the bar at Lincoln's Inn, wrote very influential tracts on behalf of Jewish emancipation in the 1830s and 1840s, and became one of the first Jewish MPs in 1860. As concerned with education as his sister, Francis established the Infant School for the Jewish poor while Anna Maria established the West Metropolitan School for Girls, the first such institutions in the community. In addition, he founded the Jews' College, a school intended to train indigenous rabbis and sermon-givers, which England sorely lacked. Along with his sister and several other prominent families, he founded the West London Synagogue for British Jews, which was not only the first reform synagogue in England, but the first joint synagogue of Sephardim and Ashkenazim. For this act, he and the other founders— called "seceders"—were temporarily expelled from the community. In the West London Synagogue, he delivered sermons in English at a time when such an act was considered heretical or Christian.[4] In other words, he very nearly fits the type of what David Sorkin calls in the German-Jewish reform context a *Gebildeter,* a reform ideologue. Because of their wealth and Ashkenazic heritage, these Goldsmids were in the unique position to bring the German reform movement to England.

But as instrumental as Francis Henry was in bringing this movement to England and interpreting it for English Jews, the initial credit really ought to go (and in standard histories never has gone) to his sister. Anna Maria Goldsmid brought the reform movement to England when she translated its main German-Jewish proponent's sermons into English in 1839, two and a half years before the founding of the West London Synagogue. The act of translation was understood to be a Jewish male activity, and undertaking such an important translation as Götthold Salomon's sermons as her first effort was shocking. Even more shocking was that she afterward suggested to her brother that he read one of the sermons before their congregation in St. Alban's Place, which he did, stirring the first serious reform/orthodox rift in the community. That rift died down, but two years later enough families wanted vernacular sermons that they "seceded" and formed the West London Synagogue. Goldsmid's choice of translation had a large impact on the community. By 1860, not only the reform, but the orthodox members of the community would be clamoring for sermons as well. As her obituary puts it, "Miss Goldsmid, among the Jewesses of her age, was quite the leader in thought."[5]

She was also the first Jew to justify her written efforts as attempts to qualify mothers as instructors, setting a trend that, as we have seen, numerous women would follow. As she says in her preface to her translation of Salomon's sermons: "To all who are engaged in the formation of the religious character of the young, but above all to mothers, whose especial vocation it is, diligently and lovingly to foster true piety in the hearts of their children, everything must be valuable, that can assist them in this, their most important duty. To mothers and instructors then, I especially offer such aid as these sermons can furnish" (iv). Perhaps because she was so involved with the West Metropolitan School for Girls and the Infant School, she was especially aware of the need for English instructional materials.[6] Although her brother officially established the Jews' Infant School, according to her obituary, he did so "largely due to [her] enthusiasm." In this effort to educate poor children, she followed in the mold of other such wealthy educators of the poor as Charlotte Montefiore. She contributed a large amount of financial support as well as time to helping Miriam Harris, her closest friend and the head mistress, to make the venture a success. She had full reason from her experiences to call for vernacular instructional materials. She did not take full credit for advocating instruction in English herself, however. She felt she had to justify her translation and her aim by saying that "My father, who has acted, both in public and private, on the opinion that religious education can be best conducted at home, shares with me this hope" (iii). She probably felt this gesture necessary for the same reason Aguilar felt it necessary to deny her desire for notoriety—if she took credit for the position herself, she would have been identified as a self-directed woman rather than as an other-directed caregiver. But whether or not Isaac Lyon shared her view, Anna Maria was the first Jew in England to articulate this position in public.

Grace Aguilar acknowledged Goldsmid's leadership in this point when she quoted the passage from the translator's preface to Salomon's sermons in *Spirit of Judaism*.[7] And Marion Hartog drew on this justification to support her *Jewish Sabbath Journal*. Although Goldsmid was not known as a woman writer so much as the translator of important texts, she showed women the way to justify entering into print by denying that as motherly women they had any agency. In addition, this passage shaped English reformist men's relationship to female education. David Woolf Marks, first preacher of the West London Synagogue, in his first sermon, also repeated this passage almost word for word without acknowledging Goldsmid. The prefatory note to his *Sermons Preached on Various Occasions at the West London Synagogue of British Jews,* citing "the dearth of Jewish discourses in the English language," says that they are for "furnishing Jewish families with the means of *home* instruction in matters that appertain to the essentials of the Mosaic faith."[8]

Goldsmid followed the reform sermons with numerous translations, each one having a large impact on the community. In her subsequent efforts, Goldsmid moved on from promoting home instruction of women to translating books that would speak primarily to Jewish men. Her translation of German reformer Ludwig Philippsohn's *Development of the Religious Idea in Judaism, Christianity, and Mahomedanism* in 1855 came at a time when the West London Synagogue was denied access to all communal funds and institutions, and constituted a plea to the Chief Rabbi to remove the ban. Her translation from French in 1872 of J. Cohen's *The Deicides. Analysis of the Life of Jesus and of the Several Phases of the Christian Church in their Relation to Judaism* was a theological and emancipationist tract much like her brother's tracts. "With the exception of Mon. Renan's 'Life of Jesus,' " one tribute says, "there is probably no work extant which throws so much light upon the vexed question of the relation of Christianity to Judaism."[9] By the time she translated the pamphlet *Persecution of the Jews of Roumania* from French in 1872, her public persona was a far cry from the meek translator hiding in her father's shadow. The translator's preface to *Persecution* shows her speaking on behalf of the entire international Jewish community, indeed, on behalf of the "whole civilized world": "While the perpetrators of Jewish wrongs in Roumania shrink not from the committal of the crimes which are here detailed, they do shrink from being held up to the merited execration of the whole civilized world. . . . The only weapons, therefore, which the advocates of my unfortunate co-religionists can wield, are those of pen and speech. I would employ them in order to declare to the Roumans once and for all, that the only course by which they can avoid the censure of mankind, is to cease to deserve it."[10] At the age of sixty-seven, she could carry off this rhetoric because she was herself a well-known figure among both Jews and Christians. She had an acquaintance with Lord Brougham, Thomas Wyse, Crabbe

Robinson, Harriet Martineau, and the composer Felix Mendelssohn. She helped the Haham (clergyman) of the Sephardic synagogue with his English sermons. She was a staunch member of the Anglo-Jewish Association, a literary association almost exclusively open to Jewish men. She regularly corresponded with such internationally renowned German-Jewish reformers as Leopold Zunz and Ludwig Philippsohn, and was friends with Moses Montefiore, with whom she worked to free persecuted Jews around the world. Indeed, one friend told her that she was "really a sort of female edition of Sir Moses,"[11] quite a comparison, considering that Montefiore has been the most lauded person in Anglo-Jewish history, and one of the most influential Jews in modern times. By comparison with this truly atypical Anglo-Jewish woman's life, Aguilar's life and fictions appear, not sui generis, but rather exemplary of her age.

Beyond advocating for home instruction in her translation of Salomon's sermons, Goldsmid maintained her distance from other Jewish women's literary forms and life paths. While Aguilar and Hartog both wrote sermons for women, they recognized that this was mainly a male form, the kind of thing that *Gebildeters* like Goldsmid's brother presented at the synagogue. While they called for emancipation, for the most part they did not write emancipation tracts—again, because emancipation tracts were a male form. Translation, whether of ancient literature or reformist writings and biographies, was also a male form; indeed, it was the prevailing form in such men's periodicals as the two *Hebrew Reviews* and the *Voice of Jacob*. While Aguilar did attempt one translation, at the request of Moses Mocatta, the "oral tradition" she hoped to transmit was one of tales. The Mosses specifically claimed that "flowery paths of romance" were female paths, but Goldsmid did not take them. She did not take a typical female life path either, at least insofar as she chose not to marry. On the other hand, like many wealthy women she did endow charities, in her case, the Jews' Deaf and Dumb Home, the University College Hospital, and the Homeopathic Hospital.

But to say that Goldsmid took atypical paths for a Jewish woman is not to say that she was unaware of, uninterested in, or unaffected by Jewish women's issues. In particular, the issue of increasing female education seems to have been one on which all the Anglo-Jewish women writers agreed that something needed to be done. Goldsmid used her unique position in the community, not only to call for changes in Jewish girls' education, but to effect them. Already in the

1830s she was working to establish the West Metropolitan School for Girls, years before the public debate on female education had taken place. By the time her translations were well known in the 1870s, she was ready to take a bolder step in advocating equal education for women. In April 1874, she was the first woman to be asked to give one of the "Lectures to Jewish Working Men," a forum sponsored by the Jews' and General Scientific and Literary Institute, a Jewish men's organization founded by some of the "seceders" of the West London Synagogue thirty years before.[12] She used the historic occasion to deliver a lecture on "What Jewish girls should learn, what Jewish wives and mothers should practice, and how fathers and husbands should help them."[13]

From the start, she calls attention to the uniqueness of the occasion—a woman being asked to lecture in a men's forum—in order to establish her credentials for speaking to this audience. She begins by placing the lecture within the framework of the debate for women's "rights" and the establishment of their "duties": "I am sure that all of you have of late heard much talk about the 'Rights of Women.' It occurred therefore to the Committee of this Association that one of these rights was that the women should have a lecture about themselves, and another was that the lecturer should be a woman also. It was thought that ladies should be spoken about and advised as to what are their rights and duties. No one can have the one without performing the other." Having set up this liberal framework of rights and duties, she goes on to give her credentials for lecturing on the subject: "There is a further reason why you see me, a woman, lecturing here instead of a man. Who knows so well to tell women how to do their duty as a woman?" If she establishes an equality with the women in her audience by appealing to their common gender, she also immediately establishes their difference in education and class. "I imagined that if I spoke to you," she tells them, "I should take those who listened to me to be sensible women, who did not care to listen to fine speeches, but who desired to do all they could do for the good of themselves." This wealthy educated woman could provide them "fine speeches," but knowing that they are working class and under-educated, she chooses not to.

Having established her aim, her credentials, and her relation to her audience, she launches into her straightforwardly feminist address: "I hope to be able to make you clearly understand that from the day the children of Israel came out of Egypt . . . , God gave to woman the same rights and duties as He gave to man." All the people, not just the men, participated in the Giving of the Law at Sinai and responded that they would perform and understand the commandments. All the people, without qualification, were commanded to gather to learn and observe the commandments. Girls and boys should receive the same education. After explaining Jewish women's continuing domestic responsibilities to care for their breadwinning husbands and educate their children, she goes on to make these domestic responsibilities yet another reason for providing equal education: "Women naturally ask how can we do and understand all that is required of us, if it is never taught at our schools or shown to us. Why should these things not be taught?" Goldsmid appears to go a great deal further than Aguilar in her calls for reforms. Still, she does not address several problems with her advocacy of equal women's education: if women are educated equally, why should they not be able to be employed equally rather than simply fulfilling their home responsibilities? And why has she herself, like Aguilar, not taken on these domestic duties if she is such a staunch advocate of them? Perhaps in a Jewish men's forum, a forum presided over by Rabbi Arthur Green and several other men who toasted her at the end of the speech, she felt she could only say so much.

By the time she gave this speech in 1874, Goldsmid's interest in education had already led her beyond the boundaries of the Jewish community to address the national issue of teacher training. She had argued that there were too few "normal schools," schools for the training of teachers, to serve the developing national education system. At the same time she had argued that, because Jews and Judaism were excluded from most Victorian normal schools and curricula, Jews should set up their own educational union for the establishment of a Jewish normal school. The *Chronicle*'s retrospective for the year 1870 remarks that Goldsmid "tried to promote an educational union in our community, but was not successful."[14] In her speech to the working women, she explains that the paucity of women's education is bound up with the poverty of the educational system as a whole, and particularly with the lack of trained teachers. She says that she desires, "before I pass away from life, the foundation of a real Jewish Normal School." In the next few years, she was to endow a trust with £2000 for the purpose, but died in 1889 before her aim was achieved.

This "Woman of Israel's" anomalous career began in 1839 with a call to increase the level of maternal home instruction by providing vernacular instructional materials. It ended some fifty years later with a broad appeal for credentialed universal education. In between, Goldsmid broke almost every rule. She spoke out on public causes. She did not marry. She employed "male" literary forms, and spoke on "male" topics to "male" institutions. She did not, after her first translation, give credit for her work to others. Yet when she died, she was one of the most lauded women in Victorian Jewish history. Why was she able to avoid the criticism for crossing established gender lines that so affected Aguilar and Hartog in their different ways? Perhaps she was shielded by her wealth and by the prominence of her family, a protection that middle-class Anglo-Jewish women writers such as Aguilar and Hartog did not have. Yet, although Goldsmid was able to transgress the domestic sphere without suffering punishment in her lifetime, history meted out the expected punishment after her death. Victorian Jews celebrated her, but they did not remember her. This short biography is the first to be published since her obituary a century ago.

The extent of Goldsmid's contribution to the development of Jewish women's awareness and education was accurately, if unwittingly, described by an anonymous Jewish antifeminist who wrote a letter to the *Chronicle* in 1879 complaining about the emergence of a group of Jewish feminists. He did not specify Goldsmid by name—perhaps her wealth, prominence, and family connections prevented him—but it seems probable that he was thinking of her: "it has recently come to my knowledge that a section (at present, happily, a small and unimportant one) of the ladies in our community are openly advocating what are known as 'Women's Rights.' . . . It is this doctrine . . . which is insinuated now-a-days into the minds of young people by some mothers and by a few school-mistresses."[15] Whether or not he had Goldsmid specifically in mind, his claim that mothers and instructors had become the primary spokeswomen for women's rights was an idea she would no doubt have embraced with pride.

The existence of such an atypical intellectual woman in the Victorian Jewish community suggests that the powerful ideologies and institutions that sought to limit and define women—conversionism and missionary societies, sexism and journalistic censorship, domestic ideology and domestic fiction—were not wholly successful. If Goldsmid managed to evade the limitations placed on women by these ideologies and institutions much of the time, other Jewish women were able to do so at least some of the time. The Moss sisters were able to imagine publicly feminist and reformist heroines in their historical romances. Aguilar found that she could bargain for at least some measure of fame, education, and emancipation. Charlotte Montefiore took refuge in anonymity to criticize Jewish and mainstream inequities toward women and the poor. Because Anglo-Jewish women were able to discover these avenues for publicizing their subjectivities, the history of their writing reveals the limits of liberal Christian and Jewish male attempts to homogenize Victorian and Jewish culture.

This insight about the limits of liberalism and Jewish patriarchy can only be won by reconstructing the inequitable dialogues that took place between dominant and marginalized groups. What has been the general approach to representations of Jews in English literature—the deconstruction of Christian writers' stereotypes of Jews by discovering their internal contradictions—is inadequate to the task of building an accurate picture of the Victorian world.[16] This is true because members of marginalized groups often name the very hegemonic strategies that the dominant cultural discourse is intent on masking. The best of such deconstructive work has started with the premise that culturally privileged writers' representations of the Other say more about those who circulate them than about those they purport to represent. But finally, such work is limited because, even if it is critical of the stereotypes, it offers no positive alternatives. Setting dominant stereotypes (even those attached to important names like Shakespeare, Scott, or Dickens) against the much more interesting and complex self-representations made by members of the marginalized group does more than reveal the inadequacy of the stereotypes, or the relations of power in which the dominant writers are engaged. This method renders audible the aspirations of actual Jews, aspirations that would otherwise remain forever lost amid the perennial and fruitless spats over whether Fagin is "true" or "false."

That the voices of actual Jews have too often been rendered inaudible is a misfortune that must be attributed, not only to Victorian scholars, but to Jewish studies scholars as well. The historiography of Jewish modernity has largely been slanted in such a way as to exclude women's experience. The prevalent emphasis on work done in so-called "Jewish languages" (e.g., Hebrew, Yiddish, Ladino, Judeo-Arabic, Aramaic) has often worked to exclude women's work that has appeared in so-called "hyphenated languages" (e.g., English). Furthermore, the organization of Jewish history exclusively around men's struggles and achievements has done a disservice both to women and men by removing the dynamic social context in which men achieved. In consequence, much of both modern Jewish women's history and the history of Jewish masculinity has been lost. But as in this case, some of the losses are recoverable. Historians need to continue to revisit the archives to reclaim what remains of the gendered experience of Jewish modernity.

Because literary critics interested in Jewish cultural studies are only now beginning the work of reconstructing voices once dismissed or unsuspected, it is easy to become discouraged by the depth of the silence that greets the researcher. But for all the ephemera, the reminiscences, and the texts that have been lost, for every image that has been forgotten or misremembered or deliberately suppressed, there are still hundreds of unique documents left to be read and reconstructed. An entire community waits to be reconstituted by the scholars to whom its debates and concerns most particularly speak. Those scholars interested in recovering the lost history of women, the diversity of English literature, and the complexity of the modern Jewish experience will find that the Victorian Jewish subculture is a place where the work may begin in earnest.

Notes

The following abbreviations are used for periodicals throughout the notes:

HCW   *Hebrew Christian Witness*
HRJ   *Hebrew Review and Magazine of Jewish Literature*
HRR   *Hebrew Review and Magazine of Rabbinical Literature*
HJ   *Howitt's Journal*
IW   *Israel's Watchman; A Hebrew Christian Magazine*
JA   *The Jewish Advocate. For the Young*
JC   *Jewish Chronicle*
JHer *Jewish Herald and Record of Christian Effort For the Spiritual Good of God's Ancient People*
JSJ   *Jewish Sabbath Journal*
VoJ   *Voice of Jacob*

INTRODUCTION

1. Statistics in this and the following paragraph on Victorian Jewish population growth are derived from V. D. Lipman, *Social History of the Jews in England, 1850–1950* (London: Watts, 1954), 65.
2. See David Feldman, *Englishmen and Jews: Social Relations and Political Culture, 1840–1914* (New Haven: Yale University Press, 1994); and M. C. N. Salbstein, *Emancipation of the Jews in Britain: The Question of the Admission of the Jews to Parliament, 1828–1860* (Rutherford, N.J.: Fairleigh Dickinson Press, 1981).
3. See Cecil Roth, *A History of the Jews in England* (London: Oxford University Press, 1941), esp. chap. 7.
4. For the growth in communal institutions, see Asher I. Meyers, *The Jewish Directory of 1874 . . . and other interesting information* (London: A. I. Meyers, 1874). Meyers lists 72 synagogues, 43 literary, burial, and friendly societies, 36 schools, 70 miscellaneous charities for the poor, 6 hospitals, a home for the deaf and dumb, a home for the blind, 3 charities for widows, 2 for lying-in women, and 2 for providing marriage portions to poor young women; at least 3146 children and adults were attending the

schools in 1874, and some 1640 persons were holding official positions in the community.

5. David Sorkin, *The Transformation of German Jewry, 1780–1840* (New York: Oxford University Press, 1987), 6. Sorkin maintains that English Jewry cannot be called a subculture because the community is too heterogeneous and small in size (175). Yet, as this study will show, the notion of a "self-contained system of ideas and symbols," borrowed from the dominant culture but altered for the English Jews' own purposes, does apply. The term "subculture" is in any case preferable to "nation," "race," or even "ethnicity." In the wake of political Zionism, "nation" is too likely to be apprehended as if it had state-building aspirations, which for most English Jews during most of the nineteenth century it did not. "Race" is likely to be confused for a genetic term, and a post-Holocaust Jewish consciousness will not permit its scholarly use. The concept of Jewish "ethnicity" did not emerge until the late nineteenth century.

6. For a new history of the *Jewish Chronicle,* see David Cesarani, *The Jewish Chronicle and Anglo-Jewry, 1841–1991* (New York: Cambridge University Press, 1994). For the centennial history, see *The Jewish Chronicle 1841–1941: A Century of Newspaper History* (London: Jewish Chronicle, 1949).

7. The most recent example of this tendency is Feldman's *Englishmen and Jews.* Other prominent histories include Lipman, *Social History;* Roth, *History of the Jews;* Todd Endelman, *Radical Assimilation in English Jewish History 1656–1945* (Bloomington: Indiana University Press, 1990); Israel Finestein, "Anglo-Jewish Opinion During the Struggle for Emancipation," *Transactions of the Jewish Historical Society of England* 20 (1964) 113–43; Albert M. Hyamson, *The Sephardim of England, A History of the Spanish and Portuguese Jewish Community, 1492–1951* (London: Methuen, 1951); Salbstein, *Emancipation of the Jews.*

8. See Cecil Roth, "Evolution of Anglo-Jewish Literature" (London: Edward Goldston, 1937), whose manifestly apologetic essay mentions only three Anglo-Jewish women writers (Aguilar, Polack, and Emma Lyons) in a list of twenty Jewish writers, and remarks, without explanation, "If we neglect . . . Grace Aguilar's romantical Vale of Cedars, etc., the earliest attempt [of Jews to give a more faithful picture of themselves] was perhaps that of Matthias Levy" (8). Todd Endelman, in the introduction to *The Jews of Georgian England, 1714–1830* (Philadelphia: Jewish Publication Society, 1989), argues that Jews produced no emancipationist theory. Also see Sorkin, *Transformation of German Jewry,* 175: "English Jewry did not generate a significant Haskala movement. And lacking the political pressures of a comprehensive emancipation process—emancipation turned on the ability to hold office . . . —English Jewry experienced no conspicuous ideological ferment." Rachel Beth Zion Lask Abrahams does attempt to reckon with the history of Anglo-Jewish women in "Grace

Aguilar: A Centenary Tribute," *Transactions of the Jewish Historical Society of England* 16 (1952): 137–48, and acknowledges Aguilar's "phenomenal popularity" and her "bearing on the period following political emancipation" (137). But her final assessment is that, though Aguilar was "gifted with great facility in the art of expressing herself, she was yet without that equipment and solid learning which could have measured up to her indomitable spirit, her phenomenal industry, and her unquestioning loyalty to her people" (147). The question of how her work influenced Jews and Christians during the emancipation period is left unresolved. A similar argument about women's subsumption under the banner of "man" appears in Marion A. Kaplan, *The Making of the Jewish Middle Class: Women, Family, and Identity in Imperial Germany* (New York: Oxford University Press, 1991), 8–9, 15.

9. Literary critics have had to be more attentive to the women's works, since these are the majority of Victorian Jews' literary production. Nevertheless, while Linda Gertner Zatlin's *The Nineteenth-Century Anglo-Jewish Novel* (Boston: G. K. Hall, 1981) is a useful survey, it characterizes the novels of Aguilar and the Mosses as "propaganda fiction" that "fail to enlighten" (40). Of Anglo-Jewish novels as a whole, Zatlin offers this assessment: "Individual Anglo-Jewish novels do not offer the kind of vision found in the 'great' works of the Victorian period. Most characters fit a Procrustean bed and fail to do more than embody a thinly disguised point. . . . [T]ogether they provide a social history of Victorian Anglo-Jews that vividly depicts problems of this minority group as it became freed from political and social restrictions" (133). Philip Weinberger, "The Social and Religious Thought of Grace Aguilar (1816–1847)" (Ph.D. diss., New York University, 1970), on the other hand, singles out Aguilar as "sui generis," making comparison between her and contemporaries impossible. Livia Bitton-Jackson's excellent *Madonna or Courtesan? the Jewish Woman in Christian Literature* (New York: Seabury Press, 1982) does not consider how Anglo-Jewish women represented themselves.

10. Beruria was the celebrated wife of Rabbi Meir. The Talmud records her great feats as a scholar, and her goodness as a wife. Later, Rashi led a medieval wave to denigrate her achievements by suggesting that she was an adulterer. See Judith Romney Wegner, "The Image and Status of Women in Classical Rabbinic Judaism," in *Jewish Women in Historical Perspective,* ed. Judith Baskin (Detroit: Wayne State University Press, 1991), 68–93. Also see Charlotte Baum, Paula Hyman, and Sonya Michel, *The Jewish Woman in America* (New York: Dial Press, 1976), 12–14. Glückel of Hameln was a medieval German-Jewish merchant's wife who had fourteen children and ran the business after her husband died. Her fascinating autobiography has been preserved as *The Memoirs of Glückel of Hameln,* trans. Marvin Lowenthal (New York: Schocken Books, 1977).

11. Rarely, Ashkenazic women such as Hester Rothschild in her *Imrei Lev, Prayers and Meditations for Every Situation and Occasion in Life* (reviewed in *JC*, Aug. 1, 1856), still did publish *tekhinot* even during the Victorian period. For a discussion of *tekhinot*, see Chava Weissler, "The Traditional Poetry of Ashkenazic Women," in *Jewish Spirituality: From the Sixteenth Century Revival to the Present*, ed. Arthur Green (New York: Crossroad, 1988), 2:245–75. Weissler carries the discussion forward in "Prayers in Yiddish and the Religious World of Ashkenazic Women," in *Jewish Women in Historical Perspective*, ed. Judith Baskin (Detroit: Wayne State University Press, 1991), 159–81. Also see Weissler's translation of several examples and her introduction in Ellen Umansky and Diane Ashton, eds., *Four Centuries of Jewish Women's Spirituality* (Boston: Beacon Press, 1992), 36–37; 51–55. For women's role in Jewish law, see Rachel Biale, *Women and Jewish Law* (New York: Schocken Books, 1984); Judith Plaskow, *Standing Again at Sinai: Judaism from a Feminist Perspective* (San Francisco: Harper Collins, 1990). The best listing of the "exceptional" women who wrote despite their "exemption" was probably made by the Victorian Jewish apologists themselves. One Dr. Carmoly published a list of short biographies of "Learned Women in Israel" in the *Jewish Chronicle*; this was subsequently republished three times, as if to ameliorate Jewish women's demand for recognition (Aug. 6, 1858; Oct. 12, 1860; Mar. 1, 1867; Feb. 18, 1887). The most thorough Victorian rereading of Jewish women's intellectual role in Jewish history is Grace Aguilar's set of biographies of biblical, Talmudic, medieval, and modern Jewish heroines, *The Women of Israel* 3 vols. (New York: D. Appleton, 1884).

12. To this lack of historical models must be superadded the "anxiety of authorship" that all women writers faced in confronting Victorian patriarchal literary culture. See Sandra Gilbert and Susan Gubar, *The Madwoman in the Attic: The Woman Writer and the Nineteenth-Century Literary Imagination* (New Haven: Yale University Press, 1979), chap. 2.

13. Deborah Hertz analyzes the salonières in *Jewish High Society in Old Regime Berlin* (New Haven: Yale University Press, 1988). Hertz argues that for the most part German-Jewish salonières were dilettantes rather than authors who gained standing in the literary community through "some combination of their social standing, occupation, personal charm, friendships, and unpublished writing" (159). Fanny Lewald began writing novels in Germany in the 1840s. See Deborah Hertz, "Work, Love and Jewishness in the Life of Fanny Lewald," in *From East and West: Jews in a Changing Europe 1750–1870*, ed. Frances Malino and David Sorkin (Oxford: Basil Blackwell, 1990), 202–20. The only work by Lewald to be translated into English is *The Education of Fanny Lewald: An Autobiography*, trans. and ed. Hanna Ballin Lewis (Albany: State University of New

York Press, 1992). In the American context, Rosa Sonneschein did not begin publishing her Jewish women's periodical *The American Jewess* until 1895. Women such as Rebekah Kohut, Emma Lazarus, and Henrietta Szold also published late in the century. For discussions of these writers, see Baum, Hyman, and Michel, *Jewish Woman in America*; Linda Gordon Kuzmack, *Woman's Cause: The Jewish Woman's Movement in England and the United States, 1881–1933* (Columbus: Ohio State University Press, 1990); and Diane Lichtenstein, *Writing Their Nations: The Tradition of Nineteenth-Century American Jewish Women Writers* (Bloomington: Indiana University Press, 1992).

14. Endelman, introduction to *Jews of Georgian England*.

15. Examples of literary criticism focusing on representations of Jews by Christian writers include Bryan Cheyette, *Constructions of "the Jew" in English Literature and Society: Racial Representations, 1875–1945* (Cambridge: Cambridge University Press, 1993); Catherine Gallagher, "George Eliot and *Daniel Deronda*: The Prostitute and the Jewish Question," in *Sex, Politics, and Science in the Nineteenth-Century Novel,* ed. Ruth Bernard Yeazell (Baltimore: Johns Hopkins University Press, 1986), 39–62; Bitton-Jackson, *Madonna or Courtesan?*; Estelle Chevelier, "Characterization of the Jew in the Victorian Novel. 1864–1876" (master's thesis, Emory University, 1962); Joseph Gaer, *The Legend of the Wandering Jew* (New York: Mentor, 1961); Montagu Frank Modder, *The Jew in the Literature of England: To the End of the Nineteenth Century* (New York: Meridian Books, 1960); Edgar Rosenberg, *From Shylock to Svengali: Jewish Stereotypes in English Fiction* (Stanford: Stanford University Press, 1960); Harold Fisch, *The Dual Image* (London: Lincolns-Prager, 1959); Harry Stone, "Dickens and the Jews," *Victorian Studies* 11 (Mar. 1959): 223–53; Lauriat Lane, Jr., "Dickens' Archetypal Jew," *PMLA* 73 (Mar. 1958): 95–101; Edgar Johnson, "Dickens, Fagin and Mr. Riah," *Commentary* 9 (1950): 47–50; M[eyer] J[ack] Landa, *The Jew in Drama* (New York: William Morrow, 1927); Edward N. Calisch, *The Jew in English Literature as Author and as Subject* (Richmond, Va.: Bell, 1909); David Phillipson, *The Jew in English Fiction* (Cincinnati: Clarke, 1889).

16. Nancy Armstrong, *Desire and Domestic Fiction: A Political History of the Novel* (New York: Oxford University Press, 1987), 23. Mary Poovey makes a similar point about turning from male representations of women to women's representations of themselves in *The Proper Lady and the Woman Writer: Ideology as Style in the Works of Mary Wollstonecraft, Mary Shelley, and Jane Austen* (Chicago: University of Chicago Press, 1984), xii.

17. Examples of this neglect of Jews' literature include almost all recent feminist readings of Victorian literary history. See Anita Levy, *Other Women: The Writing of Class, Race, and Gender, 1832–1898* (Princeton:

Princeton University Press, 1991); Armstrong, *Desire and Domestic Fiction*; Margaret Homans, *Bearing the Word: Language and Female Experience in Nineteenth-Century Women's Writing* (Chicago: University of Chicago Press, 1986); Mary Poovey, *Uneven Developments: The Ideological Work of Gender in Mid-Victorian England* (Chicago: University of Chicago Press, 1988); Dorothy Mermin, *Godiva's Ride: Women of Letters in England, 1830–1880* (Bloomington: Indiana University Press, 1993); and Susan Rubinow Gorsky, *Femininity to Feminism: Women and Literature in the Nineteenth Century* (New York: Twayne Publishers, 1992).

18. See George Mosse, *Toward the Final Solution: A History of European Racism* (New York: Harper Colophon Books, 1980). Racial representations of Jews in England began to appear somewhat later than elsewhere, especially with the rise of Disraeli to prime minister. See Cheyette, *Constructions of "the Jew."* During the period, colloquially Jews were called "blacks." These biological determinist characterizations should not be confused by the typical Victorian tendency to use the terms "race" and "nation" nonbiologically and interchangeably to describe Jews. "Nation" had the sense of a transnational community, exiled from its geographical home, the different diasporas of which shared a common language, holidays, customs, and beliefs—much the same sense as "the Jewish people" has today.

19. See Bitton-Jackson, *Madonna or Courtesan?*; Edward Said, *Orientalism* (New York: Vintage Books, 1978); and Billie Melman, *Women's Orients: English Women and the Middle East, 1718–1918* (Ann Arbor: University of Michigan Press, 1992).

20. For the necessity of understanding the differences between men's and women's experiences of Jewish history, see Plaskow, *Standing Again at Sinai.* See also Kaplan, *Making of the Jewish Middle Class,* 15.

21. Aubrey Newman, *The Board of Deputies of British Jews, 1760–1985* (London: Valentine Mitchell, 1987), 5.

22. See, however, the several emancipationist tracts by Jewish men that emerged in two waves, during the early 1830s and in the period between 1848 and 1856. A listing is in Cecil Roth, ed., *Magna Bibliotheca Anglo-Judaica: A Bibliographical Guide to Anglo-Jewish History* (London: Jewish Historical Society of England, 1937).

23. Lipman, *Social History,* 9.

24. This did not mean that Anglo-Jewish men always agreed with each other on how community-building ought to proceed. Israel Finestein, "Anglo-Jewish Opinion" identifies the major areas of dissension.

25. Barry A. Kosmin, "Nuptiality and Fertility Patterns of British Jewry 1850–1980: An Immigrant Transition?" in *Demography of Immigrants and Minority Groups in the United Kingdom,* ed. D. A. Coleman (London: Academic Press, 1982), 245–62.

26. Endelman, introduction to *Radical Assimilation.*

27. Marc Shell identifies liberalism as a specifically crypto-Jewish invention in "Marranos (Pigs), or From Coexistence to Toleration," *Critical Inquiry* 17, no. 2 (winter 1991): 306–35.

28. The famous example of a Sephardic Jew rejecting the *Ascamot* is Isaac D'Israeli, Benjamin Disraeli's father, who refused to pay a fine levied by the Haham (leader) of the Sephardic congregation. See James Picciotto, *Sketches of Anglo-Jewish History* (London: Trubner, 1875).

29. Hyamson's standard history, *Sephardim of England*, 261–64, describes the predominance of Sephardim in Anglo-Jewish literary life. Among other things, the Sephardim were instrumental in operating the Cheap Jewish Library, the Anglo-Jewish Press, and the Association for the Promotion of Jewish Literature (which became the Jews' and General Literary and Scientific Institution); along with Ashkenazi scholar Morris Raphall, Sephardic Jews translated the Mishnah and the Sephardi ritual into English; and they produced or edited a volume of traditional melodies, a history of the Sephardim, a Hebrew dictionary, a Jewish calendar, novels, polemics, and a cookbook.

30. As Arthur Hertzberg, *The French Enlightenment and the Jews: The Origins of Modern Anti-Semitism* (New York: Columbia University Press, 1968), explains, Isaac de Pinto gave modern expression to this Sephardic myth in his famous response to Voltaire, when he exclaimed "that only the Portuguese were descended from the tribe of Judah, and that they had always lived apart from all the other children of Jacob, marrying only among themselves and maintaining separate synagogues" (181). "[B]eing superior to all the rest, they deserved more consideration" in French emancipation than Ashkenazim (270). As late as 1834, an Anglo-Sephardic historian of "The Origin and Progress of Literature Amongst the Jews of Spain" argues for Sephardic nobility as compared to the Ashkenazim, and uses it to argue for removal of disabilities: "However great [the Spanish Jews'] influence may have been on the other European Jews, these latter could not, during many centuries, raise themselves to that eminence of merit and dignity which the former occupied. This difference between them affords us the most convincing proof of the great influence which the consciousness of freedom, or the feeling of degradation and slavery, exercises on the minds and actions of men" (*HRR* 2 (1834): 158). Grace Aguilar saw a downside to the Sephardic "pride," in that it sometimes manifested itself as "stubbornness" which "renders powerless every effort made" for the "Improvement" of Sephardic poor, while the Germans are "more willing to work and push forward their own fortunes . . . and are more successful as citizens, and, as a class, less difficult to guide" (*JC*, Jan. 2, 1852, "Social Arrangements of the English Jews").

31. Sorkin, *Transformation of German Jewry*, 86. Also see Endelman, *Radical Assimilation*, chap. 5; and Hyamson, *Sephardim of England*, 217.

32. The translation is accompanied by a note saying that "the laxity of modern ideas and manners may not approve of its minute precepts, or of the rigour of a morality and religion extending its inward checks over every possible action and regulation of life"—still, a "sincere" follower of the code will be "a most moral and useful member of society" (*HRR* 1 [1834]: 11).

33. Morris J. Raphall, "Introduction," *HRR* 1 (1834): 5, 3. At one point, in the "Introduction," Raphall expresses his belief that the Jewish people "has at all times and in all ages evinced a profound veneration for learning, and an eager thirst for the acquirement of true knowledge . . . ; and they possess as extensive a literature . . . as any nation that ever existed;—a literature which we may justly characterize, as expressing the profoundest thoughts, the most pious sentiments, and the best precepts for regulating the conduct of man" (1). A cross between a musar periodical based on the ideal of traditional learnedness with a modern periodical based on the Enlightenment ideal of reasoned knowledge, with its translations of Talmudic allegories and its biographies of great rabbis, the *Review* was not a Reform periodical, as Raphall made clear in his introduction. M. H. Bresslau's *Hebrew Review and Magazine of Jewish Literature,* which did not appear until 1859, conforms much more closely to the German Reformers' periodicals. Its Hebrew title, *Ma'asef,* imitated that of the original periodical of the German Haskalah, which appeared in 1784. Anglo-Jewry did not articulate a Reform platform until half a century after German Jewry. See Sorkin, *Transformation of German Jewry,* 45–55.

34. Endelman, *Radical Assimilation,* 35.

35. Roth, *History of the Jews,* 256–58. One must be a little careful with this last statement. There was substantial debate over the divinity of the Oral Law, which was not simply a matter of presentation. Roth sometimes seems to be attempting a retrospective healing between the two groups.

36. George Mosse traces the German Jews' attempt to replace their "degraded" spirit and culture with the German spirit, or *Geist,* and culture, or *Bildung,* in *German Jews Beyond Judaism* (Bloomington: Indiana University Press, 1985). Arthur Lumley Davids, "On the Emancipation of the Jews," letter to *The Times,* May 6, 1831 shows how differently Anglo-Jewish men approached the issue: "he earnestly looked for the emancipation of the Jews, as the means of developing the cramped energies of that people." Bernard Van Oven, "Ought Baron de Rothschild to Sit in Parliament? An Imaginary Conversation between Judaeus and Amicus Nobilis" (London: Effingham Wilson, 1847), likewise uses the term "cramping" to describe the effects of persecution on Jews' industriousness and argues that "Jews should be allowed to develop their energies for their own and the public good" (14). As poor Ashkenazic Jews immigrated to England, members of the Jewish aristocracy in London did invoke the German reform regeneration rhetoric. But in general the reform movement was

much less tied to the removal of disabilities in England than it was in Germany. As the *Jewish Chronicle* put it in its retrospect on "Jewish Progress in the Victorian Era" (May 14, 1897), "One body of Jews fought for political equality, while another body fought for the modifications of the arrangements made by the community for its own government. But the former movement had come to a successful end before the latter had resulted in the establishment of our communal institutions as we know them to-day. And thus, the emancipation struggle can best be regarded as a history within a history, separate and complete in itself."

37. Aguilar, *Women of Israel*, 1:12–13. Subsequent references will be cited parenthetically in the text by volume and page number.

38. Abraham Benisch, "Our Women," *JC*, Nov. 8, 1861.

39. These parties were not, however, precisely the same as German-Jewish women's salons. Just as with upper-class Anglo-Jewish women's parties, Jewish women's salons in late-eighteenth- and early-nineteenth-century Prussia functioned to increase Jews' contact with members of other estates in society, and implicitly to argue for Jews' (or at least some Jews') emancipation. But Anglo-Jewish women such as Judith Montefiore tended to feel less a need to denigrate their Jewishness in order to appeal for emancipation than did their German-Jewish counterparts. Montefiore, whose husband Moses led the Board of Deputies of British Jews, produced the first Jewish cookbook, *The Jewish Manual or Practical Information in Jewish and Modern Cookery*, intro. by Chaim Raphael (New York: NightinGale Books, 1983), so that Jewish women could present traditional Jewish foods along with "plain English dishes; and also such French ones as are now in general use at all refined modern tables" (ii). By contrast to this notion of Jewish and English coexistence at the dinner table, gentile German intellectuals of the salon era flocked to the homes of Jewish women who were marginal to the Jewish community, who had taken steps (including in many cases conversion) to place themselves outside of it, and who focused their gatherings on celebrating and analyzing works by German Christian intellectuals. The story of the salons is told in Hertz, *Jewish High Society*, esp. 101 and chap. 6 passim. Kaplan, *Making of the Jewish Middle Class*, 31–35, describes the creation later in the nineteenth century of the middle-class German-Jewish *Hausfrau*, whose homemaking activities were supported by bourgeois domestic ideology as well as by Jewish tradition. This German middle-class type seems to be closer to what the upper class Montefiore was striving to convince her readers to attain; yet, it is still not the same, for like the German salonières, the *Hausfrau* also strives to appear more "German" and less "Jewish," a goal that Montefiore would not have advocated.

40. See Joseph Kestner, *Protest and Reform: The British Social Narrative by Women, 1827–1867* (Madison: University of Wisconsin Press, 1985).

41. Michael McKeon, *The Origins of the English Novel, 1600–1740* (Balti-

more: Johns Hopkins University Press, 1987), 318–37, argues that Defoe's *Robinson Crusoe* is one of the earliest examples of what he calls "progressive narrative," the secularization of "Protestant narrative," in which the narrator steps into the role of Providence. The novel was a form unknown to traditional Jewish writers.

42. Thanks to David Biale for this joke.

43. Melman, *Women's Orients*.

44. See Endelman, *Radical Assimilation*.

45. Bitton-Jackson, *Madonna or Courtesan?* has traced the gesture of "orientalizing" the Jewish woman back to a fundamental Christian ambivalence about Jewish women's bodies. The gesture undoubtedly gained force with the rise of orientalism, as Said, *Orientalism*; and Melman, *Women's Orients*, have documented.

46. In *Uneven Developments*, 200, Poovey calls for increased attention to gender, class, race, and national identity in feminist work in order to "produce a history of ideological formulations of difference that might help us understand the impetus behind and resistances to change in ways our old histories have failed to do. This would necessarily entail . . . analyzing the competitions among various institutions for the right to articulate and legislate difference."

47. For Jewish feminism's commitment to women's various processes and experiences, see Melanie Kaye/Kantrowitz and Irena Klepfisz, eds., *The Tribe of Dina: A Jewish Women's Anthology* (Boston: Beacon Press, 1986): "Jewish feminists and lesbians are of a diverse sort. . . . Disagreements are fierce; denouncements not uncommon" (9). The editors' goal is "to express the wide range of Jewish experience and culture, and to develop more empathy and support for Jewish identities we do not share" (10). Also see Ruti Kadish, "Midrash and Feminism" (master's thesis, University of California, Berkeley, 1991). For traditional Judaism's commitment to polysemous dialogue, see Geoffrey H. Hartman and Sanford Budick, eds., *Midrash and Literature* (New Haven: Yale University Press, 1986). For a useful introduction to Jewish feminism, see Susannah Heschel, ed., introduction to *On Being a Jewish Feminist: A Reader* (New York: Schocken Books, 1983). Also see her essay "Feminism," in *Contemporary Jewish Religious Thought*, ed. Arthur A. Cohen and Paul Mendes-Flohr (New York: Charles Scribner's Sons, 1987), 255–59.

CHAPTER 1

1. For a comparison to other similar orientalist fantasies, see in particular Edward Said's discussion of the novels of Flaubert and Kipling in *Oriental-*

ism (New York: Vintage Books, 1978). Flaubert's heroines are not women, but entire worlds, emblems of oriental landscapes that are sensual yet barren, willing, and mute (187, 207); Kipling's White Men sanitize and "conquer" these sensual orientals (228).

2. The story of their parliamentary struggle is told in M. C. N. Salbstein, *Emancipation of the Jews in Britain: The Question of the Admission of the Jews to Parliament, 1828–1860* (Rutherford, N.J.: Fairleigh Dickinson Press, 1981). Also see David Feldman, *Englishmen and Jews: Social Relations and Political Culture, 1840–1914* (New Haven: Yale University Press, 1994), chap. 1. Important pamphlets and letters from the 1830s wave are Francis Henry Goldsmid, *The Arguments Advanced against the Enfranchisement of the Jews. Considered in a Series of Letters* (London: Colburn and Bentley, 1831); John E. Blunt, *A History of the Establishment and Residence of the Jews in England; with an Enquiry into their Civil Disabilities* (London: Saunders and Benning, 1830); Arthur Lumley Davids, "On the Emancipation of the Jews" (*Times*, May 6, 1831); Thomas Babington Macaulay, *Essay and Speech on Jewish Disabilities*, ed. Israel Abrahams (Edinburgh: Jewish Historical Society of England, 1909); Apsley Pellat, *Brief Memoir of the Jews in Relation to Their Civil and Municipal Disabilities* (London: Hatchard and Son, 1829).

3. Robert Grant brought most of the motions for Jewish emancipation to the House floor. Macaulay, *Essay and Speech*, 44, responds to a "friend" in the House who asks "where are we to stop, if once you admit into the House of Commons people who deny the authority of the Gospels? Will you let in a Mussulman? Will you let in a Parsee? Will you let in a Hindoo, who worships a lump of stone with seven heads? I will answer my honourable friend's question by another. Where does he mean to stop? Is he ready to roast unbelievers at slow fires? . . . When once you enter upon a course of persecution, I defy you to find any reason for making a halt till you have reached the extreme point." He also compares Jewish emancipation to Catholic emancipation (54).

4. Thomas Carlyle, "The Jew Our Lawgiver" (London: Thomas Bosworth, 1853), 10–11.

5. See Michael Ragussis, "Writing Nationalist History: England, the Conversion of the Jews, and *Ivanhoe*," *ELH* 60, no. 1 (spring 1993): 181–215. Much of the following reading of *Ivanhoe* concurs with Ragussis, but while Ragussis focuses on the meaning of Scott for English national identity, this chapter focuses on its meaning for Anglo-Jewish identity, particularly for the identity of women.

6. For a discussion of the Romantic wandering motif, see my "Blake's 'firm perswasions': the Judaic and the Jew," a paper given at the 1990 Modern Language Association convention. Important sources include: William

Blake, *The Complete Poetry and Prose,* ed. David Erdman and Harold Bloom (New York: Doubleday, 1988); Edmund Burke, *Reflections on the Revolution in France in Two Classics of the French Revolution* (New York: Doubleday, 1989); George Gordon Byron, *Byron,* ed. Jerome J. McGann (Oxford: Oxford University Press, 1986) and *Hebrew Melodies* (London: J. Murray, 1815); Maria Edgeworth, *Harrington: Tales and Novels,* vol. 9 (London: G. Routledge, 1893); Walter Scott, *Ivanhoe* (New York: New American Library, 1983); Thomas Carlyle, *Sartor Resartus,* ed. Charles Frederick Harrold (New York: Odyssey Press, 1937) and "The Jew Our Lawgiver"; Samuel Taylor Coleridge, "The Rime of the Ancient Mariner," in *English Romantic Writers,* ed. David Perkins (New York: Harcourt Brace Jovanovich, 1967), 404–13; Charles Dickens, *Oliver Twist* (New York: New American Library, 1980) and *Our Mutual Friend* (Oxford: Oxford University Press, 1989); Henry Mayhew, *London Labour and the London Poor,* 4 vols. (1861–62; reprint, New York: Dover, 1968).

7. The character of Shylock was undergoing a transformation on the stage at this time to make him seem more sympathetic. Professor Judith Rosen at UCLA pointed out to me that as late as 1891 this was still the case. The actress Lady Helena Faucit Martin, in her essays *On Some of Shakespeare's Female Characters* (London: Blackwood and Sons, 1891), rewrote *Merchant* so that Portia nurses Shylock at the end and persuades him to convert.

8. For critical discussions of the stereotypes see Bryan Cheyette, *Constructions of "the Jew" in English Literature and Society: Racial Representations, 1875–1945* (Cambridge: Cambridge University Press, 1993); Edgar Rosenberg, *From Shylock to Svengali: Jewish Stereotypes in English Fiction* (Stanford: Stanford University Press, 1960); Harold Fisch, *The Dual Image* (London: Lincolns-Prager, 1959); Lauriat Lane, Jr., "Dickens' Archetypal Jew," *PMLA* 73 (Mar. 1958): 95–101; Montagu Frank Modder, *The Jew in the Literature of England: To the End of the Nineteenth Century* (New York: Meridian Books, 1960); Joseph Gaer, *The Legend of the Wandering Jew* (New York: Mentor, 1961). See Anita Norich, "Jewish Family Images in the English Novel," in *The Jewish Family: Myths and Reality,* ed. Steven M. Cohen and Paula E. Hyman (New York: Holmes and Meier, 1986), 99–109. For a critique of the critical method of cataloguing stereotypes, see Michael Ragussis, *Figures of Conversion: "the Jewish Question" and English National Identity* (Durham, N.C.: Duke University Press, 1995). Also, see David Biale, *Eros and the Jews* (New York: BasicBooks, 1992), esp. 149–75.

9. Amy Levy, "The Jew in Fiction," *JC,* June 4, 1886. Also see the *Jewish Chronicle*'s obituary of Dickens, June 17, 1870, in which the editor refers to Fagin as "the unreal character" and Riah as "the beautiful, even if equally unreal, character."

10. Levy, "Jew in Fiction."
11. See Harry Stone, "Dickens and the Jews," *Victorian Studies* 11 (Mar. 1959): 223–53.
12. "Mr. Charles Dickens' Readings," *JC,* Nov. 27, 1868—he removed *Oliver Twist* from the scheduled program on Jan. 1, 1869.
13. In the 1880s, Scott's novel still loomed to Jews as the most influential representation of the century. See Levy, "Jew in Fiction": "Rebecca of York, with her hopeless love for the Gentile knight, and Isaac of York, divided, like Shylock, between his ducats and his daughter, remain to day the typical Hebrews of fiction."
14. Gillian Beer, *The Romance* (London: Methuen, 1970), 13. Subsequent references will be cited parenthetically in the text.
15. Other Victorian romances stitched in this pattern are *Jane Eyre* (1847), and in a slightly different way, *Wuthering Heights* (1847) and *Great Expectations* (1861), though in these, it is the man who hales from the marginalized group (gypsies or the working class, respectively). Hardy's *Tess of the D'Urbervilles* (1891) plays on the pattern in order to undermine it. In late-twentieth-century American culture, the pattern is still prevalent in Harlequin romance novels, such as Karen Percy's *In Too Deep* (Toronto: Harlequin Books, 1991), in which the wealthy Joanne Stephenson falls desperately in love with Mike Balthazar, the burly working-class man who comes to build her swimming pool.
16. Also see Michael McKeon, *The Origins of the English Novel, 1600–1740* (Baltimore: Johns Hopkins University Press, 1987), 318–37, who argues that the first "Protestant narratives," such as Defoe's *Robinson Crusoe,* leave behind the more obviously Christian romance narrative, with its allegorized types. But though Victorians may indeed have understood realism to be "progressive" in contrast to romance, the "progressive narrative" of the novel was not necessarily any more politically progressive for Jews than the romance. In the movement from romance to realism, the fantasy of erasing prejudicial barriers between different groups—one dominant, one marginal—through intermarriage yields to the fantasy of regulating the barriers that actually existed between members of different groups. As Beer in *Romance* puts it, the opposition between romance and realism was seen "in terms of a contrast . . . between the *individualism* of romance and the inexorable processes of society" (74). In terms of the non-Jewish fiction of Jewish identity, the romance fantasy of a Christian man falling in love with a Jewish woman—the plot of *Ivanhoe,* which cannot be consummated and ends in exile—is eventually brought to consummation through the woman's conversion in the philo-Semitic romances of M. G. Lewis, Thackeray, Bulwer Lytton, and others. But when romance gives way to realism, this conversionist plot of love between Jew and Christian gives way, in *Daniel*

Deronda, to the denial of love between Jew and Christian, the denial of the romance of the title character and Gwendolyn Harleth. The intermarriage fantasy of romance gives way to a "realist" fantasy that the Jew will choose exile with his aesthetic Jewess (Mirah is compared to a picture by Titian) to some unspoken place in the East. The Jew and Jewess are reorientalized. In this way the Christian novel of Jewish identity in the early and mid-Victorian periods begins and ends with Eastern exile, with the romance fantasy of consummation and conversion intervening. The century moves from an unattainable desire for eradication of barriers in Scott (and exile to Granada) to a self-chosen maintenance of barriers in Eliot. In the movement from romance to realism, Jews' options, apostasy or exile, remain limited.

17. See Jerome Mitchell, *Scott, Chaucer, and Medieval Romance* (Kentucky: Kentucky University Press, 1987), 514; Cecil Roth, *Magna Bibliotheca Anglo-Judaica: A Bibliographical Guide to Anglo-Jewish History* (London: Jewish Historical Society of England, 1937).

18. Scott, *Ivanhoe,* 403. Subsequent references will be cited parenthetically within the text.

19. The orientalization of the Jewish woman was an old trope, which Jewish women themselves constantly drew upon. For a history of the trope, see Livia Bitton-Jackson, *Madonna or Courtesan? the Jewish Woman in Christian Literature* (New York: Seabury Press, 1982), 19.

20. A biography of Gratz appears in Baum, Hyman and Michel, *Jewish Woman in America,* 30, 36–38. Also see Ellen Umansky and Dianne Ashton, eds., *Four Centuries of Jewish Women's Spirituality* (Boston: Beacon Press, 1992), 6–7, 83–85.

21. Contemporary reviewers, including Scott himself, noted historical inaccuracies in his treatment of Jews, whether in the amount of toleration, or various details, but justified them. Some later reviewers have done the same. See A. S. G. Canning, *History in Scott's Novels* (1907). Patricia Christine Hodgell, "The Nonsense of Ancient Days: Sources of Scott's 'Ivanhoe' " (Ph.D. diss., University of Minnesota, 1987), says Scott has "a very cavalier attitude toward historical facts." But the trend in most recent *Ivanhoe* criticism has been not to speak of the Jewish aspect of it at all, and sometimes to indicate a belief in Scott's realistic portrayal of Rebecca. See Mitchell, *Scott, Chaucer,* 133, who says that "Rebecca is Scott's most memorable dark-lady type," and that her "love for Ivanhoe must go unrequited" because "she could never have given up her religion." A more positive reading of Scott's historical fiction can be found in James Kerr, *Fiction against History: Scott as Storyteller* (Cambridge: Cambridge University Press, 1989): "the mixed genre of historical romance becomes a field in which perceived contradictions in history can be recreated and resolved. It is a zone of freedom . . . , the limits of which

are prescribed by the taleteller's imagination, where the ugly facts history throws in the way of the writer can be made into appealing, or at least consoling, stories about the past" (1–2).

22. This is perhaps another version of the argument Michael Ragussis makes in "Representation, Conversion, and Literary Form" in which he asserts that comedy's master trope is conversion and that the Jew's conversion literalizes the trope and thereby politicizes it. In Scott's version, romance's master trope is chivalry—but Rebecca cannot accept the terms of chivalry because she is a Jew: her very presence calls romance's master trope into question. This reading differs from Ruth Eller, "The Poetic Theme in Scott's Novels," in *Scott and His Influence,* ed. J. H. Alexander (Aberdeen: Association for Scottish Literature Studies, 1983), 81, who says of Rebecca's relating the battle at Torquilstone to Ivanhoe, that Rebecca is "an outsider, who can set in perspective the chivalric code which Ivanhoe takes for granted."

23. Walter Scott, *Ivanhoe, with Critical Appreciations, Old and New,* ed. G. K. Chesterton et al. (Cambridge: Cambridge University Press, 1919), 52.

24. James Anderson, *Sir Walter Scott and History* (Edinburgh: Edina Press, 1981) essentially agrees with this when he says that "The immense superiority of the Jewess Rebecca may be traced" to the fact that "she is really the representative in England of Mohammedan civilization" with "her Eastern unguent" (97). The sensual "noble savage" as described in European and American romances about American Indians is also relevant here.

25. "To Our Readers," the opening article of *JHer* 1, no. 1 (1846): 1 states the Society's aims: "to show the claims which the ancient people of God have on the sympathy and prayers of the Church, to diffuse information with regard to their present circumstances, both in England and elsewhere, and to record the progress of the different efforts which are made for their conversion to Christianity." Features in this and other similar periodicals included "Intelligence" reports on the conversion meetings held and missionary work, population statistics to gauge the extent of work to be done, strategies for conversion ("Aim at the parish church in every such community, and propose a special service for the evangelising of Jews. The time, the language in which to make your appeal must be wisely and carefully settled. Raise a special fund") *HCW* 1, no. 6 (1872): 83, anthropological descriptions of Jews' festivals and customs, reports of developments in the Jewish press and within the Jewish community (particularly the advent of Reform, hailed "as an indication of coming light") *JHer* 1, no. 4 (1846): 83, narratives of conversions as role models for conversionists in the field, poems by and to Jewish women, reviews of writing by Jewish women, criticism of the Jewish press for putting down Hebrew Christians, and "Historical Notices of the Wandering Jew."

26. Todd Endelman, *Radical Assimilation in English Jewish History 1656–1945* (Bloomington: Indiana University Press, 1990), 147.
27. Rev. John Harding, "Mercy for Israel, a sermon preached on behalf of the London Society for the Promotion of Christianity amongst the Jews," *Jewish Tracts* (British Museum, 1866).
28. Endelman, *Radical Assimilation*, 147–49. Endelman notes that the London Society was unlikely to appeal to wealthy would-be converts, given its reputation for working with the poor. Charlotte Montefiore provides a scathing contemporary satire of the society, questioning its motivations and methods, in *Caleb Asher* (Philadelphia: Jewish Publication Society, 1845).
29. *IW,* Mar., 1877: 42.
30. Amelia Bristow, *Rosette and Miriam: or the Twin Sisters: A Jewish Narrative of the Eighteenth Century* (London: Charles Tilt, 1837), 30. Eliphalette is the name of one of David's daughters among the children he had after he had established Jerusalem as his capital city (2 Sam. 5:16). The name does not appear to have been in use among Victorian Jews. Bristow's choice of an obscure biblical name for the Jewish woman suggests the conversionist myth that biblical Jews, not having rejected Christ, were still regenerate. For a more famous example of this idea from an ostensibly different perspective, see Eliot's depiction of Mordecai's biblical speech patterns in *Daniel Deronda*—the logic seems to be, the more easily a Jew can be identified with the prerabbinic Judaism of the Bible, the more redeemable the Jew is.
31. Bristow, *Rosette and Miriam,* 279.
32. J. K. S., review of *Spirit of Judaism* by Grace Aguilar, *JHer* 2, no. 13 (1847): 28–41. Also see Marion Moss, "Lines Written by Marion Moss, A Jewess, after attending service in a Christian Chapel, Mar. 1845," *JHer* 1, no. 2 (1845): 48.
33. J. K. S., review of *Spirit of Judaism,* 39. Also see the review of *Jewish Faith,* by Grace Aguilar, *HJ* 1 (Feb. 6, 1847): 84, "We see in it how the grand, simple faith of the ancient people of God is unfolding itself in the light of advancing intelligence; how all that was understood by them in their first ages as temporal, is becoming spiritual; all that was exclusive, widening out into universality; how they are reading their Law and their Prophets in the spirit of Him who 'revealed the Father' to us; and who in emphatic words declared that He came 'not to destroy the law, but to fulfil it.' While enlightened Judaism thus advances, we see in the progress of events the spirit of Christianity purifying the doctrines adopted by its professors, exterminating the dark errors of the times of persecution and hatred." It is significant that such a philo-Semitic statement appears in a nonmissionary journal; it suggests that philo-Semitism was mainstream.
34. *IW,* Mar., 1877: 43.
35. See Ragussis, "Representation, Conversion."

36. Götthold Ephraim Lessing, *Nathan the Wise*, trans. Bayard Quincy Morgan (New York: Continuum, 1988); Edgeworth, *Harrington*, vol. 9. For post-Scott conversionist novels, see William Makepeace Thackeray, "Rebecca and Rowena," in *Burlesques* (Boston: Houghton, Mifflin, 1895), 305–66; Edward Bulwer Lytton, *Leila, or the Siege of Granada* (London: George Routledge and Sons, 1875); M. G. Lewis, *The Jewish Maiden*, 4 vols. (London: A. K. Newman, 1830); Bristow, *Rosette and Miriam.*

37. Hereafter, all references to Lewis, *Jewish Maiden*, will be made parenthetically in the text, by volume and page number.

38. For similar discussions of this dynamic in the British colonialist context, see Said, *Orientalism*, 207: "The Oriental was linked . . . to elements in Western society (delinquents, the insane, women, the poor) having in common an identity best described as lamentably alien. Orientals . . . were seen through, analyzed not as citizens, or even people, but as problems to be solved or confined. . . . Since the Oriental was a member of a subject race, he had to be subjected. . . . [W]omen are usually the creatures of a male power-fantasy. They express unlimited sensuality, they are more or less stupid, and above all they are willing." See also Bitton-Jackson, *Madonna or Courtesan?* For a wide-ranging set of essays on minority discourse, also see *Cultural Critique*, ed. David Lloyd and Abdul JanMohammed, (spring–fall): 1987.

39. Beer, *Romance*, has shown that all these forms of romance have a common historical source.

40. For another example, see Bristow, *Rosette and Miriam*, where the condescension reaches unbearable heights: "It will be seen . . . how deep is the darkness which envelopes Israel. . . . Oh that every Christian bosom may be touched with pity . . . to remove that awful darkness!—Gentile Christians! . . . pity your exiled, dispersed, and despised elder brethren!" (76).

41. See Grace Aguilar, dedication to "Adah, A Simple Story," 1838, Grace Aguilar MSS, where she argues that Scott's Rebecca is the most positive role model she has ever read about in non-Jewish writings.

42. For a Lacanian take on the mother's absence in Western culture, see Margaret Homans, *Bearing the Word: Language and Female Experience in Nineteenth-Century Women's Writing* (Chicago: University of Chicago Press, 1986). Deborah Hertz, in *Jewish High Society in Old Regime Berlin* (New Haven: Yale University Press, 1988), 204–50, and "Emancipation through Intermarriage in Old Berlin," in *Jewish Women in Historical Perspective*, ed. Judith Baskin (Detroit: Wayne State University Press, 1991), 182–201, shows that for a tiny proportion of wealthy young Jewish women in Berlin at the end of the eighteenth century, intermarriage and social integration via conversion were possible, but women with less wealth could not use conversion as an end. By contrast, English conversionism was directed toward the poor and the middle classes. Another

point of contrast between English and German conversionism: most converts among the salonières had already been married to Jewish men through an arranged marriage and had divorced them before converting to marry gentile men in what appear to be companionate marriages (*Jewish High Society*, 156–203). English conversionists, on the other hand, depict Jewish women abandoning their families (particularly their fathers) for a companionate marriage with a gentile the first time around.

CHAPTER 2

1. Proverbs 31 was a standard passage for such defenses of Judaism's attitude toward women at the time. See Charlotte Montefiore's exposition of the same passage in *A Few Words to the Jews. By One of Themselves* (London: John Chapman, 1855), chap. 7, 161–68; also Grace Aguilar's tombstone bears the epithet from Proverbs 31, "Give her of the fruit of her hands, and let her own works praise her in the gates," according to Rachel Beth Zion Lask Abrahams, "Grace Aguilar: A Centenary Tribute," *Transactions of the Jewish Historical Society of England* 16 (1952): 137–48.

2. The Jewish notion is both similar to and different from the Victorian Christian separation of spheres. See Nancy Armstrong, *Desire and Domestic Fiction: A Political History of the Novel* (New York: Oxford University Press, 1987), 18. Differences will be described in text.

3. Jacob A. Franklin, "Position of Israel's Women," *VoJ*, Sept. 25, 1846. In a review of *Spirit of Judaism*, by Grace Aguilar, *VoJ*, Apr. 1, 1842, the editor had argued that she had "occasionally exaggerated apprehensions of the success of those who would apostasize us." Perhaps his view of Sephardic women's constancy in the Inquisition informs this position—but it seems to me Aguilar could respond that he was not on the brunt end of much of the conversionists' efforts.

4. See Isaac D'Israeli, *Genius of Judaism* (London: Edward Moxon, 1833), 170–73.

5. Jacob A. Franklin, "Women and Judaism," *VoJ*, Apr. 9, 1847. In contrast to the editor's view, the Jewish feminist translator Marcia Falk, in the preface to *The Song of Songs: A New Translation and Interpretation* (San Francisco: Harper, 1990), xiv, argues that the *Song* is really a collection of love poems in many distinct voices, that it does not narrate a single passionate affair between two lovers.

6. Jacob A. Franklin, "Israel's Women," *VoJ*, Dec. 4, 1846.

7. See Rachel Biale, *Women and Jewish Law* (New York: Schocken Books, 1984): "The life of any traditional Jew, whether a man or a woman, is

guided, even dictated, by the *mitzvot* (the commandments). The *mitzvot* encompass almost all conceivable spheres of human activity, and through prohibitions and prescriptions fashion private and public Jewish life, often down to the most minute details" (11).

8. Charlotte Baum, Paula Hyman, and Sonya Michel trace a similar motivation for the American reform movement's outreach to women in *The Jewish Woman in America* (New York: Dial Press, 1976), 17–34. The *locus classicus* of the mainstream Victorian separation of spheres is John Ruskin, "Of Queens' Gardens," in *The Literary Criticism of John Ruskin,* ed. Harold Bloom (New York: Da Capo Press, 1965), 182–213.

9. Billie Melman speaks of the effects of Evangelicalism on the gender coding of religion in "Evangelical Travel and the Evangelical Construction of Gender," in *Women's Orients: English Women and the Middle East, 1718–1918* (Ann Arbor: University of Michigan Press, 1992), 166.

10. B. H. A., "On the Necessity of the Religious Instruction of Females," *HRJ,* Nov. 2–Dec. 9, 1859.

11. Ibid.

12. David Sorkin, *The Transformation of German Jewry, 1740–1880* (New York: Oxford University Press, 1987), cites a similar shift in German-Jewish attitudes.

13. A new selective reading of Proverbs 31 is developed by the Victorians, still pointing to her role in the home, but now deemphasizing her role in the marketplace and bringing into relief her special charitable role among the poor: "she stretcheth out her hand to the poor; yea, she reacheth forth her hands to the needy." Proverbs 31 turns out to be a flexible document.

14. *JC,* May 5, 1865. For a more thorough discussion of the traditionalist position, see my reading of Nathan Meritor's scathing critique of Jewish women's education in *The Hasty Marriage; A Sketch of Modern Jewish Life* (London: Mann Nephews, 1857), to follow.

15. "Social Condition of Jewish Females," *VoJ,* Apr. 1, 1842.

16. This was also a central point of the German-Jewish reform movement, as Philip M. Weinberger points out in his discussion of Abraham Geiger in "The Social and Religious Thought of Grace Aguilar (1816–1847)" (Ph.D. diss., New York University, 1970). Indeed, German-Jewish reformers may have been more likely to provide their daughters with a privately tutored education, if the evidence of salonières like Dorothea Veit (daughter of Moses Mendelssohn) and Henriette Herz is any indication. See Deborah Hertz, *Jewish High Society in Old Regime Berlin* (New Haven: Yale University Press, 1988), 172–75.

17. Nehemiah 8:2–3: "And Ezra the priest brought the law before the congregation both of men and women, and all that could hear with understanding. . . . And he read therein . . . before the men and the women, and

those that could understand; and the ears of all the people were attentive unto the book of the law."

18. David Woolf Marks, *Sermons Preached on Various Occasions at the West London Synagogue of British Jews* 4 vols. (London: R. Groombridge and Sons, 1851), esp. vol. 1.

19. Abraham Benisch, review of "Imrei Lev" by Hester Rothschild, *JC*, August 1, 1856.

20. In this, reformers were similar to their German-Jewish brethren. See Marion A. Kaplan, "Tradition and Transition: Jewish Women in Imperial Germany," in *Jewish Women in Historical Perspective,* ed. Judith Baskin (Detroit: Wayne State University Press, 1991), 211.

21. The list first appeared Aug. 6, 1858; it was subsequently reprinted three times: Oct. 12, 1860; Mar. 1, 1867; Feb. 18, 1887. "Our Communal Weekly Gossip" appears on Oct. 26, 1860.

22. Michaelis Silberstein, "The Women of Israel," *JC,* Apr. 2, 1852. For a similar sentiment among German-Jewish men, see Kaplan, "Tradition and Transition," 213.

23. Indeed, at the end of the period, one M. Gaster wrote "Jewish Sources of and Parallels to the Early English Metrical Romances of King Arthur and Merlin" and *Papers Read at the Anglo-Jewish Historical Exhibition, Royal Albert Hall* (London: Jewish Chronicle, 1888), proving that Arthur is based on King David and that Merlin is based on the Talmudic tale of Solomon and Ashmedai. "This new epical literature soon conquered Europe, and brought about a great change in social life, through the spirit of refined chivalry it breathed. . . . Fairies, and all that is akin to them, appeared for the first time; the exaggerated fantastic worship of women; in one word, romantic fiction came into the world." Perhaps the great change in social life is the change in Jewish men, who at first disclaimed chivalry absolutely and here claim to have invented it.

24. "Our Women," *JC,* Nov. 8, 1861.

25. The debate around the divinity of the Talmud and of subsequent rabbinical commentaries was at the heart of the reform movement. An enormous conflict took place in the 1840s and 1850s over the question of whether the Oral Law was divine or human made. See Cecil Roth, *Magna Bibliotheca Anglo-Judaica: A Bibliographical Guide to Anglo-Jewish History* (London: Jewish Historical Society of England, 1937) for examples.

26. "On the Education of Israelitish Girls," *JC,* Apr. 18, 1862.

27. Feminist Jews are debating the same issue today. Judith Plaskow, *Standing Again at Sinai: Judaism from a Feminist Perspective* (San Francisco: Harper Collins, 1990), asks: "are there feminist reasons why law . . . should or should not be a central religious category in a feminist Judaism? What considerations are relevant to the question of whether, when

'women add our voices to tradition, halakhah will be our medium of expression and repair?' " (61).

28. Quoted in Diane Lichtenstein, *Writing Their Nations: The Tradition of Nineteenth-Century American Jewish Women Writers* (Bloomington: Indiana University Press, 1992), 27.

29. Grace Aguilar, *The Spirit of Judaism,* ed. Isaac Leeser, 3d ed. (Philadelphia, 1864), 6. For a biography of Leeser, see Maxwell Whiteman, "Isaac Leeser and the Jews of Philadelphia: A Study in National Jewish Influence," in Abraham J. Karp, ed., *The Jewish Experience in America III: The Emerging Community* (New York: KTAV Publishing House, 1969), 27–62.

30. See *JA,* 209. See *JHer* 2, no. 13 (1847): 39.

31. Abrahams, "Grace Aguilar," says the episode "makes it all the easier for us to observe Grace Aguilar's straining at the leash of traditional or Rabbinical Judaism with Leeser pulling her back time and again" (142). Weinberger, "Religious Thought of Grace Aguilar," views this episode in a different light, suggesting that Leeser "rid Miss A. of her misunderstandings about certain aspects of tradition, Jewish tolerance, consistency, and ideals" (39). In his view, their work on *Spirit of Judaism* was "a collaboration," though it is difficult to see how both benefited from the exchange. Weinberger argues that Aguilar's thought changed because of Leeser's editorial criticisms on her views of Moses, the Oral Law, need of an English Bible, free vs. fixed prayer, Judaism's attitude toward Christianity, and other issues. This would seem to me to argue both that Aguilar learned something and that the censorship was effective. A certain range of experience—that of a middle-class reformist Jewish woman who was an avid reader—was systematically altered to fit a traditionalist line.

32. The effect of translation on women's educational options will be discussed more fully in chap. 4.

33. "Notice for *Jewish Sabbath Journal,*" *JC,* July 7, 1854.

34. *JC,* Aug.–Oct., 1854.

35. Tribute, Ladies of the Society for the Religious Instruction of Jewish Youth, Charleston, South Carolina, Nov. 23, 1847, Grace Aguilar MSS.

36. This apathy was a characteristic feature of all new literary pursuits in the community, including such men's projects as the Jews' and General Literary and Scientific Institution, and was yearly bewailed by Benisch in his annual retrospective. See the lead article, *JC,* May 28, 1869: "Jewish literature has been too long and too needlessly neglected in England. The generation which has at this epoch attained maturity has . . . shown too little regard for the monumental intellect of its ancestry."

37. Marion Hartog, letter, *JC,* Nov. 17, 1854.

38. See "To My Daughter, aged 6 years teaching her little brother to Pray": "O ever let him learn from thee/Such lessons of holy truth," *JC,* Nov. 24, 1854.

39. Linda Gordon Kuzmack, *Woman's Cause: The Jewish Woman's Movement in England and the United States, 1881–1933* (Columbus: Ohio State University Press), 1990, has argued that Rosa Sonneschein's *American Jewess,* which first appeared in 1895, was the first Jewish women's periodical. Presumably, the *Jewish Sabbath Journal* was unfamiliar to her.

40. Marion Hartog, *JSJ,* Mar. 22, 1855.

41. See Ruth, "Zillah," *JSJ,* Apr. 19, 1855. See A Lady of the Jewish Faith, "A Lesson for the Israelites," *JSJ,* Apr. 11, 1855. See Marion Hartog, "Hannah Rosenheim," *JSJ,* June 8, 1855.

42. See *JSJ,* Apr. 4, 1855: "Stella—Your tale has some pretty incidents, but is too disjointed. Do not be discouraged; try again, and most likely you will succeed better." She uses the correspondence section to communicate directly with submitters and readers.

43. *JSJ,* Mar. 22, 1855: "We have much gratification in informing you, that the Rev. Chief Rabbi has personally expressed to us his entire approbation of the Sabbath Journal and its objects."

44. A biographical sketch of Marion Hartog, which appeared on the Golden Anniversary of her marriage to Alphonse, *JC,* Aug. 23, 1895, gave somewhat different reasons for the end of her career: "She . . . tried to combine her literary and scholastic pursuits by editing the *Jewish Sabbath Journal,* but cares of her school and her young and growing family absorbed all her time. She was ambitious to train up a set of high-minded girls and boys who should be ornaments to the nation from which they sprang, and who, by their culture, refinement, and enthusiastic love of the good and the beautiful, would be known as 'Madame Hartog's pupils' wherever they were to be met. To this aim she devoted her life. It was a choice between her literary ambition and the still nobler one, and she chose the latter, and so we find her soon giving up the *Sabbath Journal* and devoting herself to her pupils and children." The biographer omits the debacle with Benisch and places Hartog's motivations back in the realm of the ideologically dominant—the realm of the moral governess choosing her proper sphere over the male sphere of "literary ambition."

45. *JC,* Apr. 11, 1856.

46. *JC,* May 5, 1871.

47. *JC,* Jan. 1, 1864.

48. "Faith and Its Influence on Women," *JC,* Mar. 12, 1875. Grace Aguilar responded directly to the question of whether women's participation in the public sphere (the mind) was consistent with refinement of the heart in "The Authoress," *Home Scenes and Heart Studies* (London: G. Routledge and Sons, 1894), 243: her heroine, Clara Stanley, proves "to the full how very possible it is for woman to unite" literary pursuits in the public sphere with domesticity in the private sphere.

49. *JC*, Jan. 15, 1875.
50. *JC*, Feb. 25, 1876.
51. See "Jewish Literature in England," *HRJ*, June 29, 1860. Also see Michael McKeon, *The Origins of the English Novel, 1600–1740* (Baltimore: Johns Hopkins University Press, 1987), esp. chaps. 1–3.
52. "The Memory of Arthur Lumley Davids," *HRR* 1 (1834): 145–52.
53. See David Woolf Marks and Rev. A. Lowy, *Memoir of Sir Francis Henry Goldsmid*, ed. Louisa Goldsmid, 2d ed. (London: Kegan Paul, Trench, 1882). Isaac founded the Association for Removing Civil Disabilities. Francis wrote several emancipationist pamphlets, became the first Jew called to the Bar, and founded the first Reform synagogue in England.
54. *VoJ*, Apr. 12, 1844, Nov. 7, 1845.
55. *JC*, Aug. 10, 1855.
56. *JC*, lead article, Mar. 8, 1850. Also see Hertz Ben Pinchas, "Encouragement of Literature among the Jews," *JC*, Mar. 27, 1850; lead article, "Jewish Literary Society," *JC*, May 31, 1850; lead article, "Progress of Literature Among the Jews," *JC*, Oct. 18, 1850. Only the last mentioned article includes women writers among its concerns.
57. For a reading of Disraeli's theories of Jewish racial superiority, see Michael Ragussis, "The Birth of a Nation in Victorian Culture: The Spanish Inquisition, the Converted Daughter, and the 'Secret Race,'" *Critical Inquiry* (spring 1994): 493–95.
58. For a history of the break, see James Picciotto, *Sketches of Anglo-Jewish History* (London: Trubner, 1875).
59. Isaac D'Israeli, *Works, with a view of the life and writings of the author, by his son, the Right Hon. B. Disraeli* (New York: A. C. Armstrong and Son, 1881), 2:33.
60. D'Israeli, *Genius of Judaism*. Subsequent references will be cited by page number parenthetically in the text. For some reason, this volume is not included in his son's edition of his *Works*.
61. Philip Abraham, *Curiosities of Judaism, Facts, Opinions, Anecdotes, and Remarks Relative to the Hebrew Nation* (London: Wertheimer, Lea, 1879).
62. Benjamin Disraeli, *Alroy and Ixion* (London: Longmans, Green, 1846); and *Tancred, or, The New Crusade* (London: Longmans, Green, 1880).
63. Sarah Bradford, *Disraeli* (New York: Stein and Day, 1982), chap. 1.
64. See "Earl Beaconsfield," lead article, *JC*, Aug. 18, 1876. Five years earlier, an article acknowledged that earlier generations of English Jews had criticized Disraeli, but championed him for having "honoured the race from which he sprung. . . . He did for us Jews what we Jews had not the courage or intelligence or perhaps the opportunity to do for ourselves— he lifted the veil which concealed our glorious past from our worldly present" (*JC*, Aug. 11, 1871). While claiming a connection, this still asserts a distance. The recuperation took some time.

65. See Joseph Heinemann, "The Nature of the Aggadah," and Judah Goldin, "Freedom and Restraint of Haggadah," in *Midrash and Literature,* ed. Geoffrey H. Hartmann and Sanford Budick (New Haven: Yale University Press, 1986), 41–76.

66. "The Sun and the Moon," *HRR* 2, (1835): 41–42.

67. Louis Ginzberg, *Legends of the Jews* 7 vols. (Philadelphia: Jewish Publication Society of America, 1928–66), 5:34, 36; 1:23–24. See also Grace Aguilar's use and revision of this legend, "The Spirit of Night," in *Home Scenes,* 369–74.

68. *JC,* Mar. 22, 1861.

69. See the phenomenal cross-cultural lifework of Wilbur Owen Sypherd, *Jephthah and His Daughter: A Study in Comparative Literature* (Newark: University of Delaware, 1948), which covers virtually every reference to the story from antiquity to the 1950s, anywhere in the world. It shows that there was an explosion of references in England in the nineteenth century.

70. "Heroism of Jeptha's Daughter," *JC,* July 29, 1864. Also, the tale appeared five years later in a poetic rendition as "Jephtha's Daughter," *JC,* Jan. 1, 1869. For other contemporary versions of the story, see Lord Byron, "Jephtha's Daughter," in *Hebrew Melodies* (London: J. Murray, 1815), 13–14, a remarkable poem, written in the daughter's voice. See Celia and Marion Moss, "The Slave," *Romance of Jewish History,* 3 vols. (London: A. K. Newman, 1843), 135, in which the floor of the queen's chamber is decorated by a "carpet, worked in various colours, with the spectacle of Jeptha sacrificing his daughter." Later, a murder is very nearly committed on the carpet.

71. *JC,* Apr. 21, 1871.

72. Matthias Levy [Nathan Meritor], *The Hasty Marriage; A Sketch of Modern Jewish Life* (London: Mann Nephews, 1857), 41. All subsequent references will be made parenthetically in the text.

73. See Maria Polack, *Fiction without Romance; or, the Locket-Watch,* 2 vols. (London, 1830): her heroine Eliza Desbro receives a proposal from a man she does not love, but "she was not so romantic, as to suppose there could be no happiness for her, independent of him" (2:85)—especially since by marrying him she can please her uncle. The antiromance replaces individualistic attachments with duty to family and community. Also see Judith Montefiore, *The Jewish Manual or Practical Information in Jewish and Modern Cookery,* intro. Chaim Raphael (New York: NightinGale Books, 1983), iii.

74. Steven S. Schwarzschild, "Aesthetics," in *Contemporary Jewish Religious Thought,* ed. Arthur A. Cohen and Paul Mendes-Flohr (New York: Charles Scribner's Sons, 1987), 1–6.

75. Celia and Marion Moss, dedication to *Romance.*

76. Polack, *Fiction without Romance,* 1:42.

77. "Cramped" was the word often chosen by English Jews to describe to non-Jews the damaging effects of generations of persecution. See Arthur Lumley Davids, "On the Emancipation of the Jews," letter to *The Times*, May 6, 1831: "he earnestly looked for the emancipation of the Jews, as the means of developing the cramped energies of that people." Bernard Van Oven, "Ought Baron de Rothschild to Sit in Parliament? An Imaginary Conversation between Judaeus and Amicus Nobilis" (London: Effingham Wilson, 1847), likewise uses the term "cramping" to describe the effects of persecution on Jews' industriousness and argues that "Jews should be allowed to develop their energies for their own and the public good" (14).

CHAPTER 3

1. In these public calls for increased female education, middle-class Anglo-Jewish women both resembled and differed from their German counterparts. As Marion A. Kaplan argues in *The Making of the Jewish Middle Class: Women, Family, and Identity in Imperial Germany* (New York: Oxford University Press, 1991), 42–57, for German-Jewish women of the 1890s as for Anglo-Jewish women of the 1850s, "motherhood was central to the definition of Jewish womanhood." And just as for the earlier generation of Anglo-Jewish women, the responsibility for child rearing and a child's moral education was central to the definition of Jewish motherhood. Both groups attempted to pass on middle-class notions of respectability to their children. But while Anglo-Jewish women desired and were expected to pass on Jewish religious knowledge and values, German-Jewish women were expected to pass on the value of self-education or cultivation called *Bildung* rather than religious knowledge. In this "secular" knowledge of Dickens, Scott, and Goethe, German-Jewish women were self-taught, so they did not feel the need to call for the extension of female education. Also, women in Germany were responsible for the "informal transmission of Judaism—affective, private, and personal, including foods, family, and hearth" (70–71) while Anglo-Jewish women seem to have been responsible also for introducing daughters and sons to Jewish texts. The greater existence of anti-Semitism in Germany than in England seems to have led German-Jewish mothers to downplay the elements of their education that were specifically Jewish. At the same time, German liberalism and emancipation lagged behind by about forty years. For a discussion of men's relation to *Bildung*, see George L. Mosse, *German Jews beyond Judaism* (Bloomington: Indiana University Press, 1985).

2. "Miss Abigail Lindon's Dictionary," *JC*, Apr. 3, 1846. Götthold Salomon, *Twelve Sermons Delivered in the New Temple of the Israelites, at Ham-*

burgh, trans. Anna Maria Goldsmid (London: John Murray, 1839). Goldsmid believes "that religious education can be best conducted at home" (iii) by "mothers, whose especial vocation it is, diligently and lovingly to foster true piety in the hearts of their children" (iii). Her argument is that female education is needed to fulfil maternal duties.

3. See Marion Hartog, "To the Reader," *JSJ,* Feb. 22, 1855: "Alone, at present, in this onerous undertaking, I hope soon to see myself surrounded by a band of friends and cooperators. Israel has gifted sons, and daughters too, with minds full of high and holy aspirations for the benefit of the rising generation. To these I appeal for aid" (1). Several men wrote, but by far the majority of contributors to the *Journal* were women.

4. *JC,* Apr. 11, 1856.

5. *VoJ,* July 2, 1847. "The Two Pictures" also appears in the *JSJ,* Apr. 19 to May 10, 1855.

6. See Celia and Marion Moss, dedication to *Romance of Jewish History,* 3 vols., 2nd ed. (London: A.K. Newman, 1843); and see Grace Aguilar, in the dedication to her third novel-length tale, "Adah, A Simple Story," 1838, Grace Aguilar MSS. Maria Polack responded to *Ivanhoe* with an antiromance, *Fiction without Romance; or, the Locket-Watch* (1830).

7. "Marion Hartog, from a Correspondent," *JC,* Aug. 23, 1895.

8. Ibid.; "Death of Marion Hartog," *JC,* Nov. 1, 1907. Numa Hartog, Marion's son, was a community hero for having won the seat of Senior Wrangler at Cambridge after challenging the University Tests Act. Her daughter, Helena Darmesteter, was a well-known portrait painter, and Marcus Hartog, her son, was known for scientific studies.

9. Celia Levetus, introduction to *The King's Physician and Other Tales* (Birmingham: T. Hinton, 1865).

10. Livia Bitton-Jackson, *Madonna or Courtesan? the Jewish Woman in Christian Literature* (New York: Seabury Press, 1982), 33.

11. Maria Polack, preface to *Fiction Without Romance; or, the Locket-Watch,* 2 vols. (London, 1830): "endeavoured, as much as possible, to keep within the limits of simplicity; for, were I to soar above the mediocrity of my power, my ignorance would soon be detected and despised. . . . I shall receive [criticism] as the wholesome chastisement which a judicious tutor bestows on the pupil whom he wishes to train towards proficiency."

12. See Sara Aguilar, "Memoir of Grace Aguilar," in Grace Aguilar, *The Vale of Cedars, or, the Martyr* (New York: D. Appleton and Company, 1851).

13. Salomon, preface to *Twelve Sermons,* trans. Anna Maria Goldsmid.

14. Celia and Marion Moss, dedication to *Romance.*

15. Ibid.

16. Celia and Marion Moss, preface to *Romance.*

17. For cramping as an emancipationist term, see intro., n. 35; and chap. 2, n. 76.

18. One could almost choose any of the tales to illustrate this point. In Levetus, "Jacob; a Tradition," *King's Physician,* Jacob's father has been taken prisoner by Ernest Von Adheim, Count of Wolfstein, for lending him money and requiring repayment. Jacob sets about trying to free him, a dangerous task both for himself and the community. He gets an audience with the duke, who agrees to send his guards to look for Jacob's father at Wolfstein's castle. The guards search but cannot find Jacob's father, and Jacob is about to be delivered to Wolfstein as a liar, but says the Shema and prays that his father's "spirit may reveal itself to me for one moment; so that I may know I die not accusing the innocent" (166). His prayer is granted: when he stamps his foot on the ground a secret trap door is sprung, revealing his father's dead body. Wolfstein is punished. Jacob settles down and "his descendants are still to be found, amongst whom his history is still told, with pride in his courage and filial piety" (167). The story of the search for the dead father is what is passed down here; a literary folk tradition replaces study of Torah.

19. Marion Moss, "The Twin Brothers of Nearda, A Tale of the Babylonian Jews," in *Tales of Jewish History,* by Celia and Marion Moss, 3 vols. (London: Miller and Field, 1843), 1:225. Subsequent references will be cited by volume and page number within the text.

20. See Bitton-Jackson, *Madonna or Courtesan?* esp. 69–80. Bitton-Jackson does not identify the characteristics of La Belle Juive as "oriental," but does remark that her "perfection of feminine beauty" was supposed to have originated "in the 'cradle of mankind'"—that is, the East. The fictional Jewish woman's "ultimate function without exception is that of dispensing love" (72), and like Mary Magdalene, she is the sensual woman redeemed. The Mosses adopt this tradition uncritically as romantic. It is one aspect of their assimilation.

21. This theme had been with the Mosses since they published *Early Efforts. A Volume of Poems By the Misses Moss, of the Hebrew Nation. Aged 18 and 16* (London: Whittaker, 1839), in such poems as "The Jewish Captive Song" and these lines from "The Conclusion" (144):

> 'Tis long since Judah's children sung
>   Their songs within a stranger-land;
> Too long her harp hath been unstrung,
>   Awakened by no minstrel hand.
>
> Tho' all unskill'd to strike the string,
>   Tho' all as yet unknown to fame,
> Scorn not the offering that we bring,
>   Though poor and lowly be the strain.

O do not spurn our untaught lay,
   Though clad in simple garb it seem;
For Judah's bards are pass'd away,
   And we are not what they have been.

22. Dorothy Mermin, *Godiva's Ride: Women of Letters in England, 1830–1880* (Bloomington: Indiana University Press, 1993), 108, points out that while religion could bind women to their father's authority, it could also "authorize resistance to patriarchal authority, including husbands' and fathers'," as it does here.

23. Also see Celia Moss, "The Pharisee, or, Judea Capta," in *Tales*, Moss, 2:203–3:186; discussion to follow in text.

24. See "Jewish Women's Work in Philanthropy and Education," *JC*, June 13, 1902, which says the Mosses produced "works on Jewish history . . . at a time when the literature on this subject was almost *terra incognita*." Grace Aguilar mined the one potential source, the renditions of Aggadot, or Talmudic apologues, to be found in Morris Raphall's periodical *HRR*. In particular, she chose to base two tales on Aggadot that focused on gender relations, rewriting the Aggadah's gender politics to her satisfaction—see chap. 4.

25. Marion Moss, "Malah, the Prophet's Daughter," in *Romance,* 317.

26. Celia and Marion Moss, preface to *Romance.* Also see Aguilar, preface to "Adah": "'I know but one Author,' you once said, 'whose portrait of a Jewess pleased me, and that was Sir Walter Scott. The modern tales in which that race is introduced, are written by Christians, who know nothing of, and are consequently prejudiced against them.' From the hour that observation was made Adah has been present to my imagination."

27. Perhaps the best contemporary statement of the function of these tales as exercises in self-definition can be found in the review of *King's Physician,* by Levetus, *JC,* Aug. 4, 1865. The reviewer first gives a historical overview of popular vernacular Jewish literature, directed toward unlettered men, women, and children, and then applies the notion of a vernacular Jewish literature to his own day:

> Although for centuries excluded from all participation in the movements of the nations among which the Jews lived, yet did they enjoy an inner life stirred up by powerful currents of its own. . . . Theology, science, and poetry were alike cultivated by them; but . . . these were generally treated in an idiom unintelligible to the unlettered among them and to women and children. . . . The mass only understood the language of the country, and the literature . . . had consequently to be presented to them in the vernacular; and such a literature every larger section of Israel possessed. *And even as this*

literature was the creation of a popular mind, so it was its reflection. . . . [I]n those countries in which Israel had entered the general human family no special literature was needed for it. The general national life also throbbed in its veins. *But what of those matters constituting Israel as a race and a creed, with a history, a mission, hopes, and aspirations of its own?* Israel's special life, which could no longer partake of the mental food of bygone ages, required savoury meat suitable to the new taste. And this savoury meat is now being prepared. Here are some morsels. . . . "The King's Physician" will meet with the approbation of those who feel the want of *that special Jewish literature tending to bring out the latent Jewish feeling, to foster and intensify it.* (emphasis added)

Although Linda Gertner Zatlin, *The Nineteenth-Century Anglo-Jewish Novel* (Boston: G. K. Hall, 1981), 40, claims the Mosses' work did not address a Jewish audience, this reviewer seems to feel otherwise.

28. Celia Moss, "The Slave," in *Romance,* 1: 128, 142.
29. Celia and Marion Moss, *Tales,* 2:280, 236.
30. Celia Moss, "Storming of the Rock," in *Romance,* 14. See also Levetus, "The Martyrs of Worms: A German Tale," *King's Physician,* in which the father is described as "of a despised and degraded nation, and although yet in the prime and vigour of life, the bowed head and stooping body of him who stood before the haughty noble showed a consciousness of humiliation and self-abasement" (85). Here the father is the very opposite of a tyrant—but in his humiliated state, still untrustworthy in time of crisis, as far as the daughter is concerned. From a sociological perspective, it might be possible to explain this emphasis on fathers' absence and powerlessness by suggesting that since fathers' major roles in the separation of spheres were outside the home, the daughters would have felt abandoned by them whose primary commitments were in the public rather than the private sphere. For a similar argument, see Kaplan, *Making of the Jewish Middle Class,* 53. An approach focused less on the effect of economic specialization within middle-class families in general and more on the effect of the Mosses' father's personality might suggest that his burning of their books indicated to his daughters that he could not be trusted to understand their emotional needs.
31. See in particular, Levetus, "Martyrs of Worms," *King's Physician,* 82–121. Zillah's father has been killed in a pogrom in Frankfort and she has been brought up by Judah, a wealthy Jew. In his crisis with the authorities she gives him her inheritance, saying, "Am I not . . . thy child? when the cruel people of Frankfort slew my father, didst thou not protect my mother and myself . . . ? and when I called for my father, didst thou not say, 'I will be thy father, poor or orphan?' and since that day have I not

been as a child to thee? have not I looked upon thee with the love and reverence I should have paid to the dead?' " In one after another of these tales, the biological father must be dead so that a truly loving father/daughter bond can be established by contract.

32. By contrast Zatlin, *Anglo-Jewish Novel,* claims that the Mosses' "weakly executed" (31) tales only address a non-Jewish audience and are purely "propaganda fiction" (40) without relevance to the Jews' own community. "Female Jews are always noble. . . . Noble Jews receive a temporal reward. The men conquer their enemies; the women are rescued" (32). This unrealistic propaganda fiction is characterized, Zatlin argues, by a "reliance on stereotypes, didacticism, and heavy-handed direct address" (4) and the characters lack a deep characterization. But to fault the tales for not conforming to the standards of novelistic realism is to fault them for achieving exactly what they set out to do. One must understand the development of their historical romance genre, with all its conventions, in its own rich soil, as a particularly Jewish female response to a particular set of historical conditions. Not to attempt this is to condescend to history and set a critic's own literary critical limits on the past. Besides being remarkable documents of early reform, written in a decade of Victorian women's leadership in reform (see *Joseph Kestner, Protest and Reform: The British Social Narrative by Women, 1827–1867* [Madison: University of Wisconsin Press, 1985]), many of these tales are immensely enjoyable.

33. See Gillian Beer, *The Romance* (London: Methuen, 1970), speaking of Don Quixote as the emblem of romance: "Don Quixote represents the idealization of the self, the refusal to doubt inner experience, the tendency to base any interpretation of the world upon personal will, imagination and desire, not upon an empirical and social consensus of experience" (42).

34. Marion Hartog, "Milcah: A Tale of the Spanish Jews in the Fifteenth Century," *JSJ,* Mar. 22, 1855.

35. For Jephtha's daughter, see chap. 2. This pattern of the self-controlled Jewish woman is reversed in portraits of Jewish women that appear at the end of the century. Zatlin, *Anglo-Jewish Novel,* argues that with respect to the novels of Mrs. Alfred Sidgwick, Samuel Gordon, and Isidore Ascher, their work "indicates the Jewish woman's need to control herself" (54). She has become a domineering social climber, busybody, and henpecker—the misogynist take on the "New Woman," in fact.

36. Celia Moss, "Gertrude, or, Clouds and Sunshine," *King's Physician,* 61. Subsequent references will appear in the text. Also see Aguilar, *Vale of Cedars,* in which the Jewish heroine, Marie Henrique Morales, never dares breathe her affection for Arthur Stanley the Christian Englishman but dutifully marries a Jewish man and dies for love.

37. Nina Auerbach, "Women on Women's Destiny: Maturity as Penance,"

Romantic Imprisonment: Women and Other Glorified Outcasts (New York: Columbia University Press, 1986), 84–85.

38. Examples of texts directed exclusively at Jewish audiences include Grace Aguilar, *Women of Israel,* 3 vols. (New York: D. Appleton, 1884); Marion Hartog's *Jewish Sabbath Journal*; and Charlotte Montefiore, *A Few Words to the Jews. By One of Themselves* (London: John Chapman, 1855).

39. See Zaire in Celia Moss, "The Storming of the Rock," *Romance,* who tells "those sweet tales of our people which none can tell so well as thou" (1:24). Rachael, in Celia Moss, "The Priest's Adopted," *Romance,* inspires the deformed grandson of a king to speak against his Babylonian oppressors by "pour[ing] into his eager ears the tales of past power and splendour of Judea" (2:26). Ramah, in Marion Moss, "The Promise; A Tale of the Restoration," *Romance,* has a "high and intellectual" forehead, and a "gifted and sensitive mind" (2:84). Mattathias, father of the Maccabees, in Celia Moss, "The Asmoneans," *Romance,* tells his daughter Imla that "I have instructed thee in all the truths of our blessed religion. I have taught thee to revere the will of the Almighty, and honour his laws" (2:134). Kesiah, in Celia Moss, "The Pharisee, or, Judea Capta," *Tales,* is a slave who is a "woman of strong understanding . . . who, while preserving a warm attachment to her native country and her own religion, had not disdained to adorn her mind with the beauties of Greek and Latin authors" (2:217). She teaches the children all she knows, and in the crisis of the narrative, she captures the traitor Elias, an orthodox man who would have betrayed her to the Romans.

40. In the Bible, Tamar is Absalom's sister. Abia seems to be Celia Moss's invention.

41. Celia Moss, "The Slave," *Romance* 1:132. See Grace Aguilar, "The Escape," in *Home Scenes and Heart Studies* (London: G. Routledge and Sons, 1894), 162–85, in which the heroine, Almah, cross-dresses as her husband's servant, the male Moor Hassan Ben Ahmed, in order to save her husband Alvar from death in the Inquisition. While Abia is rewarded for her adventure, the result of Almah's transvestism is much more ambiguous—first, because she dresses the part of a servant, and of a member of another race, and second, because as soon as Alvar is freed she basically is rendered unconscious for the duration of the tale.

42. Celia Moss, "The Asmoneans," *Romance,* 2:137–39.

43. If there is any doubt on this point, see Marion Moss's response to the conversionists in "Lines Written By Marion Moss, a Jewess after attending Service in a Christian Chapel," *JHer* 1, no. 2 (1846): 48.

44. The full story of the oath of abjuration is told in M. C. N. Salbstein, *Emancipation of the Jews in Britain: The Question of the Admission of the Jews to Parliament, 1828–1860* (Rutherford, N.J.: Fairleigh Dickinson Press, 1981).

45. Celia Moss, "The Slave," *Romance*, 1:67–68.
46. Levetus, "Gertrude; or Clouds and Sunshine," *King's Physician*, 59–80. Note the similarity to Charlotte Brontë's *Jane Eyre*, written approximately at the same time. Both texts attempt to offset women's powerlessness by disempowering the suitor, opening the way for what Sandra M. Gilbert and Susan Gubar call "the marriage of true minds," *The Madwoman in the Attic: The Woman Writer and the Nineteenth-Century Literary Imagination* (New Haven: Yale University Press, 1979), 371.
47. Celia Moss, "The Priest's Adopted," *Romance*, 23–25. Subsequent references will be cited parenthetically in the text.
48. Throughout their tales, the Mosses claim the "Eastern" quality of their Jewish female characters. It was a long-standing tradition of anti-Semitic discourse to orientalize the Jewish woman, but the Mosses seem to adopt that convention uncritically themselves.
49. For a brief history of the organization, see Aubrey Newman, *The Board of Deputies of British Jews, 1760–1985* (London: Valentine Mitchell, 1987).
50. Kaplan, *Making of the Jewish Middle Class*, 108, suggests that the transition from arranged marriages to "modern" marriages based on love and "accident" was also taking place among German Jews, perhaps a bit more slowly than in the more liberal English atmosphere.
51. The reviewer in the *VoJ*, Apr. 9, 1847, the year of Aguilar's death, assumes her history was written by a man: "The writer is evidently perfectly acquainted with his subject."
52. Beth Zion Lask Abrahams, "Grace Aguilar: A Centenary Tribute," *Transactions of the Jewish Historical Society of England* 16 (1952): 137–48.
53. Salomon, *Twelve Sermons*, trans. Anna Maria Goldsmid. Goldsmid calls (1) for publication of sermons to promote "home instruction" and "the formation of the religious character of the young," citing the need for vernacular religious education; and (2) for more English explanations of Judaism, in the "hope, that from their perusal, many of my Christian countrymen may derive a better knowledge than they previously possessed, of the actuating faith of the Jew" (iv). David Woolf Marks, *Sermons Preached on Various Occasions at the West London Synagogue of British Jews*, 4 vols. (London: R. Groombridge and Sons, 1851), in a prefatory note, calls (1) for vernacular sermons to furnish "Jewish families with the means of home instruction," citing the "dearth of Jewish discourses in the English language;" and (2) for the "setting forth a fair exposition of the doctrines which are taught in our synagogue," citing "misrepresentations concerning our opinions and practices" (v), both among other Jews and Christians. That is, he repeats Goldsmid's terms exactly.
54. Kaplan, *Making of the Jewish Middle Class*, 72, points out that German-Jewish women had been producing cookbooks since 1815.
55. Rev. Abraham de Sola, a respected man in the community, revealed

Montefiore's responsibility for the *Cheap Jewish Library* after her death. See "The Late Charlotte Montefiore," *JC,* Sept. 23, 1864. In the same article he reveals the correspondence between her and Grace Aguilar.

56. Marion Hartog, "Lines Written on the Death of Grace Aguilar," *JC,* Nov. 10, 1854; "Lines on the Death of Lady Montefiore," *JC,* Oct. 24, 1862; the "Correspondence" section of each issue of the *JSJ.*

57. Linda Gordon Kuzmack, introduction to *Woman's Cause: The Jewish Woman's Movement in England and the United States, 1881–1933* (Columbus: Ohio State University Press), 1990.

58. For Anglo-Jewish women's charitable work, see William Gilbert, "Jewish Ladies and Their Charities in London," *JC,* July 1, 1864, reprinted from *Christian Work,* June 1864; and "Jewish Women's Work in Philanthropy and Education," *JC,* June 13, 1902, a retrospective, primarily on the Mosses. For the pressure Jewish women could bring to bear on men, see for example American reform founder Isaac Mayer Wise, *Reminiscences,* ed. David Philipson (Cincinnati: Leo Wise and Company, 1901), 215, who records a meeting with a "bevy of Portuguese Jewesses" who convince him to edit the Reform journal the *Asmonean,* and later convince him to write a volume of Jewish history.

59. Caroline L. Samuel and Rachel Simon, Letter, *JSJ,* May 24, 1855.

60. Mrs. R. Hyneman, Philadelphia, Nov. 8, 1847; Female Hebrew Benevolent Society of Philadelphia, Philadelphia, Nov. 3, 1847; Ladies of the Society for the Religious Instruction of Jewish Youth, Charleston, South Carolina, Nov. 23, 1847. All from Grace Aguilar MSS.

61. The tribute has been reprinted in full in Abrahams, "Grace Aguilar" 16 (July 12, 1947): 137–45. The Jewish Chronicle regrets that no Montefiore, Rothschild, Goldsmid, Cohen, or Mocatta—no wealthy Jewish woman—was involved in the tribute, arguing that Aguilar was shunned because she "was not rich" (*JC,* Oct. 8, 1847).

62. Todd Endelman, introduction to *The Jews of Georgian England, 1714–1830* (Philadelphia: Jewish Publication Society, 1989). Also see David Sorkin, *The Transformation of German Jewry, 1780–1840* (Oxford: Oxford University Press, 1987), 175: "English Jewry did not generate a significant Haskala movement. And lacking the political pressures of a comprehensive emancipation process—emancipation turned on the ability to hold office . . . — English Jewry experienced no conspicuous ideological ferment."

CHAPTER 4

1. See Ellen Umansky and Dianne Ashton, eds., *Four Centuries of Jewish Women's Spirituality* (Boston: Beacon Press, 1992). Also see Sondra

Henry and Emily Taitz, *Written Out of History: Our Jewish Foremothers* (Sunnyside, New York: Biblio Press, 1990), 229–35.

2. Unless otherwise noted, all biographical details come from Rachel Beth Zion Lask Abrahams, "Grace Aguilar: A Centenary Tribute," *Transactions of the Jewish Historical Society of England* 16 (1952): 137–45.

3. Traditional Judaism always focused women's roles in the home as Marion A. Kaplan points out in "Tradition and Transition: Jewish Women in Imperial Germany," in *Jewish Women in Historical Perspective*, ed. Judith Baskin (Detroit: Wayne State University Press, 1991), 205–6. But the hegemonically valued space was the public space of the synagogue and yeshiva. The mother-centered nature of the crypto-Jewish tradition is well documented. See Renée Levine Melammed, "Sephardi Women in the Medieval and Early Modern Periods," *Jewish Women in Historical Perspective*, ed. Judith Baskin (Detroit: Wayne State University Press, 1991), 115–34. Lynn Gottlieb, "The Secret Jew: An Oral Tradition of Women," in *On Being a Jewish Feminist*, ed. Susannah Heschel (New York: Schocken Books, 1983) writes: "The women of the Marrano communities thought of themselves as Queen Esther, living a secret existence very different from the reality perceived by the outside world. . . . [W]omen did assume major leadership roles in the community. They led communal prayers, performed marriage ceremonies, and developed rituals around the Fast of Esther, which became a major conversos holiday" (274). Also see Cecil Roth, *A History of the Marranos* (Philadelphia: Jewish Publication Society of America, 1947); and the recent film *The Last Marranos*, which made a rare appearance at the Jewish Film Festival in Berkeley, Aug. 1992, and vividly depicts the continuance of the matriarchal tradition in the late twentieth century among Portuguese crypto-Jews.

4. In the United States as well as in England, the cultural designation of "Mother in Israel" resonated with the particularly Jewish functions of True Womanhood. For a discussion of the American meaning of this phrase, see Diane Lichtenstein, *Writing Their Nations: The Tradition of Nineteenth-Century American Jewish Women Writers* (Bloomington: Indiana University Press, 1992), 23–35. Also see Rachel Adler, "A Mother in Israel: Aspects of the Mother Role in Jewish Myth," in *Beyond Androcentrism: New Essays on Women and Religion*, ed. Rita M. Gross (Missoula, Mont.: Scholars Press for the American Academy of Religion, 1977), 237–55.

5. Linda Gertner Zatlin, *The Nineteenth-Century Anglo-Jewish Novel* (Boston: G. K. Hall, 1981), 35–37.

6. An example of a conversionist's thick description can be found in Madam Brendlah, *Tales of a Jewess; Illustrating the Domestic Customs and Manners of the Jews: Interspersed with Original Anecdotes of Napoleon* (London: Simpkin and Marshall, 1838).

7. A. J. Isaacs, *Young Champion* (New York, 1933).
8. Grace Aguilar, *The Spirit of Judaism,* ed. Isaac Leeser, 3d ed. (Philadelphia, 1864), 121–22. Subsequent references will be cited by page number parenthetically in the text.
9. Christian women had in the figure of Mary a prime example of a woman who literally transmitted "the Word" of cultural tradition without displaying subjectivity. See Margaret Homans, *Bearing the Word: Language and Female Experience in Nineteenth-Century Women's Writing* (Chicago: University of Chicago Press, 1986), 156.
10. The consistency with which Aguilar and virtually all her Anglo-Jewish colleagues spoke out against conversion presents a striking contrast with the consistency with which German-Jewish writers saw conversion as a viable entry ticket. Fanny Lewald, *The Education of Fanny Lewald: An Autobiography,* trans. and ed. Hanna Ballin Lewis, SUNY Series, Women Writers in Translation (Albany: State University of New York Press, 1992), makes for interesting comparison. Both Aguilar and Lewald were home-educated and from the middle class. To use domesticity to defend against conversion was a specifically Jewish take on the idea that the home was to be "a way of drawing a line around culture in order to preserve it in the face of a competitive marketplace," as Nancy Armstrong comments in *Desire and Domestic Fiction: A Political History of the Novel* (New York: Oxford University Press, 1987), 163.
11. In England, the persistence of the severe *Ascamot,* or regulations of the Sephardic synagogue, produced such resistance as the famous rebellion of Isaac D'Israeli. For the nobility myth, see "The Origin and Progress of Literature Amongst the Jews of Spain," *HRR* 2 (1835): 158: "we find the Spanish Jews of the middle ages perfectly similar to their brethren in Germany, France, or England of that period, as far as their religious doctrines and observances are concerned: But they are animated by another spirit: Freedom, and the feeling of their own dignity, assign to them a station in the scale of society which their brethren could not attain." The writer contrasts them with "French usurers torn from their money-bags" (158). Also see Grace Aguilar's critical assessment of this Sephardic "pride of birth" in the excerpt from her history of the English Jews in "Social Arrangements of the English Jews," *JC,* Jan. 2, 1852: Sephardic "pride . . . not only prevents their advancing themselves, either socially or mentally, but renders powerless every effort made for their improvement. The Germans, more willing to work and push forward their own fortunes, and less scrupulous as to the means they employ, are more successful as citizens, and, as a class, are less difficult to guide. Both parties would be improved by the interchange of qualities."
12. Marc Shell, "Marranos (Pigs), or From Coexistence to Toleration," *Critical Inquiry* 17, no. 2 (winter 1991): 306–35. Sephardim who had fled the

Inquisition had a "unique philosophical stance . . . which was skeptical and liberal" (321).

13. Aguilar's novels were distributed in America as well as England, as was Charlotte Montefiore's *Caleb Asher*. Beyond these few texts, however, the exchange would have been paltry had it not been for Isaac Leeser, the rabbi of Mikve Israel Congregation in Philadelphia and editor of the *Occident*, which served as a conduit for reciprocal influence throughout the period. It was Leeser who encouraged Rebecca Gratz to found the Jewish Sunday school movement in America in 1838 and published her achievements; Leeser who published many of Grace Aguilar's and Marion and Celia Moss's tales in the *Occident*; Leeser who edited Aguilar's *Spirit of Judaism* and distributed it on both sides of the Atlantic; and Leeser who revealed Charlotte Montefiore's editorship of the *Cheap Jewish Library* after her death (*JC*, Sept. 23, 1864). The *Occident* must be seen as a conduit (male-mediated, to be sure) for Jewish women's interaction in the absence of their own publications. Until 1855, when Marion Hartog's periodical *Jewish Sabbath Journal* briefly appeared, only to be put out of business by the very man who helped promote it, and then until 1895, when Rosa Sonneschein's *American Jewess* appeared, there were no Jewish woman's publications in existence.

An interesting case of the English/American Jewish women's reciprocal influence is that of Rebbeca Gratz and Grace Aguilar. Rebecca Gratz was the prototype for what Grace Aguilar considered as the most important text about Jews to have come out of the dominant culture in early Victorian England. Since *Ivanhoe* was the founding text against and through which Aguilar defined the terms of the debate around Anglo-Jewish reform, then indirectly Rebecca Gratz could be said to have been the mother of Aguilar's writing in England. But the influence went both ways, for Rebecca Gratz later took Grace Aguilar as a role model when she refused to marry in order to pursue a career. See Linda Gordon Kuzmack, *Woman's Cause: The Jewish Woman's Movement in England and the United States, 1881–1933* (Columbus: Ohio State University Press, 1990), 20.

14. See Isaac Mayer Wise, *Reminiscences,* ed. David Philipson (Cincinnati: Leo Wise and Company, 1901): "Ancestral pride of birth has been beaten out of the German and the Polish Jews with whip and knout; but it has persisted in these American Portuguese." Wise's assessment of Ashkenazic Jews does not hold for those Ashkenazim whose ancestors had lived in England for several generations. These tended to display a similar penchant for romance as their Sephardic coreligionists, the prime example being the Mosses, whose family arrived in the middle of the eighteenth century.

15. Wise, *Reminiscences,* argued that Sephardic women were interested both

in historical romances and in liberal reform in the Jewish community. In his *Reminiscences,* Wise records a meeting with a group composed of "Portuguese Jewesses," among whom were a Mrs. F., who according to Wise had earlier convinced him to edit the Reform journal the *Asmonean;* and Rebecca Gratz. The women's purpose—to convince Wise to write a volume of Jewish history: "These ladies, all of whom were Portuguese Jewesses, importuned me to write a history of the Jews instead of a history of the Middle Ages. I had communicated my purpose to Mrs. F. some time before, and she had requested me to devote myself rather to writing Jewish history. Upon my refusal, she sent her well-instructed agents to convince me. When I persisted in the pursuance of my original plan, she came with this bevy of Portuguese Jewesses to persuade me.

"Any one who does not know this peculiar class of American women may consider this proceeding strange. American women exercise great influence in religious matters. This is also the case often with the native-born Jewesses of Portuguese descent. . . . [They] are very proud of their descent. They lay the greatest stress on the genealogical tree. They are Jews and Jewesses from pride of ancestry. Hence Jewish history is of prime importance in their eyes. Then, as now, there were but few works on Jewish history in the English language, and therefore Mrs. F. desired that I, willy nilly, should undertake this task. I expressed my doubts as to my powers and protested my inability, but all to no avail; I had to submit. . . . Mrs. F. and her bodyguard would not desist until I promised to begin my studies in Jewish history at once. Therefore I had to begin with *B'reshith* once again in the winter of 1852. May God forgive this woman all her sins, and also this one! First she made a Jewish editor of me, and then also a Jewish historian" (215–17).

He goes on to say that "They like to hear about the Jewish worthies of aforetime. The princes of Judah and the heroes of the olden days are of great interest to them, because their blood flows through the veins of the present generation of Jews." The shift from religious affiliation with Judaism to a cultural or ancestral affiliation was one of the most significant transitions brought about by reformers on both sides of the Atlantic. These Portuguese Jewesses are on the forefront of reform—indeed, they are the ones who push Wise to undertake the task of writing Jewish history in the first place. Perhaps it is Portuguese women who ought to be called the founders of Reform Judaism in America.

16. Grace Aguilar, "The Friends, a Domestic Tale," 1834, Grace Aguilar MSS.
17. Grace Aguilar, "Social Arrangements of the English Jews," *JC,* Jan. 2, 1852.
18. Aguilar, dedication to "Friends."
19. Grace Aguilar, "Adah, A Simple Story," 1838, Grace Aguilar MSS.
20. Aguilar, dedication to "Friends."

21. The debate over her authenticity has extended to the critics. Abrahams, "Grace Aguilar," writes: "a great deal of her Jewish knowledge was derived largely from Christian Studies of Jewish learning, rarely from the original sources, and certainly never from a direct study of the Talmud or the Codes. . . . Her frequent decrying of traditional usages represents a form of Jewish Protestantism" (142). Philip M. Weinberger, "The Social and Religious Thought of Grace Aguilar (1816–1847)" (Ph.D. diss., New York University, 1970), has attempted to counter such an attack on her Jewish authenticity by comparing her work to Maimonides' thirteen tenets. Because he finds her to agree with almost all of them, he calls her "orthodox." In fact, she was acutely aware of her lack of traditional Jewish knowledge. This was one of the reasons she called for the translation of the Bible and for Jewish female education. In these calls, she was a reformer, not a traditionalist.

22. Grace Aguilar, *Women of Israel,* 3 vols. (New York: D. Appleton, 1884), 2:34. Subsequent references will be cited parenthetically in text by volume and page number.

23. She made at least one certain borrowing from the *HRR.* In "Spirit of Night," a homily "founded on a Hebrew Apologue," published in *Home Scenes and Heart Studies* (London: G. Routledge and Sons, 1894), Aguilar rewrote the midrash on the "Sun and the Moon," which first appeared in the *HRR.* For analysis of the midrash as an allegory of women's secondary status in creation, see chapter 2. Aguilar revises the gender politics of the tale, so that the argument over status takes place between two male angels, and rather than "the spirit of night" being humiliated, he is cleansed by the angel of Love and restored before God's eyes. The moon herself remains throughout an orb of "pale but lovely lustre" (373). Aguilar displaces the argument over hierarchy from male sun and female moon to two male angels, removes any humiliation or loss of dignity from the moon, and invokes what must have looked like a Christian solution to the dispute—Love. "The Spirit of Night" is thus a perfect emblem of all that made Aguilar seem important and contradictory to her readers: her willingness to revise tradition on behalf of women, her introduction of heretofore unknown Christian elements, her search for Jewish knowledge in whatever form she could find it.

24. Letter, *VoJ,* Sept. 2, 1842.

25. Aguilar, *Women of Israel,* 1:143.

26. See Exod. 2:9.

27. See Aguilar's biographies in *Women of Israel* of Leah and the Daughters of Zelophehad; Rebekah; Deborah and Huldah; and Miriam, respectively.

28. Armstrong, *Domestic Fiction,* 201, comments: "The Victorian novel [transforms] household space into an instrument that can be used to classify any social group and keep it under observation. . . . The promi-

nence of domestic fiction [in the 1840s] suggests the degree to which such power did not in fact rely on overtly juridical or economic means so much as on cultural hegemony, that is, on the notion of the family, norms of sexual behavior, the use of language, the regulation of leisure time, and all those microtechniques that constitute the modern subject." D. A. Miller discusses the "disciplinary power" and "social surveillance" practiced in the novel in *The Novel and the Police* (Berkeley: University of California Press, 1988), 17–18. Both critics owe much to Michel Foucault's discussion of Jeremy Bentham's Panopticon in *Discipline and Punish* (New York: Pantheon, 1977).

29. Tribute, Ladies of the Society for the Religious Instruction of Jewish Youth, Charleston, South Carolina, Nov. 23, 1847, Grace Aguilar MSS.

30. Tribute, Camilla Toulmine, *La Belle Assemblée,* Nov. 1, 1847, Grace Aguilar MSS.

31. Jacob Franklin, "A Memoir of the Late Grace Aguilar," *VoJ,* Dec. 3, 1847.

32. See Weinberger, "Religious Thought of Grace Aguilar": "Miss Aguilar is here viewed as a case study. But she is in a category all her own, *sui generis.* There have been Jewish women writers in all areas of competence. . . . But none compares in either scope or character with Grace Aguilar whose major concern was to educate the Jewess and to define and heighten her status and station" (258). Only Zatlin, *Anglo-Jewish Novel,* eschews this label, placing Aguilar in context with her contemporaries.

33. In a letter to the *VoJ,* Sept. 2, 1842, she "disclaims any intention either of interfering in the spiritual questions at issue between the different parties of Jews, or of attempting to throw any discredit on rabbinical or traditional law." Nonetheless, in both *Spirit of Judaism* and *Women of Israel,* she strikes explicit positions against the divinity of the rabbis and halacha and for religious reforms.

34. Maria Polack, *Fiction Without Romance; or, the Locket-Watch,* 2 vols. (London, 1830), describes Sabbath and kashrut forms in detail rather than arguing for the "spirit" of the law, and denigrates the romance form as un-Jewish. Judith Montefiore, *The Jewish Manual or Practical Information in Jewish and Modern Cookery,* intro. Chaim Raphael (New York: NightinGale Books, 1983), takes up issues of kashrut, and argues against female education, except in culinary and domestic arts.

35. Obituary and leader, *Occident,* Dec., 1847, Grace Aguilar MSS.

36. Review of *The Works of Grace Aguilar, New Edition,* by Grace Aguilar, *JC,* Sept. 1, Oct. 27, Nov. 24, 1871.

37. See Ellen M. Umansky, *From Vision to Vocation: Lily H. Montagu and the Advancement of Liberal Judaism* (Lewiston, N.Y.: Edwin Mellen Press, 1983), 61; and Amy Levy, *The Complete Novels and Selected Writings of Amy Levy, 1861–1889,* ed. Melvyn New (Gainesville: University Press of Florida, 1993). A notable exception to this pattern of tokenizing Aguilar is

the recent study of the Anglo-Jewish novel by Linda Gertner Zatlin. In Zatlin's study, Aguilar receives nearly the same treatment as the Mosses, and they are compared to each other and to other novelists, male as well as female. The problem here is that, although Zatlin recognizes some differences in presentation style, her comparison basically equates all the early novelists as "propaganda" writers who idealize their Jews for a cause, and she does not differentiate their productions by gender. Within an analytic framework that seeks to understand these novels as positioned participants in ongoing exo- and endo-cultural dialogues, the designation "propaganda," with its negative connotation and lack of differentiation, is not useful.

38. Obituary, *VoJ*, Nov., 1847, Grace Aguilar MSS.; obituary, *Athenaeum*, Nov., 1847, Grace Aguilar MSS.

39. Abrahams, "Grace Aguilar."

40. Jacob Franklin, "Memoir of the Late Grace Aguilar," *VoJ*, Dec. 3, 1847, front page.

41. Tribute, Ladies of the Society for the Religious Instruction of Jewish Youth. In another tribute, her Christian friend Mrs. S. C. Hall, *Art Union*, Nov. 1, 1847, Grace Aguilar MSS, likewise wrote that "she paid the penalty of over-exertion."

42. Felicia Hemans's friends had the same problem. See Norma Clarke, *Ambitious Heights: Writing, Friendship, Love—The Jewsbury Sisters, Felicia Hemans, and Jane Welsh Carlyle* (New York: Routledge, 1990), 37. That she did serve as a role model to some young women is indisputable, as in the case of the most famous early American Jewish "spinster," Rebecca Gratz, and even Marion Hartog. For her influence on Gratz, see Kuzmack, *Woman's Cause.* Her influence on Marion Hartog is evident in Hartog's addresses to Aguilar in her poems and in the *Jewish Sabbath Journal.* For biographies of American Jewish "spinsters," including Rebekah Kohut, Emma Lazarus, Ernestine Rose, and Henrietta Szold, see Charlotte Baum, Paula Hyman, and Sonya Michel, *The Jewish Woman in America* (New York: Dial Press, 1976), 34–46.

43. Amy Levy, "Jewish Women and 'Women's Rights,' " *JC*, Jan. 31, 1879.

44. Hemans's friends resolved the issue in a similar way. See Clarke, *Ambitious Heights,* 45. As did Christian writers Charlotte Elizabeth Tonna and Charlotte M. Yonge, for as Dorothy Mermin suggests in *Godiva's Ride: Women of Letters in England, 1830–1880* (Bloomington: Indiana University Press, 1993), 109, "An avowedly religious purpose justified literary self-display" in a woman, especially if allied with social protest. Yet, in Aguilar's case, the other possibility (that she did not like the company of men) may hold true. Many of Aguilar's books, especially *Woman's Friendship,* focus on the beauties of relationships between women. When, in a curious epilogue to that book that reads as if it were tacked on, Florence

does marry, her wedding appears to be quite a disappointment to her rather than the fulfillment of her lifetime dream. Also see Marion A. Kaplan, *The Making of the Jewish Middle Class: Women, Family, and Identity in Imperial Germany* (New York: Oxford University Press, 1991), 126, who speaks of a "female world of sociability" in which Jewish women moved. Such a world was consonant with Victorian Christian women's experience as well. See Carroll Smith-Rosenberg, *Disorderly Conduct: Visions of Gender in Victorian America* (New York: A. A. Knopf, 1985); and Valerie Sanders, *The Private Lives of Victorian Women: Autobiography in Nineteenth-Century England* (New York: St. Martin's Press, 1989).

45. Amy Levy, "Jewish Children, by a Maiden Aunt," *JC,* Nov. 5, 1886.

46. Mary Poovey, in an essay on Jane Eyre and governesses in *Uneven Developments: The Ideological Work of Gender in Mid-Victorian England* (Chicago: University of Chicago Press, 1988), 127, argues that the figure of the governess is inherently ambivalent, similar to both "the figure who epitomized the domestic ideal, and the figure who threatened to destroy it"— that is, similar to the middle-class mother and the working-class woman who commits the sin of receiving wages for productive, rather than reproductive, labor. In Aguilar's selfless (yet nevertheless public) caregiving, she also bears resemblance to the figure of Florence Nightingale as constructed by Victorian domestic ideologists. See Poovey, *Uneven Developments,* chap. 6.

47. Aguilar, *Home Scenes,* 229. Subsequent references will be cited parenthetically in the text by page number.

48. The tension between writing and marriage displayed here could be found among Christian women writers as well and in Germany as well as in England. See Clarke, *Ambitious Heights,* 14; Homans, *Bearing the Word,* 223; and Deborah Hertz, *Jewish High Society in Old Regime Berlin* (New Haven: Yale University Press, 1988), 171.

49. Geraldine Jewsbury and other Christian writers, including the Brontës, Christina Rossetti, Elizabeth Barrett, and even George Eliot, engaged in similar renunciation of public ambition. See Mermin, *Godiva's Ride,* 17–20.

50. "The Late Charlotte Montefiore," *JC,* Sept. 23, 1864.

51. Grace Aguilar, "Notes on Excursion," Oct. 1843, Grace Aguilar MSS.

52. She seemed also to resemble German Christian women writers from a generation past. Hertz, *Jewish High Society,* 163–65, describes writers of the 1790s such as Helene Unger and Caroline de la Motte Fouqué who published prolifically while opposing salonières as too public an example for women. German-Jewish women of the same era, such as Dorothea Veit, were so cautious about gaining notoriety that they issued their publications anonymously, as Hertz shows (172).

53. In this tradition, as Jane Spencer puts it in *The Rise of the Woman*

Novelist: From Aphra Behn to Jane Austen (London: Basil Blackwell, 1986), the writer "could express the fears and anger that could not be openly acknowledged; and equally, romance allowed for the expression of women's hopes and desires. The novelist creating an ideal romantic world might run the risk of escapism but also had the chance to create visions of a better future, and these are an essential part of feminist thought" (210).

54. Aguilar, "Adah."

55. In her history of the English Jews ("Social Arrangements of the English Jews," *JC*, Jan. 2, 1852), Aguilar writes "The characteristics so often assigned to [Jews] in tales professing to introduce a Jew or a Jewish family, are almost all incorrect, being drawn either from the impressions of the past, or from some special case. . . . These great errors in delineation arise from the supposition that, because they are Hebrews, they must be different from any other race. They are distinct in feature and religion, but in nothing else." In each case, she is explicitly concerned with presenting a liberal view of Jews as ethical monotheists. She goes on to describe their good qualities, in accordance with her domestic ideology: "The virtues of the Jews are essentially of a domestic and social kind. . . . From the highest classes to the most indigent, affection, reverence, and tenderness mark their domestic intercourse." Taken together, all these prefaces and essays constitute a fairly complete theoretical model with which to read Aguilar's early works.

56. Aguilar, *Spirit of Judaism,* 179. This passage comes from chap. 7, "The Spirit and the Forms of Judaism Considered Separately and Together": "The Bible and reason are the only guides to which the child of Israel can look in security. The laws for which we can find no foundation in the one, and which will not stand the test of the other, need no farther proof; they are not the dictates of the law, they are wanderings from the true and only law, the inventions of man, and not the words of God. The Bible gives us a cause, a reason for every statute it enjoins." Also see *Women of Israel,* 1:165: "The law, in form, like the human frame, may die for a time, but the spirit of the ordinances, like the soul of the body, is immortal, and will revive again the shell from which awhile it may have flown."

57. For a substantially similar reading, see Michael Ragussis, "The Birth of a Nation in Victorian Culture: The Spanish Inquisition, the Converted Daughter, and the 'Secret Race,' " *Critical Inquiry* (spring 1994): 477–508. For a theory of the historical romance novel, see Avrom Fleishman, introduction to *The English Historical Novel: Walter Scott to Virginia Woolf* (Baltimore: Johns Hopkins University Press, 1971).

58. Grace Aguilar, *The Vale of Cedars and Other Stories* (London: J. M. Dent, 1902). Critics have puzzled over Aguilar's depiction of Isabella, who signed the Expulsion Edict, as a sympathetic mother who is only tricked into expelling the Jews by Torquemada the evil Inquisitor (223). The

difficulty is explained by seeing Isabella as a substitute for Victoria. There is evidence that Aguilar idealized Queen Victoria as a great mother. See her "Notes on Excursion," where she describes two pictures of the queen and concludes "both are sweet touching pictures of our gentle Queen— whom I never felt so much inclined to love as when listening to anecdotes of her happy domestic life from the lips of her own retainors." (Here she was only replicating the idealization of the queen as mother common in the culture: see Susan Rubinow Gorsky, *Femininity to Feminism: Women and Literature in the Nineteenth Century* [New York: Twayne Publishers, 1992], 26.) Ragussis, "Birth of a Nation," 487, points out that Isabella is more philo-Semitic than sympathetic, attempting to use "gentle" means to convert Marie.

59. Ragussis concurs in "Birth of a Nation," 486.

60. "The Example of Israel," *JSJ*, Feb. 22, 1855.

61. Aguilar, *Spirit of Judaism,* 74. Ragussis rightly emphasizes Aguilar's attention to the "secret race" and to "woman's heart" in *Vale of Cedars,* but underemphasizes how much the secrecy of gender and subculture resembled one another structurally.

62. While Aguilar's belief that Jews and women each ought to hide a piece of themselves seems to suggest that she understands the categories of ethnicity and gender as congruent, in at least one sense she understands these two categories as divergent. For Jews have to hide in order to convince Christians of their essential similarity and therefore of their right to equality; women have to hide in order to convince men of their essential inferiority and therefore of their need for subordination. To pass as members of the dominant group, Jews have to convince Christians of their intelligence as measured by their ability to ape dominant cultural conventions. But intelligent, ambitious women have to "dumb down" to pass as fully feminine members of the "second sex."

63. Aguilar, "The Escape," *Home Scenes.* As noted, all references will appear parenthetically in the text.

64. See Zatlin, *Anglo-Jewish Novel*: "To minimize doctrinal differences [between Jews and Christians], the narrator skims over actual practices, while highlighting similarities to Christian customs. . . . Each description employs adjectives such as 'peculiar' and 'mysterious,' which distance rather than reveal anything about the spiritual significance of Jewish practices" (36).

65. It would be interesting to speculate on why, when Almah cross-dresses, she dons the garb of another persecuted minority in Spain, a Moor, rather than a Christian. Perhaps Aguilar could not bring her character to sympathize with her persecutors enough to impersonate one of them, while she could allow Almah to sympathize with a member of a persecuted race.

66. See Abia in Celia Moss, "The Slave," *Romance of Jewish History* 3 vols.

(London: A. K. Newman and Co., 1843), 1:55–162, who cross-dresses as a male minstrel in order to deliver a message to King David.

67. Cecil Roth, in "The Evolution of Anglo-Jewish Literature" (London: Edward Goldston, 1937) demonstrates how Aguilar's efforts to depict and think through the problems of Victorian Jewish identity in the romance could be trivialized and misunderstood: "If we neglect Benjamin Disraeli's exuberances in *Alroy* and *Coningsby,* and Grace Aguilar's romantical *Vale of Cedars,* etc., the earliest attempt [of Jews to give a more faithful picture of themselves] was perhaps that of Matthias Levy" (8). Although Roth gives a reason for neglecting Disraeli, he gives none for neglecting Aguilar—as if the adjective "romantical" were reason enough.

68. Grace Aguilar, Preface to *Records of Israel* (London, 1844), Grace Aguilar MSS. Interestingly, this is almost word for word the justification used by the director of the *Holy Office,* the 1970s Mexican film depicting Jews during the Inquisition, which was shown at the Jewish Film Festival in Berkeley, California, Aug. 2, 1992.

69. Grace Aguilar, Preface to *Records of Israel,* Grace Aguilar MSS.

70. In *Spirit of Judaism* and *Women of Israel,* her tone is not at all self-deprecating even though she addresses only Jews in those works. But in the first case, she suffered for her boldness by having Leeser administer harsh editorial correctives to the body of her text, which Philip M. Weinberger argues were decisive in the later, milder tone of her work. In the case of *Women of Israel,* she was directing her text primarily to Jewish women only, and did not have to fear that she was ignorant relative to them.

71. Grace Aguilar, Preface to *Home Influence: A Tale for Mothers and Daughters* (London: James Nisbet, 1855).

72. A favorable review in *HJ* 1 (May 1, 1847): 251, shows that at least some of her Christian audience agrees. "The works of Grace Aguilar prove of how little vital consequence are the differences of creed, where the heart is influenced by the spirit of true religion. In this spirit, the Jew and the Christian are one."

73. See William Gilbert, "Jewish Ladies and Their Charities in London," *Christian Work* (June 1864); reprinted in *JC,* July 1, 1864.

74. "The Late Charlotte Montefiore," *JC,* Sept. 23, 1864.

75. Charlotte Montefiore, *A Few Words to the Jews. By One of Themselves* (London: John Chapman, 1855). Subsequent references will be cited parenthetically in the text.

76. Quoted in letter to D. A. de Sola, "The Late Charlotte Montefiore."

77. *JC,* Feb. 2, 1855.

78. "The Late Charlotte Montefiore."

79. Celia Levetus identifies this materialism—with its ultimate end, conversion—particularly with Montefiore's own upper class in "The Two Pic-

tures: A Sketch of Domestic Life," *JSJ,* Apr. 19, 1855: "Mrs. Emanuel was in name, and as far as mere outward observance went, a Jewess; that is to say, she never rode in her carriage on the feast days, never touched fire on the Sabbath, kept the two principal fasts, and had her house cleansed from leaven for the Passover; but beyond this she never thought of religion at all. Her children had been brought up by Christian nurses, educated by a Christian governess; of their own faith they knew nothing. What marvel, then, if their minds were open to any impression which their instructress thought fit to make on them?" (131) This worry over the conversionist tendencies of Christian domestics was quite different than the worry expressed by middle-class German Jews about their domestics: German Jews, who suffered more intense anti-Semitism, worried instead that Christian domestics would refuse to work for them. This is the difference between a philo-Semitic and an anti-Semitic milieu. See Kaplan, *Making of the Jewish Middle Class,* 38.

80. Celia and Marion Moss, preface to *Romance,* 1843.
81. "The Late Charlotte Montefiore."
82. Ibid.
83. Ibid.
84. The obituary for Grace Aguilar, *JC,* Oct. 8, 1847, regrets that the Montefiores, Rothschilds, Goldsmids, Cohens, and Mocattas—all members of the Cousinhood—were not among the ladies who presented the testimonial, because Aguilar "was not rich."
85. Grace Aguilar, "The Perez Family," *Home Scenes and Heart Studies* (London: G. Routledge and Sons, 1894), 11. Subsequent references will be cited parenthetically in the text.
86. Kaplan, *Jewish Middle Class,* 25, suggests that German-Jewish domestic ideology is by contrast concerned with increasing "permeability"—that is, increasing the Germanness of the Jewish home in the form of paintings and books, artifacts visible to the German eye. Theoretically, high permeability would convince gentile Germans that Jews had achieved *Bildung* and were worthy of social integration.
87. An example was the Sandy's Row Synagogue, established as a friendly society for Jewish working men in 1860.
88. In being transitional yet woman-centered she was much like Felicia Hemans, as Clarke's description shows in *Ambitious Heights,* 35.
89. Roth, "Anglo-Jewish Literature," mentions with Aguilar only Emma Lyons and Maria Polack, and neglects the Montefiores, the Mosses, and Goldsmid altogether.
90. An example of the latter appeared when her work was reissued in 1871. The reviewer of the *Jewish Chronicle* used it as an example of the days when "the rights of women were not talked of, and the strong-minded women of our day were unknown. At least," the reviewer continued, "in

that era, a strong-minded woman was one whose *mind* was strong; and its strength seemed all the brighter for the relief afforded to it by the tender *womanly* heart and the gentle *womanly* manner. . . . Not so, now. Now, the model strong-minded woman tries to do her deeds in a manly way, and the best charm of womanhood is lost in a graceless mimicry of manhood" (*JC*, Sept. 1, 1871). Simply put, it was Grace's "grace"—with that word's feminine and Christian resonance intact—that helped her work survive the partisan debates between feminists and antifeminists, between Jewish men and conversionists. In her capacity to appeal to competing constituencies, she resembles Florence Nightingale again. See Poovey, *Uneven Developments,* 198: while Nightingale was widely read as a selfless comforter, she could also "be appropriated by feminists who sought proof of women's capabilities. For Harriet Martineau and others, Florence Nightingale planted a flag upon a new territory, a 'woman's battle-field' that others could now defend. . . . She . . . proved beyond a doubt that women could work in the public sphere. Because her image displaced her own antifeminist sentiments, the name of Florence Nightingale could be enlisted in the feminist cause the woman herself refused to support."

91. *JC,* Aug. 16, 1872.

EPILOGUE

1. Along with studies of West Indian, Gypsy, Catholic, and Arab Victorian writing, Anglo-Jewish women's writing can help to determine what kind of "minority discourse" was developing during the period. Such comparisons would make it possible to work out the relations between gender, ethnicity, religion, and race on a comparative basis. They would also help to determine the attitudes and institutions English Protestants adopted toward minorities living on what the Protestants considered their own shores. These attitudes and institutions toward domestic minorities could in turn be compared with imperial Britain's "orientalist" strategies toward its dominions abroad. The similarities and disjunctions between its imperialist and domestic strategies for dealing with the Other would no doubt reveal a great deal about the tensions within Victorian liberalism and English national identity.

2. The best sources for late-nineteenth-century Anglo-Jewish women writers are Amy Levy, *The Complete Novels and Selected Writings of Amy Levy, 1861–1889,* ed. Melvyn New (Gainesville: University Press of Florida, 1993); Ellen M. Umansky, *Lily Montagu and the Advancement of Liberal Judaism: From Vision to Vocation* (New York: Edwin Mellen,

1983); Ellen M. Umansky, ed., *Lily Montagu: Sermons, Addresses, Letters, and Prayers* (New York: Edwin Mellen, 1985); and Linda Gertner Zatlin, *The Nineteenth-Century Anglo-Jewish Novel* (Boston: G. K. Hall, 1981). For the Anglo-American crossover, see Linda Gordon Kuzmack, *Woman's Cause: The Jewish Woman's Movement in England and the United States, 1881–1933* (Columbus: Ohio State University Press, 1990). For the American women's writing community, see Charlotte Baum, Paula Hyman, and Sonya Michel, *The Jewish Woman in America* (New York: Dial Press, 1976); and Diane Lichtenstein, *Writing Their Nations: The Tradition of Nineteenth-Century American Jewish Women Writers* (Bloomington: Indiana University Press, 1992).

3. "Death of Miss Goldsmid," *JC*, Feb. 15, 1889.

4. David Woolf Marks and Rev. A. Löwy, *Memoir of Sir Francis Henry Goldsmid*, ed. Louisa Goldsmid, 2d ed. (London: Kegan Paul, Trench, 1882). Also see F. H. Goldsmid, *The Arguments Advanced against the Enfranchisement of the Jews. Considered in a Series of Letters* (London: Colburn and Bentley, 1831), and *Reply to the Arguments Advanced against the Removal of the Remaining Disabilities of the Jews* (London: John Murray, 1848).

5. "Death of Miss Goldsmid." Also see Götthold Salomon, *Twelve Sermons Delivered in the New Temple of the Israelites, at Hamburgh*, trans. Anna Maria Goldsmid (London: John Murray, 1839). Subsequent references will be cited by page number parenthetically in the text.

6. The lack of instructional materials was to continue to be a problem for the next thirty years. In 1860, a major controversy in the community took place when it was discovered that class books at the Jews' Free School contained a passage that children were supposed to repeat out loud, saying that God "sent Christ to save me." Neither the Head Master, Moses Angel, nor the educational committee claimed to understand how the passage made it into the class book undiscovered—but because of the dearth of vernacular materials, and because Angel had wanted "to provide a set of books on general subjects," the class books had actually been taken from Christian classrooms. Attempts were made to paste over the offending passages, but this only led one writer, who wanted Jewish books by Jewish writers, to threaten to "paste my name over in the list of subscribers" to the Free School. *The Hebrew Review and Magazine of Jewish Literature* held the Chief Rabbi himself responsible, while the *Jewish Chronicle* tried to smooth things over, until a second offending passage was found. See lead article, "Revision of Our School Books," *HRJ*, Apr. 27, 1860; lead article, "The Forthcoming New Class-Book for our Schools," *HRJ*, May 4, 1860; and letters, *HRJ* Apr. 13, 20, 27, and May 4, 1860.

7. Grace Aguilar, *Spirit of Judaism*, ed. Isaac Leeser, 3d ed. (Philadelphia, 1864), 29.

8. David Woolf Marks, *Sermons Preached on Various Occasions at the West London Synagogue of British Jews* (London: R. Groombridge and Sons, 1851).

9. "Death of Miss Goldsmid," review in *JC* appeared July 19, 1872.

10. Quoted in review of *Persecution of the Jews of Roumania,* trans. Anna Maria Goldsmid, *JC,* Aug. 23, 1872.

11. "Death of Miss Goldsmid."

12. The *VoJ* records the founding of the *JGLSI* Apr. 12, 1844. By Nov. 1845, the institute is studying Mendelssohn, doing philology on Job, discussing whether man is a carnivore, debating the effect of Henry VIII's destruction of the monastic establishment on the English community at large, opining on the politics of Pitt, etc.

13. "Lectures to Jewish Working Men," *JC,* Apr. 3, 1874. All subsequent references to the lecture are taken from this article.

14. *JC,* Sept. 23 1870.

15. *JC,* Feb. 7, 1879.

16. For a similar argument, see Michael Ragussis, "The Novel of Jewish Identity," *Critical Inquiry* (fall 1989): 113–43; Bryan Cheyette, *Constructions of "The Jew" in English Literature and Society: Racial Representations, 1875–1945* (Cambridge: Cambridge University Press, 1993); and Michael Galchinsky, "The New Anglo-Jewish Literary Criticism," *Prooftexts* 15, no. 13 (1995).

Bibliography

PRIMARY SOURCES

1. Grace Aguilar MSS

[The Grace Aguilar MSS are held at University College London, on loan from the Jewish Museum.]

Published Volumes Included among the MSS

Aguilar, Grace. *Jewish Faith*. London, 1846.
———. *Records of Israel*. London, 1844. Contains a series of reviews of Aguilar's work.
———. *Sabbath Thoughts and Sacred Communings*. London, 1853.
———. *Vale of Cedars*. London, 1851. With many deletions in ink and pencil.

Handwritten Documents

Aguilar, Grace. "Adah, A Simple Story." 1838.
———. "The Charmed Bell and Other Poems." 2 vols. 1836.
———. "Francoise." A Fragment. 1834.
———. "The Friends, a Domestic Tale." 1834.
———. "Leila, A Poem in Three Cantos with Notes."
———. "Notes on Chonchology."
———. "Notes on Excursion." Oct. 1843.
———. "Notes upon C. C. Clarke's Hundred Wonders of the World."
———. Poems. 1834–35.
———. "Sabbath Thoughts." Lecture on the Psalm 32 by Rev. R. A. Feb. 1837.
"The Late Miss Aguilar's Case." Translation of German doctor's description of the stages of her illness.
"Proctor's Account of the Administration of the Estate of Grace Aguilar, Spinster."

Tributes Collected by Sara Aguilar

Bowles, Caroline A. "Reminiscences of Grace Aguilar." Jan. 1848.
Female Hebrew Benevolent Society of Philadelphia. Philadelphia. Nov. 3, 1847.
Friend from Devonshire. "Her love for many Christian friends . . ."
Hall, Mrs. S[amuel]. C[arter]. *Art Union*. Nov. 1, 1847.

Hebrew Benevolent Society of Charleston, South Carolina. Apr. 1848.

Hesse, G. "Grace Aguilar." *Archives Israelites.* Nov. 1847.

Hyneman, Mrs. R. Philadelphia. Nov. 8, 1847.

Ladies of the Society for the Religious Instruction of Jewish Youth. Charleston, South Carolina, Nov. 23, 1847.

Luria, S. "Elegy."

Meldola, David. "Is This My Place of Rest?" 1848.

Michell, Nicolas. "Lines of the Death of Grace Aguilar." *La Belle Assemblée.* 1847.

Millbourne, W. "Elegy."

Obituary. *Athenaeum.* Nov. 1847.

Obituary. *Voice of Jacob.* Nov. 1847.

Obituary and Leader. *Occident.* Dec. 1847.

Toulmine, Camilla. *La Belle Assemblée.* Nov. 1, 1847.

Unattributed. Jamaica. Nov. 1847.

2. Periodicals

Hebrew Christian Magazine. No. 1–7. London: Hall, Virtu. May 1852–Nov. 1852.

Hebrew Christian Witness, an Anglo-Judaeo-Christian Magazine, under the Entire Management of the Editor and Contributors from Patriotic Jewish Believers. London: Elliot Stock, 1872.

Hebrew Review and Magazine of Jewish Literature. Ed. Marcus H. Bresslau. London: M. H. Bresslau. Oct. 1859–July 1860.

Hebrew Review and Magazine of Rabbinical Literature. Ed. Morris J. Raphall. London: Simpkin and Marshall. Oct. 1834–July 1836.

Howitt's Journal. 1 (Feb.–May 1847).

Israel's Watchman; A Hebrew Christian Magazine. Ed. Alfred Edersheim. Mar. 1877.

The Jewish Advocate. For the Young. London: London Society for the Promotion of Christianity Amongst the Jews, 1845.

Jewish Chronicle. 1841–1907.

Jewish Herald and Record of Christian Effort For the Spiritual Good of God's Ancient People. London: British Society for the Propagation of the Gospel among the Jews, 1846–47.

Jewish Sabbath Journal. Ed. Marion Hartog (née Moss). no. 1–11, Feb.–June 1855.

Voice of Jacob. Ed. Jacob A. Franklin. London: B. Steill, 1841–47.

3. Other Published Primary Sources

Abraham, Philip. *Curiosities of Judaism, Facts, Opinions, Anecdotes, and Remarks Relative to the Hebrew Nation.* London: Wertheimer, Lea, 1879.

Aguilar, Grace. *Collected Works.* 8 vols. London: R. Groombridge, 1861.
———. *Home Influence: A Tale for Mothers and Daughters.* London: James Nisbet, 1855.
———. *Home Scenes and Heart Studies.* London: G. Routledge and Sons, 1894.
———. *The Jewish Faith.* Philadelphia: 1864.
———. *The Spirit of Judaism.* Ed. Isaac Leeser. 3d ed. Philadelphia, 1864.
———. *The Vale of Cedars; or, the Martyr.* New York: D. Appleton, 1851.
———. *Woman's Friendship: A Story of Domestic Life.* New York: D. Appleton, 1867.
———. *The Women of Israel.* 3 vols. New York: D. Appleton, 1884.
Arnold, Matthew. *Culture and Anarchy.* Ed. J. Dover Wilson. Cambridge: Cambridge University Press, 1971.
Blake, William. *The Complete Poetry and Prose.* Ed. David Erdman and Harold Bloom. New York: Doubleday, 1988.
Blunt, John E. *A History of the Establishment and Residence of the Jews in England; with an Enquiry into their Civil Disabilities.* London: Saunders and Benning, 1830.
Brendlah, Madam. *Tales of a Jewess; Illustrating the Domestic Customs and Manners of the Jews: Interspersed with Original Anecdotes of Napoleon.* London: Simpkin and Marshall, 1838.
Bristow, Amelia. *Emma de Lissau: A Narrative of Striking Vicissitudes and Peculiar Trials: with Explanatory Notes Illustrative of the Manners and Customs of the Jews.* 2 vols. London: T. Gardiner, 1828.
———. *The Orphans of Lissau and Other Interesting Narratives Immediately Connected with Jewish Customs Domestic and Religious: with Explanatory Notes.* 2 vols. London: T. Gardiner, 1830.
———. *Rosette and Miriam: or the Twin Sisters: A Jewish Narrative of the Eighteenth Century.* London: Charles Tilt, 1837.
———. *Sophia De Lissau: A Portraiture of the Jews, of the Nineteenth Century: Being an Outline of Their Religious and Domestic Habits: with Explanatory Notes.* 4th ed. London: T. Gardiner, 1833.
The British Jew to His Fellow Countrymen. London: James Ridgeway, 1833.
Browning, Robert. "Rabbi Ben Ezra," "Saul," "Holy Thursday." In *Robert Browning's Poetry,* ed. James F. Loucks. New York: W. W. Norton, 1979.
Bulwer Lytton, Edward. *Leila, or the Siege of Granada.* London: George Routledge and Sons, 1875.
Burke, Edmund. *Reflections on the Revolution in France in Two Classics of the French Revolution.* New York: Doubleday, 1989.
Byron, Lord George Gordon. *Byron.* Ed. Jerome J. McGann. Oxford: Oxford University Press, 1986.
———. *Hebrew Melodies.* London: J. Murray, 1815.
Carlyle, Thomas. "The Jew Our Lawgiver." London: Thomas Bosworth, 1853.

————. *Sartor Resartus*. Ed. Charles Frederick Harrold. New York: Odyssey Press, 1937.

Cobbett, William. *Good Friday: Or the Murder of Jesus Christ by the Jews*. 1830.

Coleridge, Samuel T. "The Rime of the Ancient Mariner." In *English Romantic Writers*, ed. David Perkins, 404–13. New York: Harcourt Brace Jovanovich, 1967.

Davids, Arthur Lumley. "On the Emancipation of the Jews." Letter to *Times*. May 6, 1831.

De Quincey, Thomas. *Confessions of An English Opium-Eater and Other Writings*. Oxford: Oxford University Press, 1985.

Dickens, Charles. *Oliver Twist*. New York: New American Library, 1980.

————. *Our Mutual Friend*. Oxford: Oxford University Press, 1989.

Disraeli, Benjamin. *Alroy and Ixion*. London: Longmans, Green, 1846.

————. *Coningsby*. Ed. Sheila M. Smith. Oxford: Oxford University Press, 1982.

————. *Sybil*. Ed. Thom Braun. New York: Penguin Classics, 1987.

————. *Tancred*. New York: Penguin Classics, 1987.

————. *Tancred, or, the New Crusade*. London: Longmans, Green, 1880.

D'Israeli, Isaac. *Genius of Judaism*. London: Edward Moxon, 1833.

————. *Works, with a view of the life and writings of the author, by his son, the Right Hon. B. Disraeli*. 6 vols. New York: A. C. Armstrong and Son, 1881.

Edgeworth, Maria. *Castle Rackrent*. Oxford: Oxford University Press, 1969.

————. *Harrington: Tales and Novels*. Vol. 9. London: G. Routledge, 1893.

Eliot, George. *Daniel Deronda*. Oxford: Oxford University Press, 1988.

Glückel of Hameln. *The Memoirs of Glückel of Hameln*. Trans. Marvin Lowenthal. New York: Schocken Books, 1977.

Goldsmid, Francis Henry. *The Arguments Advanced against the Enfranchisement of the Jews. Considered in a Series of Letters*. London: Colburn and Bentley, 1831.

————. *Reply to the Arguments Advanced against the Removal of the Remaining Disabilities of the Jews*. London: John Murray, 1848.

Harding, John. "Mercy for Israel, a sermon preached on behalf of the London Society for the Promotion of Christianity amongst the Jews." *Jewish Tracts*. British Museum, 1866.

Harris, Emily Marian. *Estelle*. 2 vols. London: George Bell, 1878.

Isaacs, A. J. *Young Champion*. New York, 1933.

Kaufman, David. *George Eliot and Judaism*. William Blackwood and Sons, 1877.

Lessing, Götthold Ephraim. *Nathan the Wise*. Trans. Bayard Quincy Morgan. New York: Continuum, 1988.

Levetus, Celia (Moss). *The King's Physician and Other Tales.* Birmingham, England: Hinton, 1865.

Levy, Amy. *The Complete Novels and Selected Writings of Amy Levy, 1861–1889.* Ed. Melvyn New. Gainesville: University Press of Florida, 1993.

———. "The Jew in Fiction." *Jewish Chronicle.* June 4, 1886.

———. "Jewish Women and 'Women's Rights.'" *Jewish Chronicle.* Jan. 31, 1879.

Levy, Matthias [Nathan Meritor]. *The Hasty Marriage; A Sketch of Modern Jewish Life.* London: Mann Nephews, 1857.

Lewald, Fanny. *The Education of Fanny Lewald: An Autobiography.* Trans. and ed. Hanna Ballin Lewis. SUNY Series, Women Writers in Translation. Albany: State University of New York Press, 1992.

Lewis, M. G. *The Jewish Maiden.* 4 vols. London: A. K. Newman, 1830.

Macaulay, Thomas Babington. "Civil Disabilities of the Jews." *Edinburgh Review* 52 (Jan. 1831): 366–67.

———. *Essay and Speech on Jewish Disabilities.* Ed. Israel Abrahams. Edinburgh: Jewish Historical Society of England, 1909.

Marks, David Woolf. *Sermons Preached on Various Occasions at the West London Synagogue of British Jews.* 4 vols. London: R. Groombridge and Sons, 1851.

Marks, David Woolf and Rev. A. Löwy. *Memoir of Sir Francis Henry Goldsmid.* Ed. Louis Goldsmid. 2nd ed. London: Kegan Paul, Trench, 1882.

Martin, Helena Faucit, Lady. *On Some of Shakespeare's Female Characters.* London: William Blackwood and Sons, 1891.

Marx, Karl. "On the Jewish Question." In *The Marx-Engels Reader,* ed. Robert C. Tucker, 26–53. New York: W. W. Norton, 1978.

Mayhew, Henry. *London Labour and the London Poor.* 4 vols. 1861–62. Reprint, New York: Dover Publications, 1968.

Mendelssohn, Moses. *Jerusalem, or, On Religious Power and Judaism.* Trans. Allan Arkush. Hanover: University Press of New England, 1983.

Meyers, Asher I. *The Jewish Directory for 1874, containing a complete list of Metropolitan and Provincial Synagogues, Jewish schools, associations, charitable and other institutions, societies, etc., with names and addresses of all persons holding official positions (honorary and salaried) in the Anglo-Jewish community, and other interesting information.* London: A. I. Meyers, 1874.

Montefiore, Charlotte. *Caleb Asher.* Philadelphia: Jewish Publication Society, 1845.

———. *A Few Words to the Jews. By One of Themselves.* London: John Chapman, 1855.

Montefiore, Lady Judith. *The Jewish Manual or Practical Information in Jewish and Modern Cookery with a Collection of Valuable Recipes and Hints Relating to the Toilette. Edited by a Lady.* (A Facsimile of the First

Jewish Cookbook in English Published in 1846). Intro. Chaim Raphael. London: T. and W. Boone, 1846. Reprint, New York: NightinGale Books, 1983.

———. *Diaries of Sir Moses and Lady Judith Montefiore.* Ed. Dr. L. Loewe. London, 1883.

Moss, Celia, and Marion Moss. *Early Efforts. A Volume of Poems By the Misses Moss, of the Hebrew Nation. Aged 18 and 16.* London: Whittaker, 1839.

———. *The Romance of Jewish History.* 3 vols. 2nd ed. London: A.K. Newman, 1843.

———. *Tales of Jewish History.* 3 vols. London: Miller and Field, 1843.

Moss, Marion. "Lines Written by Marion Moss, A Jewess, after attending service in a Christian Chapel, March 1845." *The Jewish Herald and Record of Christian Effort For the Spiritual Good of God's Ancient People* 1, no. 2 (1846): 48. London: British Society for the Propagation of the Gospel among the Jews, 1846–47.

Pellat, Apsley. *Brief Memoir of the Jews in Relation to Their Civil and Municipal Disabilities.* London: Hatchard and Son, 1829.

Picciotto, James. *Sketches of Anglo-Jewish History.* London: Trubner, 1875.

Polack, Maria. *Fiction without Romance; or, the Locket-Watch.* 2 vols. London, 1830.

Raphall, Morris J. "Eighteenth Anniversary of the Jews' Free School, Bell-Lane, Spitalfields, for the education and clothing of 600 boys and 300 girls." London: James Nichols, 1835.

Ruskin, John. "Of Queens' Gardens." In *The Literary Criticism of John Ruskin,* ed. Harold Bloom, 182–213. New York: Da Capo Press, 1965.

Salomon, Götthold. *Twelve Sermons Delivered in the New Temple of the Israelites, At Hamburgh.* Trans. Anna Maria Goldsmid. London: John Murray, 1839.

Scott, Sir Walter. *Ivanhoe.* New York: New American Library, 1983.

———. *Ivanhoe, with Critical Appreciations, Old and New.* Ed. G. K. Chesterton, et al. Cambridge: Cambridge University Press, 1919.

Stern, Charlotte Elizabeth. *Eliezer: or, Suffering for Christ.* London: Partridge, 1877.

Sue, Eugene. *The Wandering Jew (Le Juif Errant).* 1844–45.

Thackeray, William Makepeace. *Vanity Fair.* Oxford: Oxford University Press, 1983.

———. "Rebecca and Rowena." *Burlesques,* 305–66. Boston: Houghton, Mifflin, 1895.

Van Oven, Bernard. "Ought Baron de Rothschild to Sit in Parliament? An Imaginary Conversation between Judaeus and Amicus Nobilis." London: Effingham Wilson, 1847.

Wise, Isaac Mayer. *Reminiscences.* Ed. David Philipson. Cincinnati: Leo Wise, 1901.

SECONDARY SOURCES

1. Anglo-Jewish Historiography and Literary Criticism

Abrahams, Rachel Beth Zion Lask. "Grace Aguilar: A Centenary Tribute." *Transactions of the Jewish Historical Society of England* 16 (1952): 137–48.

Black, Eugene C. "The Anglicization of Orthodoxy: The Adlers, Father and Son." In *From East and West: Jews in a Changing Europe 1750–1870*, ed. Frances Malino and David Sorkin, 295–325. Oxford: Basil Blackwell, 1990.

————. *The Social Politics of Anglo-Jewry 1880–1920*. Oxford: Basil Blackwell, 1988.

Bradford, Sarah. *Disraeli*. New York: Stein and Day, 1982.

Cesarani, David. *The Jewish Chronicle and Anglo-Jewry, 1841–1991*. New York: Cambridge University Press, 1994.

Endelman, Todd. *The Jews of Georgian England, 1714–1830*. Philadelphia: Jewish Publication Society, 1989.

————. *Radical Assimilation in English Jewish History 1656–1945*. Bloomington: Indiana University Press, 1990.

Farjeon, Eleanor. *A Nursery in the Nineties*. London: Oxford University Press, 1960.

Feldman, David. *Englishmen and Jews: Social Relations and Political Culture, 1840–1914*. New Haven: Yale University Press, 1994.

Finestein, Israel. "Anglo-Jewish Opinion During the Struggle for Emancipation (1828–1858)." *Transactions of the Jewish Historical Society of England* 20 (1964): 113–43.

Freedman, Maurice, ed. *A Minority in Britain: Social Studies of the Anglo-Jewish Community*. London: Vallentine, Mitchell, 1955.

Galchinsky, Michael. "Blake's 'firm perswasions': The Judaic and the Jew." Paper presented at the annual convention of the Modern Languages Association, 1990.

————. "The New Anglo-Jewish Literary Criticism." *Prooftexts* 15, no. 13 (1995): 272–82.

————. "Romancing the Jewish Home," in *Homes and Homelessness in Dickens and the Victorian Imagination*. Eds. Murray Baumgarten and Bill Daleski. New York: AMS Press, 1995.

Gartner, Lloyd P. *The Jewish Immigrant in England 1870–1914*. London: George Allen and Unwin, 1960.

Hyamson, Albert M. *A History of the Jews in England*. 2d ed. London: Metheun, 1928.

————. *The Sephardim of England: A History of the Spanish and Portuguese Jewish Community, 1492–1951*. London: Methuen, 1951.

Jacobs, Joseph, and Lucien Wolf, eds. and comps. *Bibliotheca Anglo-Judaica:*

A Bibliographical Guide to Anglo-Jewish History. London: Publication of the Anglo-Jewish Historical Exhibition, 3, 1888.

The Jewish Chronicle 1841–1941: A Century of Newspaper History. London: Jewish Chronicle, 1949.

Kosmin, Barry A. "Nuptiality and Fertility Patterns of British Jewry 1850–1980: An Immigrant Transition?" In *Demography of Immigrants and Minority Groups in the United Kingdom*, ed. D. A. Coleman, 24562. London: Academic Press, 1982.

Kuzmack, Linda Gordon. *Woman's Cause: The Jewish Woman's Movement in England and the United States, 1881–1933*. Columbus: Ohio State University Press, 1990.

Lipman, V. D. *Social History of the Jews in England: 1850–1950*. London: Watts, 1954.

——, ed. *Three Centuries of Anglo-Jewish History*. Cambridge: Jewish Historical Society of England, 1961.

Marks, Lara. "Carers and Servers of the Jewish Community: The Marginalized Heritage of Jewish Women in Britain." In *The Jewish Heritage in British History*, ed. Tony Kushner, 106–27. London: Frank Cass, 1992.

Newman, Aubrey. *The Board of Deputies of British Jews, 1760–1985*. London: Valentine Mitchell, 1987.

Norich, Anita. "Jewish Family Images in the English Novel." In *The Jewish Family: Myths and Reality*, ed. Steven M. Cohen and Paula E. Hyman, 99–109. New York: Holmes and Meier, 1986.

Ragussis, Michael. "The Birth of a Nation in Victorian Culture: The Spanish Inquisition, the Converted Daughter, and the 'Secret Race.'" *Critical Inquiry* (spring 1994): 477–508.

Roth, Cecil. "The Evolution of Anglo-Jewish Literature." London: Edward Goldston, 1937.

——. *A History of the Jews in England*. London: Oxford University Press, 1941.

——. *A History of the Marranos*. Philadelphia: Jewish Publication Society of America, 1947.

——. "The Jew in the Literature of England." *Menorah Journal* 28, no. 1 (1940): 122–25.

——. "Wellsprings of European Literature." *Menorah Journal* 25, no. 3 (1937): 340–49.

——, ed. *Magna Bibliotheca Anglo-Judaica: A Bibliographical Guide to Anglo-Jewish History*. London: Jewish Historical Society of England, 1937.

Salbstein, M. C. N. *Emancipation of the Jews in Britain: The Question of the Admission of the Jews to Parliament, 1828–1860*. Rutherford, N.J.: Fairleigh Dickinson Press, 1981.

Salomon, Sidney. *The Jews of Britain*. London: Jerrolds, 1938.

Umansky, Ellen M. *Lily Montagu and the Advancement of Liberal Judaism: From Vision to Vocation.* New York: Edwin Mellen, 1983.

————, ed. *Lily Montagu: Sermons, Addresses, Letters, and Prayers.* New York: Edwin Mellen, 1985.

Weinberger, Philip M. "The Social and Religious Thought of Grace Aguilar (1816–1847)." Ph.D. diss., New York University, 1970.

Williams, Bill. *The Making of Manchester Jewry: 1740–1875.* New York: Manchester University Press, 1976.

Zatlin, Linda Gertner. *The Nineteenth-Century Anglo-Jewish Novel.* Boston: G. K. Hall, 1981.

2. Jewish Women's Historiography and Jewish Feminist Criticism

Adler, Rachel. "A Mother in Israel: Aspects of the Mother Role in Jewish Myth." In *Beyond Androcentrism: New Essays on Women and Religion,* ed. Rita M. Gross, 237–55. Missoula, Mont.: Scholars Press for the American Academy of Religion, 1977.

Baskin, Judith. Introduction to *Jewish Women in Historical Perspective.* Detroit: Wayne State University Press, 1991.

Baum, Charlotte, Paula Hyman, and Sonya Michel. *The Jewish Woman in America.* New York: Dial Press, 1976.

Biale, Rachel. *Women and Jewish Law.* New York: Schocken Books, 1984.

Gottlieb, Lynn. "The Secret Jew: An Oral Tradition of Women." In *On Being a Jewish Feminist,* ed. Susannah Heschel, 273–77. New York: Schocken Books, 1983.

Greenberg, Blu. "Women and Judaism." In *Contemporary Jewish Religious Thought,* ed. Arthur A. Cohen and Paul Mendes-Flohr, 1039–53. New York: Charles Scribner's Sons, 1987.

Henry, Sondra, and Emily Taitz. *Written Out of History: Our Jewish Foremothers.* Sunnyside, New York: Biblio Press, 1990.

Hertz, Deborah. "Emancipation through Intermarriage in Old Berlin." In *Jewish Women in Historical Perspective,* ed. Judith Baskin, 182–201. Detroit: Wayne State University Press, 1991.

————. *Jewish High Society in Old Regime Berlin.* New Haven: Yale University Press, 1988.

————. "Work, Love and Jewishness in the Life of Fanny Lewald." In *From East and West: Jews in a Changing Europe 1750–1870,* ed. Frances Malino and David Sorkin, 202–20. Oxford: Basil Blackwell, 1990.

Heschel, Susannah. "Feminism." In *Contemporary Jewish Religious Thought,* ed. Arthur A. Cohen and Paul Mendes-Flohr, 255–59. New York: Charles Scribner's Sons, 1987.

———, ed. *On Being a Jewish Feminist: A Reader.* New York: Schocken Books, 1983.

Kadish, Ruti. "Midrash and Feminism." Master's thesis, University of California, Berkeley, 1991.

Kaplan, Marion A. "Bertha Pappenheim: Founder of German-Jewish Feminism." In *The Jewish Woman: New Perspectives,* ed. Elizabeth Koltun, 149–63. New York: Schocken Books, 1976.

———. *The Making of the Jewish Middle Class: Women, Family, and Identity in Imperial Germany.* New York: Oxford University Press, 1991.

———. "Tradition and Transition: Jewish Women in Imperial Germany." In *Jewish Women in Historical Perspective,* ed. Judith Baskin, 202–21. Detroit: Wayne State University Press, 1991.

Kaye/Kantrowitz, Melanie and Irena Klepfisz, eds. *The Tribe of Dina: A Jewish Woman's Anthology.* Boston: Beacon Press, 1986.

Koltun, Elizabeth, ed. *The Jewish Woman: New Perspectives.* New York: Schocken Books, 1976.

Lichtenstein, Diane. *Writing Their Nations: The Tradition of Nineteenth-Century American Jewish Women Writers.* Bloomington: Indiana University Press, 1992.

Melammed, Renée Levine. "Sephardi Women in the Medieval and Early Modern Periods." In *Jewish Women in Historical Perspective,* ed. Judith Baskin, 115–34. Detroit: Wayne State University Press, 1991.

Plaskow, Judith. *Standing Again at Sinai: Judaism from a Feminist Perspective.* San Francisco: Harper Collins, 1990.

Umansky, Ellen M., and Dianne Ashton, eds. *Four Centuries of Jewish Women's Spirituality.* Boston: Beacon Press, 1992.

Wegner, Judith Romney. "The Image and Status of Women in Classical Rabbinic Judaism." In *Jewish Women in Historical Perspective,* ed. Judith Baskin, 68–93. Detroit: Wayne State University Press, 1991.

Weissler, Chava. "Prayers in Yiddish and the Religious World of Ashkenazic Women." In *Jewish Women in Historical Perspective,* ed. Judith Baskin, 159–81. Detroit: Wayne State University Press, 1991.

———. "The Traditional Poetry of Ashkenazic Women." In *Jewish Spirituality from the Sixteenth Century Revival to the Present,* ed. Arthur Green, 2:245–75. New York: Crossroad, 1988.

3. Other Jewish Historiography, Literary Criticism, and Theory

Baldwin, Edward Chauncey. "The Jewish Genius in Literature, A Study of Three Modern Men of Letters." *Menorah Journal* 1, no. 3 (June 1915): 164–72.

Bauman, Zygmunt. "Exit Visas and Entry Tickets: Paradoxes of Jewish Assimilation." *Telos* (fall 1988): 45–77.

Biale, David. *Eros and the Jews.* New York: Basic Books, 1992.

———. *Power and Powerlessness in Jewish History.* New York: Schocken Books, 1987.

Gilman, Sander. *Jewish Self-Hatred: Anti-Semitism and the Hidden Language of the Jews.* Baltimore: Johns Hopkins University Press, 1986.

Ginzberg, Louis. *Legends of the Jews.* Trans. Henrietta Szold. 7 vols. Philadelphia: Jewish Publication Society of America, 1928–66.

Hartman, Geoffrey H. "On the Jewish Imagination," *Prooftexts* 5, no. 3 (Sept. 1985): 201–220.

Hartman, Geoffrey H., and Sanford Budick, eds. *Midrash and Literature.* New Haven: Yale University Press, 1986.

Hertzberg, Arthur. *The French Enlightenment and the Jews: The Origins of Modern Anti-Semitism.* New York: Columbia University Press, 1968.

Kraemer, David, ed. *The Jewish Family: Metaphor and Memory.* New York: Oxford University Press, 1989.

Mosse, George L. *German Jews beyond Judaism.* Bloomington: Indiana University Press, 1985.

———. *Toward the Final Solution: A History of European Racism.* New York: Harper Colophon Books, 1980.

Petuchowski, Jakob. "On the Validity of German-Jewish Self-Definitions." *Leo Baeck Institute Memorial Lecture* 29, 1985.

Postal, Bernard, and Lionel Koppman. *Guess Who's Jewish in American History.* New York: Shapolsky, 1988.

Rotenstreich, Nathan. *Jews and German Philosophy: The Polemics of Emancipation.* New York: Schocken Books, 1984.

Sartre, Jean-Paul. *Anti-Semite and Jew.* Trans. George J. Becker. New York: Schocken Books, 1965.

Schwarzschild, Steven S. "Aesthetics." In *Contemporary Jewish Religious Thought,* ed. Arthur A. Cohen and Paul Mendes-Flohr, 1–6. New York: Charles Scribner's Sons, 1987.

Shell, Marc. "Marranos (Pigs), or from Coexistence to Toleration." *Critical Inquiry* 17, no. 2 (winter 1991): 306–35.

Sorkin, David. *The Transformation of German Jewry, 1780–1840.* Oxford: Oxford University Press, 1987.

Tal, Uriel. *Christians and Jews in Germany: Religion, Politics, and Ideology in the Second Reich, 1870–1914.* Trans. Noah Jonathan Jacobs. Ithaca: Cornell University Press, 1975.

Whiteman, Maxwell. "Isaac Leeser and the Jews of Philadelphia: A Study in National Jewish Influence." In *The Jewish Experience in America III: The Emerging Community,* ed. Abraham J. Karp, 27–62. New York: KTAV Publishing House, 1969.

Yerushalmi, Yosef Hayim. "Assimilation and Racial Anti-Semitism: The Iberian and the German Models." *Leo Baeck Institute Memorial Lecture* 26, 1982.

4. Studies of Christian Representations of English Jews

Bitton-Jackson, Livia. *Madonna or Courtesan? the Jewish Woman in Christian Literature.* New York: Seabury Press, 1982.

Calisch, Edward N. *The Jew in English Literature as Author and as Subject.* Richmond, Va.: Bell, 1909.

Chevelier, Estelle. "Characterization of the Jew in the Victorian Novel. 1864–1876." Master's thesis, Emory University, 1962.

Cheyette, Bryan. *Constructions of "the Jew" in English Literature and Society: Racial Representations, 1875–1945.* Cambridge: Cambridge University Press, 1993.

Fisch, Harold. *The Dual Image.* London: Lincolns-Prager, 1959.

Gaer, Joseph. *The Legend of the Wandering Jew.* New York: Mentor, 1961.

Gallagher, Catherine. "George Eliot and *Daniel Deronda*: The Prostitute and the Jewish Question." In *Sex, Politics, and Science in the Nineteenth-Century Novel,* ed. Ruth Bernard Yeazell, 39–62. Baltimore: Johns Hopkins University Press, 1986.

Johnson, Edgar. "Dickens, Fagin and Mr. Riah." *Commentary* 9 (1950): 47–50.

Landa, M[eyer] J[ack]. *The Jew in Drama.* New York: William Morrow, 1927.

Lane, Lauriat, Jr. "Dickens' Archetypal Jew." *PMLA* 73 (Mar. 1958): 95–101.

Modder, Montagu Frank. *The Jew in the Literature of England: To the End of the Nineteenth Century.* New York: Meridian Books, 1960.

Phillipson, David. *The Jew in English Fiction.* Cincinnati: Clarke, 1889.

Ragussis, Michael. *Figures of Conversion: "The Jewish Question" and English National Identity.* Durham, N.C.: Duke University Press, 1995.

———. "The Novel of Jewish Identity." *Critical Inquiry* (fall 1989): 113–43.

———. "Writing Nationalist History: England, the Conversion of the Jews, and *Ivanhoe*." *ELH* 60, no. 1 (spring 1993): 181–215.

Rosenberg, Edgar. *From Shylock to Svengali: Jewish Stereotypes in English Fiction.* Stanford: Stanford University Press, 1960.

Schneider, Rebecca. *Bibliography of Jewish Life in the Fiction of America and England.* Albany: New York State Library School, 1916.

Stone, Harry. "Dickens and the Jews." *Victorian Studies* 11 (Mar. 1959): 223–53.

Sypherd, Wilbur Owen. *Jephthah and His Daughter: A Study in Comparative Literature.* Newark: University of Delaware, 1948.

Trachtenberg, Joshua. *The Devil and the Jews: The Medieval Conception of the Jews and Its Relation to Modern Anti-Semitism.* New Haven: Yale University Press, 1983.

5. General English Literary Criticism, Historiography, and Theory

Anderson, James. *Sir Walter Scott and History.* Edinburgh: Edina Press, 1981.

Armstrong, Nancy. *Desire and Domestic Fiction: A Political History of the Novel.* New York: Oxford University Press, 1987.

Auerbach, Nina. *Romantic Imprisonment: Women and Other Glorified Outcasts.* New York: Columbia University Press, 1986.

Bakhtin, M. M. *The Dialogic Imagination.* Ed. Michael Holquist. Trans. Caryl Emerson and Michael Holquist. Austin: University of Texas Press, 1981.

Beer, Gillian. *The Romance.* London: Methuen, 1970.

Canning, A. S. G. *History in Scott's Novels.* 1907.

Clarke, Norma. *Ambitious Heights: Writing, Friendship, Love—The Jewsbury Sisters, Felicia Hemans, and Jane Welsh Carlyle.* New York: Routledge, 1990.

Colby, Robert. *Fiction with a Purpose: Major and Minor Nineteenth-Century Novels.* Bloomington: Indiana University Press, 1967.

Cultural Critique. Ed. David Lloyd and Abdul JanMohammed. (Spring–Fall): 1987.

Eller, Ruth. "The Poetic Theme in Scott's Novels." In *Scott and His Influence,* ed. J. H. Alexander, 75–86. Aberdeen: Association for Scottish Literature Studies, 1983.

Fleishman, Avrom. *The English Historical Novel: Walter Scott to Virginia Woolf.* Baltimore: Johns Hopkins University Press, 1971.

Foucault, Michel. *Discipline and Punish.* New York: Pantheon, 1977.

George, M. Dorothy. *London Life in the Eighteenth Century.* New York: Knopf, 1925.

Gilbert, Sandra, and Susan Gubar. *The Madwoman in the Attic: The Woman Writer and the Nineteenth-Century Literary Imagination.* New Haven: Yale University Press, 1979.

Gorsky, Susan Rubinow. *Femininity to Feminism: Women and Literature in the Nineteenth Century.* New York: Twayne Publishers, 1992.

Hodgell, Patricia Christine. "The Nonsense of Ancient Days: Sources of Scott's 'Ivanhoe.'" Ph.D. diss., University of Minnesota, 1987.

Homans, Margaret. *Bearing the Word: Language and Female Experience in Nineteenth-Century Women's Writing.* Chicago: University of Chicago Press, 1986.

Irigaray, Luce. "When Our Lips Speak Together." *This Sex Which Is Not One.* Trans. Catherine Porter. Ithaca: Cornell University Press, 1985.

Kerr, James. *Fiction against History: Scott as Storyteller.* Cambridge: Cambridge University Press, 1989.

Kestner, Joseph. *Protest and Reform: The British Social Narrative by Women, 1827–1867.* Madison: University of Wisconsin Press, 1985.

Levy, Anita. *Other Women: The Writing of Class, Race, and Gender, 1832–1898.* Princeton: Princeton University Press, 1991.

McKeon, Michael. *The Origins of the English Novel, 1600–1740.* Baltimore: Johns Hopkins University Press, 1987.

Maison, Margaret M. *The Victorian Vision: Studies in the Religious Novel.* New York: Sheed and Ward, 1961.

Melman, Billie. *Women's Orients: English Women and the Middle East, 1718–1918.* Ann Arbor: University of Michigan Press, 1992.

Mermin, Dorothy. *Godiva's Ride: Women of Letters in England, 1830–1880.* Bloomington: Indiana University Press, 1993.

Miller, D. A. *The Novel and the Police.* Berkeley: University of California Press, 1988.

Mitchell, Jerome. *Scott, Chaucer, and Medieval Romance.* Kentucky: Kentucky University Press, 1987.

Poovey, Mary. *Uneven Developments: The Ideological Work of Gender in Mid-Victorian England.* Chicago: University of Chicago Press, 1988.

———. *The Proper Lady and the Woman Writer: Ideology as Style in the Works of Mary Wollstonecraft, Mary Shelley, and Jane Austen.* Chicago: University of Chicago Press, 1984.

Said, Edward. *Orientalism.* New York: Vintage Books, 1978.

Sanders, Valerie. *The Private Lives of Victorian Women: Autobiography in Nineteenth-Century England.* New York: St. Martin's Press, 1989.

Smith-Rosenberg, Carroll. *Disorderly Conduct: Visions of Gender in Victorian America.* New York: A. A. Knopf, 1985.

Spencer, Jane. *The Rise of the Woman Novelist: From Aphra Behn to Jane Austen.* London: Basil Blackwell, 1986.

Williams, Raymond. *Marxism and Literature.* Oxford: Oxford University Press, 1977.

INDEX

Abraham, Philip: *Curiosities of Judaism,* 87
"Adah, A Simple Story." *See* Aguilar, Grace
Aggadah: Anglo-Jewish women's use of, 33. *See also* Midrash
Aguilar, Grace, 135–89; as Anglo-Jewish historian, 139, 192; appeal to multiple audiences, 135, 150–51, 173–75, 185–87, 247–48n.90; appeal to patriarch for legitimacy, 108; assessment of, 185–89; association with *Cheap Jewish Library,* 131, 171–85; attitude toward Christians, 136, 143–46, 166–67; attitude toward England, 165, 166, 168, 171; attitude toward Queen Victoria, 244–45n.58; attitude toward romance, 140, 161, 164, 171–73, 179; attitude toward Sephardic "pride," 209n.30; awareness of women's exclusion from tradition, 30, 145–46; biographical sketch and literary history, 136–41; call for mothers to be instructors, 141–42; call for vernacularization of the Bible, 73, 105, 130; children's book based on her life, 140; compared with Maria Edgeworth, 153, 185; compared with Maimonides' thirteen articles of faith, 152; compared with Marion and Celia Moss, 160–71; compared with Florence Nightingale, 243n.46, 247–48n.90; comparison of gender and Jewishness by, 30, 167, 245n.62; compromises of, 136, 145, 166–67, 185–86, 187; contents of mss., 137–38; contributions unacknowledged, 130; correspondence with Charlotte Montefiore, 131, 159, 179; criticism of Jewish patriarchy, 136; crypto-Jewish influence on, 136–37, 149–50, 159–60, 177–78; designation as sui generis, 18, 140, 151–56, 186, 193, 197; domestic fiction of, 140, 156–58, 171–85, 192; domestic ideology of, 136, 145, 148–50, 169–70, 182–85; double consciousness of, 173–74; education of, 141, 145–46; feminism of, 150, 186, 187, 188–89, 192–93; and Anna Maria Goldsmid, 193; influence of Walter Scott on, 162; influence on Christian readers, 187; influence on Jewish men, 67–68, 186; influence on Jewish women, 77, 131–32, 139, 186, 188–89; Jewish authenticity of, 144, 146, 150, 152–53, 240n.21; liberalism of, 143, 162–63, 166, 171, 185; mother/daughter plots of, 137, 139; myth of her life, 154–56, 158, 160; perception of by conversionists, 52, 218n.33; reciprocal influence with Rebecca Gratz, 238n.13; reformism of, 152, 183–84; remembrance of, 135, 171, 187, 188–89; snubbed by Jewish aristocracy, 179–80; spirit vs. forms in works, 137, 144, 150, 163–64, 164, 174, 244n.56, 246n.72. Works: "Adah, A Simple